FLOODLIT DREAMS

FLOODLIT DREAMS

How to Save a Football Club

IAN RIDLEY

SIMON & SCHUSTER

London • New York • Sydney • Toronto

First published in Great Britain by Simon & Schuster UK Ltd, 2006
A CBS COMPANY

'Fix You' written and composed by Berryman/Buckland/
Champion/Martin. Published by BMG Music Publishing Ltd.
Used by permission. All rights reserved.

'One', Hewson/Evans/Clayton/Mullen. Published by
Blue Mountain Music Ltd

1 3 5 7 9 10 8 6 4 2

Simon & Schuster UK Ltd
Africa House
64–78 Kingsway
London WC2B 6AH

www.simonsays.co.uk

Simon & Schuster Australia
Sydney

A CIP catalogue record for this book is available from the British Library

ISBN: 0–7432–7626–4
EAN: 9780743276269

Typeset by Rowland Phototypesetting Ltd, Bury St Edmunds, Suffolk
Printed and bound in Great Britain by The Bath Press, Bath

*In memory of Dad, who gave me football,
and Mum, who gave me books*

Contents

*But until I heard the voice, I'd never done a crazy
thing in my whole life.*

Kevin Costner as Ray Kinsella,
Field of Dreams

Prologue

The brilliant and celebrated American broadcaster Ed Murrow developed his own style of reporting when sent to London during the Second World War to cover the Blitz. He liked to capture the human interest story as he interviewed the stoic survivors in the capital, from the bombed-out corner-shop owner to the woman who drove the big red buses through the rubble. 'By telling the little story,' he said, 'I can tell the big one.'

This may be a little story but I hope it tells a bigger one, of a personal journey and a game that occupies a position at the very heart of English, indeed worldwide, culture.

It is the tale of a football fan with every man's dream of playing for his home-town team, the one given to him by his father who took him along to watch for the first time when he was five. Perhaps he might even become the club's manager. The dream of playing, because of lack of talent and experience, was not a feasible fantasy. However, becoming its chairman, through contacts and knowledge, was possible.

It came to pass. Amid boardroom power-struggles, I became chairman of Weymouth, then a Southern League club, now promoted to the Nationwide Conference. Having lived on the periphery of the game by writing about it as a football journalist on national newspapers for twenty-five years, it was an eye-opener to be at the eye of football's storm for a while.

It may only have been Weymouth but I quickly learned that running a non-League football concern differs only from running, say, Manchester United in the number of noughts on the balance sheet. Politics, economics and personalities are the same at Old Trafford as the Wessex Stadium simply because human nature is the same.

For a hundred years and more clubs have been booming and busting. There has been corruption and malpractice, clubs making fortunes out of players treated as slaves, players now making fortunes out of clubs treated as cash cows. What went on at Weymouth in my time as chairman was occurring in every club up and down the country, and is probably still going on and will surely continue to.

So this is the story of a believer in all that is good in the game, who wanted to make a difference, to run a club in an enlightened atmosphere, one that would empower people and enable them, and the club, to flourish. It is the story of how a fan's eyes were opened, by being in the eye of a storm, to the real world inside the game; the story of dream and reality, of one small club and one huge business.

There are people I must thank at the outset. First, my partner, Vikki Orvice, a talented sports writer for the *Sun*, put up with much but offered huge help and support beyond the duties of love. My son and daughter, Jack and Alex, helped make much of it fun. Then there is my generous sister Melanie, without whose emotional backing and cooking I would not have survived.

On the Weymouth board, there were some good men and true whose integrity I could depend on, notably Charlie Lesser, Nigel Winship and Andrew Brown. Dave Higson, too, showed himself a decent man and bridge between tradition and progress. Sarah Redford was a rock in the office, Bob Lucas, Tim Davis and Bob Mowlem great supporters.

Then Steve Claridge, maddening at times but a man who enriches the life of anyone who knows him. The group of players he assembled, men like Paul Buckle and Lee Philpott, give a lie to many preconceptions about footballers.

I am extremely grateful to the wonderfully supportive Ian Chapman at Simon and Schuster for his belief in this book, a publisher with a real feel for words, along with Suzanne Baboneau. Rochelle Venables was a perceptive and sensitive editor. Thanks also to my literary agent David Godwin. The adjective literary suits him.

Above all, my gratitude goes to the people and football fans of Weymouth, mostly good, some bad, for all the memories, mostly good, some bad. All human life was here.

PART ONE

It had to start somewhere …

But if you never try, you'll never know
Just what you're worth.
Lights will guide you home,
And ignite your bones,
And I will try,
To fix you

Coldplay, 'Fix You'

The dawning of the age

In *As You Like It*, Shakespeare – who once described football as 'base' – noted the seven ages of man. For those captivated at a young age by the game's jumpers-for-goalposts simplicity there are, more probably, three.

First the child, desperately dreaming of becoming a professional, perhaps lining up for Manchester United or Arsenal, and of course England. Or full of reverie about turning out for his home-town team. When growing up, particularly in a small town, the outside world seems distant. You see United and Arsenal on the telly now and then, catch a glimpse of stuff about them in your Mum and Dad's newspaper (at that time in the mid-sixties that working-class bible called the *Daily Mirror*), but your heroes are really those you see in the flesh, performing every other Saturday afternoon, or, joy of joys, at a midweek game.

In my case, these heroes were the yeomen of Weymouth Football Club, hearts-of-oak representatives of the seaside town in Dorset where I was born. Weymouth, with its nuffin'-ever-'appens nature which all but closed down in the winter to its population then, in the 1960s, of around 50,000.

My primary school, St John's, was a hundred yards from a beach kissing what was once described as England's Bay of Naples, curving safely and beautifully, beloved of the sailing fraternity. It will become the venue for the yachting events of London's 2012 Olympic Games. We learned to swim in the freezing April English Channel and in the lively summers there was a variety of seasonal jobs to be had. I did them all in my teens: waiting tables, selling lilo water beds in a beachshop or newspapers on the promenade, packing wines and spirits in the local brewery.

The winter was beautiful, although the wind from angry seas ripped through you and the town could be bleak and gloomy. No wonder out of this landscape and its surrounding countryside grew the intense, portentous writing of Thomas Hardy, who named the town Budmouth in his lexicon of Wessex. He captured perfectly the tendency towards melancholia of the region's people.

Besides the pub, darts and skittles, there was little to divert in mid-winter except for football. The Recreation Ground by the harbour was my second home. Weymouth Football Club's home, it seemed at the time a massive theatre of dreams: floodlit nights of Southern League Championships and stirring FA Cup ties and huge crowds of 5000 and more firing the imagination and filling me with excitement.

I always thought I would play for them one day, despite going to a rugby-playing grammar school eight miles away in the county town of Dorchester, Thomas Hardy's Casterbridge. I would surely get spotted playing for my Sunday morning club side – Southill Dynamoes, Westham, or even Weymouth Wrestling Club (no, I didn't wrestle, it was just a collection of mates loosely connected). Instead, it took me until about the age of thirty to realize I was never going to play for England Under 21s.

The age of seventeen and university in London came and went, so I had to settle for playing for my college and watching Weymouth whenever I could as a career in newspapers and sports writing developed. Saturdays were then taken up with covering Football League games, so it was a question mainly of midweeks, travelling the A roads to Kettering, Nuneaton and Maidstone as a founder member of the London Supporters' Club.

As the decrepitude of thirty arrived, so, too, did the second age. With the arrogance of every fan, I thought I knew better than the manager. He didn't play the right system or formation, recruited the wrong players, played them out of position, chose the wrong team. As for his tactics, don't get me started. We didn't have radio phone-ins or websites for all the grumbles in those days so the phrase 'tactical naivety' had not yet gained currency. Had it, he would have suffered from it.

I once even applied to be manager of Weymouth during the eighties as the days of stability ended and ashen-faced supremos came and went, rather than stayed for five years and more. The game was now more transient, the culture more quick-fix and lacking in patience as attention spans dwindled with the arrival of the computer, Playstation and the fast-food age. It was a tongue-in-cheek application really, and received the standard, sober 'thank you but the position has been filled' letter in reply, but I guess it showed the way I was thinking.

Then, at some point around the turn of the millennium, the hair now grey and middle age approaching, the third age dawned. It occurred to me that the real power lay with the chairman. He hired and fired – plenty of them at Weymouth – and determined the policy and direction of the club. He was the figure who recruited the pivotal person in any club – the manager – and, with the board of directors, set the budget which determined the quality of player to be brought in. He also established the mood of the club with his leadership and personality. And the mood of the fans, for better or worse.

As a young supporter, you don't even know who the

chairman is, let alone other board members. They are men in suits and overcoats who stalk the corridors in club ties, rather than scarves and bobble hats, looking important. They drink whisky in smoke-filled boardrooms uninhabited by anyone who calls him or herself a true fan. If true fans, why don't they just dip into their bulging pockets more often? They are rich, after all, aren't they?

Occasionally as a kid, I became conscious of men like the autocratic Bob Lord at Burnley, a gruff butcher who ran his club with an iron fist and dabbled in football politics. There was also Louis Edwards at Manchester United, another who traded in meat, which seemed appropriate given the players' contracts of the early sixties, so heavily weighted in favour of the clubs before the abolition of the maximum wage.

There were bakers and candlestick-makers, too, altruistic men in some cases wanting to give back something to their town, symbolized in a football club that brought a bit of national recognition. How else would anyone have heard of Mansfield or Darlington? And where exactly were Tranmere and Port Vale? Undoubtedly, these men also liked the local kudos, as big egos swimming in a small pond. There might even be a bit of increased business and brass thrown in.

There was the odd toff, too. At Ipswich Town in the seventies (patron Lady Blanche Cobbold), Patrick Cobbold became known as the perfect chairman, benevolent and with an unperturbed perspective on the game that enabled Bobby Robson's tyro management to flourish. A crisis for Mr Patrick, whose family-owned brewing company dovetailed neatly with Saturday afternoons, arrived when the boardroom ran out of white wine. On a trip back from a European tie, he once instructed the pilot to return to the airport shortly after take-off as the champagne had been shamefully forgotten in the departure lounge.

In the eighties came Ken Bates. He bought debt-ridden

Chelsea for £1 and, with his mixture of old-fashioned one-man-band stubbornness and, shall we say, modern creative business methods, proceeded to turn the club into a brand. When Roman Abramovich finally arrived with his zillions, Bates had run up a £100 million debt but walked away himself with £18 million.

He was the precursor to the faces of the nineties, men who scented huge sums were to be made from the arrival of the Premiership. No longer were chairmen benefactors, as were Elton John at Watford, Sir Jack Hayward at Wolverhampton Wanderers and Jack Walker at Blackburn Rovers – patriarchs prepared to bankroll their clubs just to achieve boyhood dreams.

The new breed of barrow boys in Armani two-pieces were paid chief executives, insisting that the books must be balanced so that they could justify huge salaries and share options. Most football clubs still lost money, were still underwritten or loaned money by directors who would take it back whenever there was the windfall of a cup run, but with the formation of the Premier League everything had changed.

Back in the eighties, the game was down on its uppers, blighted by hooliganism and playing to dwindling audiences in crumbling stadiums. There had been the Bradford City fire in May 1985 when fifty-six people died, the very same month as the Heysel disaster, in which thirty-nine Juventus *tifosi* lost their lives as a result of a charge by Liverpool fans at the European Cup final. Finally came the Hillsborough disaster of 1989 when ninety-six Liverpool supporters died, crushed against fences before the FA Cup semi-final against Nottingham Forest.

The subsequent Taylor report recommended the phasing out of concrete terraces and introduction of all-seater stadia. The availability of funds to rebuild stadia coupled with the arrival of Rupert Murdoch's British Sky Broadcasting, which threw millions at the game in return for live coverage that would shift satellite dishes and sell subscriptions, turned the fortunes around. A young lad by the name of Paul Gascoigne, bursting on to the scene with Newcastle United and England, helped raise football's profile anew.

Up at Newcastle, a businessman by the name of Freddy Shepherd saw the opportunities. A friend of the Hall family, Sir John Hall having saved the club, Shepherd grew in power at St James's Park as the nineties turned into the new millennium. As the stadium was rebuilt, as the TV, merchandising and sponsorship money rolled in on the back of the new explosion of interest in the game, he became chairman and chief executive. His salary rose to £500,000 a year, around £700,000 with bonuses and pension contributions, and he accumulated shares giving him some 22 per cent of the club and dividends of around a £1 million a year.

Not that any of that was ever feasible at Weymouth, nor was there any money to be made, nor did I want to. But the same structure, the same hierarchy, existed throughout the game, from Newcastle in the north-east to Weymouth in the south-west. Players could influence results, managers could influence teams. But chairmen could plot the course of an entire club, turn its fortunes around. After the Fantasy Football games of the nineties, one national newspaper had even caught up and was running a Fantasy Chairman game. Now there *was* a fantasy . . .

My favourite film is *Field of Dreams* and it touches me more than is healthy. At the time of its release in 1989, I was thirty-four, with two children, wondering what else there might be in life. It was too early for a mid-life crisis that would arrive in its own good time more than a decade later but an enlightening seed – an appropriate image, given the setting for the movie – was sown.

In the film, a 36-year-old married father-of-one, an Iowa farmer named Ray Kinsella, played by Kevin Costner, is working his corn field one day when he hears a voice. 'If you build it, he will come,' it says.

At first frightened, then baffled, Ray gets the idea that if he digs up part of his land and builds a baseball diamond, the ghost of 'Shoeless' Joe Jackson, a legend in the game, will appear. It comes to pass when Ray, risking bankruptcy, ploughs up his field and creates the diamond, floodlights and all.

Something else magical occurs. Ray has always regretted the fiery relationship he had with his father, the only thing they had in common being sport. His father returns, too, to this sports field in the middle of nowhere as a proud and strong young man, to bring about a measure of healing, reconciliation and redemption.

It is a film to touch the spirit, about having the courage to follow a dream, no matter the material cost to oneself, about finding one's path and journey. And about a game that can be a bond between father and son, between people seeking connection and reassurance through the good and simple pleasures of life.

A fantasy? Perhaps. We would see. Life has been known to imitate art.

CHAPTER ONE

Bored, bored, board

I am sitting in my car on a cold January night outside a deserted football ground on the edge of a deserted seaside town, waiting for my mobile phone to ring. Not just any football ground, but an ugly, badly designed and badly built, breeze-block stadium. Still, I love it because it is home to the club I have followed with a passion all my life.

Tonight, only the lights of the boardroom pierce a Bible-black scene. They might at least have offered me a cup of tea.

I have tired of seeing the club I support lurch from crisis to crisis, through seasons of mediocrity to ones of abject awfulness. This is one of the latter. Crowds are down to around 600, which is still good for the Southern League Premier Division but bad for Weymouth, and the team is in danger of relegation. The manager is being lambasted for a long ball game at odds with the tradition of the club and the directors appear to have run out of ideas save for using the local evening paper, the *Dorset Echo*, to call for more fans to come to games and put a quid in a bucket to stave off financial crisis.

About a year earlier, in February 2002, as the latest crisis set in, I had asked to meet the board, believing I could help in some way, perhaps using some contacts I had built up in the game through my years of writing about football, perhaps by getting a few sponsors in.

I had told an old mate, Steve Claridge, stalwart of count-less clubs including Birmingham City and Leicester, of the club's plight. After starting his career at Bournemouth, in 1985 he had transferred to Weymouth, playing at the charming, atmospheric old Recreation Ground by the harbour before the club moved to its new concrete Wessex Stadium on the edge of town in 1987. He was saddened. It had been a Conference club on the verge of the Football League when he was there.

He reckoned he might be able to invest a few bob, might be interested in becoming director of football when his days at his current club, Millwall, his fourteenth, were up. He was nearing thirty-six now and thinking of the future.

The board, probably star-struck by Steve, agreed to the meeting and so we met at a hotel near Steve's Portsmouth home. It was not a pretty sight. The chairman Terry Bennett was a downbeat, gruff character, portly and conversation-ally crass. There had been tales of him telling potential sponsors to get their 'effin chequebooks out. Beer foam sometimes sat on his moustache. He owned a fish and chip shop on the quayside. Nicknamed Fishy by the fans, he was the Codfather.

There were several others at the meeting, which had been arranged by James Murphy, the supporters' representative on the board. Dave Higson, half-owner of a local company, Park Engineering, who were the club sponsors, and his business partner, Mick Archer, also a director of the club, began to sound like the real power brokers. Higson, a Bolton Wanderers fan, was silver-haired and affable; Archer, from the Tamworth area, appeared less approachable.

We talked, chewed the fat for an hour or so. Claridge was not impressed with the group, particularly their fondness for away trips on the team bus. Directors should not travel with the team, Claridge believed. He would not trust his money to these men, he told me afterwards. The meeting came to nothing. I was getting my first glimpse of the sort of men who run football clubs, of the politics and personalities that inhabit boardrooms.

In a career loitering on the fringes of the game, I had seen all types of director: some altruistic, well meaning and good natured, some ridiculous, some dangerous. Some who were a mixture of all of the above. Probably frustrated footballers themselves, they enjoyed the cocktail of power and ego. At this level of the game, the autocratic Bob Lord breed of director was definitely the more prevalent.

Now, on this January night a year later, a group of them was sitting upstairs – Murphy now replaced by one Nigel Beckett, a loyal and obedient supporter – deciding on my role, if any, in Weymouth's future. I sat in my car wondering whether to turn the engine on for heat, before deciding that it might sound as if I was about to do a runner.

That first meeting might have deterred Claridge but it had only made me more determined. I was sure I could do better than this lot. But how to get control of the club to turn things around? How to get turkeys to vote for Christmas? After that first meeting, I had earmarked Higson as the key figure and stayed in touch with him.

The season had only got worse. The directors had decided to go for the Southern League Championship and promotion to the Conference, just one rung below the full-time professional game on English football's ladder. But results had gone against them around Christmas. They had overstretched themselves and they decided to rein in. The best players were all sent out on loan to cut costs. From a position near the top of the table they finished well off the pace.

The manager Fred Davies was in his second spell with the club, leading it to promotion from a regional league it had criminally slipped into a few years earlier. He had wanted time off to be with his sick wife, the board allegedly refusing. The dispute led to his departure. Clearly his wages, believed to be £600 a week, were a factor.

For the 2002/2003 season the board had taken on Geoff Butler, who had been at Salisbury City for almost twenty years, his time there ending in acrimony and a court case. He came cheap, at £200 a week and £112 guaranteed expenses. Once a defender at Chelsea and Sunderland, Butler was a no-nonsense dinosaur of the sort who somehow keeps managing to get jobs at struggling clubs. I was taken by how his clumpy shoes never matched his suit.

He did not have an easy start, being told by the board to slash the wage bill, his willingness to do so obviously a reason why he was hired. With his curt manner, he antago-nised the players, particularly those now being asked to tear up their contracts and cut their money by 50 per cent. Some players even refused to play for a while. One pinned him to a wall in the dressing room after a particularly heated exchange of views.

Butler did have a knack of recruiting some decent players cheaply, though, including a former Exeter City goalkeeper, Jason Matthews, and a pacy right back in Steve Tully from Torquay. But the side overall was ugly and uncompro-mising. Results were poor, fans voted with their feet. There was a pall of gloom over the Wessex.

My job was to cover Premiership football for *The Observer* on Saturdays but I got to pretty much every midweek Weymouth game. My dad, now seventy, was ill, his breathing worsening because of lungs clogged by years of smoking and working on building sites, though he was in remission from prostate cancer. I liked to come back to visit him in Weymouth, spend more time with him after my mum's sudden death in her sleep the previous year, which shocked us and knocked the stuffing out of him.

Dad and I detested the football, the state of the club. But then we were football fans, and fans of one club. Good and bad, thick and thin and all that. It beat *Coronation Street* on the telly, got Dad out of the house, brought us closer. And the good thing was you could park right outside the turnstiles, get a table in the bar easily enough and not have to queue. It was especially enjoyable in school holidays when my son Jack could come too, three generations bound together by the game.

An idea insinuated itself inside me. If I could just get together a consortium of people willing to invest, perhaps we could turn this thing around. Clearly the club was in debt, with some pressing creditors to be paid off, and needed some cash to assemble a better team. I didn't have enough money myself, but then I believed it to be about knowledge, about expertise, rather than just cash. If you knew people in the game, men of quality, you could raise the profile and revenue, surely.

Claridge said he would put up £10,000, with more to follow. I could match that. Another old friend, Tony Adams, of Arsenal and England fame, agreed to become a consultant to the club and said he might be able to find me investors. I also went to a trusted man with the club at heart, Matthew McGowan.

I had known Matt for years. I had come to know him better latterly because my father had worked part-time as a porter and potman at a seafront hotel, the Russell, which Matt formerly owned. My sister Melanie had worked behind the bar there.

Matt had been player, manager and chairman of Weymouth before a falling-out with the current board in one of the many off-field battles that had beset the club over the previous decade. He had not been to the ground since, despite some seven years having passed. That bitterness seemed to me at odds with his nature. He had always seemed to me a thoughtful, decent man, full of wisdom.

'As my old man used to tell me', his pronouncements

always began, his old man being Sammy, another player for the club, a lively left-winger who had come down from Scotland to play, and who had gone on to become physio. My favourite was: 'As my old man used to tell me: never argue with an idiot as bystanders won't know the difference.'

Matt was wary, but said he would back me and lend me some money if I needed it. Having sold the Russell to another local hotelier and holiday camp owner, a man named Martyn Harrison, for almost £1 million, he had a bit of money and plenty of time on his hands. His main occupation these days seemed to be sitting in the kitchen of his harbourside house drinking coffee. That and risking a dodgy hip that gave him gyp on a motorcycle.

As I left his house and walked across the Town Bridge with my partner Vikki, a rainbow appeared over the harbour. I asked her if she thought I was mad to want to take on my local football club. 'You should follow your dream,' she said. But yes, she would say later, she thought I was mad.

I requested another meeting and the board sent Steve McDonald to that same Portsmouth hotel. I told him of an initial £30,000 to pay off pressing debt, with more to follow in the summer. I added that I thought I could shake things up, bring some – slightly – younger energy, get the feel-good factor back into the club and the town, attract sponsors back on board, increase the gates. I would raise money from sporting dinners, with people like Tony Adams coming down, and auctions of signed memorabilia that I could obtain. I reckoned we would have £100,000 of new money for next season. It was a five-year plan aimed at getting us into the Conference and then the Football League, something achievable, I believed, because the club had a good fan base. McDonald wrote my plans and figures down on the back of an envelope.

A year of stability, maybe, building the crowds back up to that magic 1000 mark, which not many clubs at our level could reach, and we could go for promotion from the Southern League, I went on. That gave us three years to get out of the Conference. Our main rivals, Yeovil Town, had shown that it could be done. Clubs much smaller than us not so long ago, like Cheltenham Town and Kidderminster Harriers, had also managed it and, at the time, on lower gates than we had been getting then. What did they have that we didn't? It was a question of getting the right manager, the right players, I said. It was a question of bringing some knowledge and expertise to the place.

My motives, I insisted, were honourable. I simply wanted to see my underachieving, home-town team finally fulfil its potential. I had some time, some money and many ideas to invest. I felt passionately about it, I added. I expected to lose my money, I told him, but it would be a price worth paying to turn the club around. Some people bought racehorses, paid the price of their training, and rarely saw any winnings. They simply enjoyed a day at the races and seeing it run. Weymouth would be my racehorse.

I knew that the club could see a light at the end of the tunnel, in the shape of the Asda supermarket chain, now owned by the giant American company Walmart. They had moved the club to its present location, the Wessex Stadium, on the edge of town, in 1987, taking over the harbourside Rec for a new store. Now they had outgrown that outlet and wanted the Wessex location. In return, they would build the club a 6000-capacity new stadium on adjacent land and give them £1.5 million on top. I did not wish to profit in any way, I said. But if the club was not careful, the stadium could become a white elephant. They could move there as a relegated club, instead of one on the upturn. McDonald took note and said he agreed.

I also spoke on the phone to Higson about the rescue

package, making it clear that I wanted to become chairman, on the principle that if I was going to make changes, I needed the authority to do so. I wanted to put together a team, on and off the field, and create a more buoyant mood. I knew, though, that if I failed, I would be blamed. And if I was going to fail, I was willing to stand up and take responsibility for that. But only if I was given the authority.

It meant Bennett stepping down. I had never warmed to him after an incident at Chelmsford City the previous season. I was in the bar with my then 12-year-old son, Jack, when Bennett emerged from the dressing room half an hour before kickoff and in a loud I'm-in-charge voice, as he ordered himself a large one, announced to a knot of nearby fans that he had told the team that he needed a result to boost the gate for Saturday. It struck me as showy, crass and unprofessional.

I also wanted another board member, Peter Shaw, slightly younger and less grey than the rest, to resign. A former chairman, Shaw was a publisher of small-circulation maga-zines and on the odd occasion I had met him before seemed to see himself as a cut above the others, above most people, in fact. The fans I spoke to seemed to have little trust in him. In addition, I wanted to replace Geoff Butler with a new manager.

Higson came back to me one Sunday night. The board were willing to meet me. He believed in my plan, he said, had canvassed opinion and was certain that the vote would go my way. And so, the next night, I was meeting them here at the ground.

Bennett, Shaw, Higson, Archer, McDonald and Beckett sat around the boardroom table, a lovely old piece of oak donated to the club by HMS *Ark Royal*, a regular visitor to the port, when they refurbished their officers' mess in the 1950s. I noticed that the carpet was red, perhaps to conceal all the bloodstains from board meetings down the years.

I outlined the plan and my manifesto. Higson had told me that the club's debts were about £250,000 and that they were losing around £2000 a week. The money I was offering was not a huge sum, I admitted, but it would meet immediate needs. Besides, this was more about regenerating interest in the club, getting the buzz back so that new investors and sponsors would materialize, I repeated to them.

They heard me out. Bennett smoked even more heavily than I did. Shaw said nothing. I was then asked to leave the room, leave the building, in fact, while they mulled everything over. Mick Archer, scruffy and puffing on roll-ups, darting unconvincing smiles beneath his moustache, was leading the meeting to show that he and Higson were the real powers and Bennett just a figurehead. I would be summoned back when they had reached a decision, Archer said.

And so I am sitting in my car on a cold January night outside a deserted football ground on the edge of a deserted seaside town, waiting for my mobile phone to ring. I could kill for a cup of tea.

CHAPTER TWO

Roots

It is surprising how much comes to mind, how many memories flood your brain, when you have time on your hands and you think about your football club. How much, usually unnoticed, you observe about the ground when you are sitting in a car on your own. There was nothing much on the radio and I hadn't brought anything to read.

The town really is a backwater, with little else for miles around. Bournemouth to the east is about thirty miles away and Exeter around fifty to the west. We were famous for very little, apart from references in Hardy, though we did not have the resonance of his Casterbridge, even if our bigger town and bigger football club had always outshone its own team, Dorchester Town.

We did have a Miss World, Lesley Langley, in 1965 and we were allowed out of our primary school on to the seafront to wave flags as she passed in a Jaguar on her way to a civic reception. Actually, we had a notoriety rather than a fame, a shame that the town preferred to keep quiet. The Black Death, that would wipe out a third of the population of the nation, entered England in 1348 through Weymouth.

More recently, the celebrated travel writer Paul Theroux, getting there ahead of Bill Bryson, had ventured into our town for his book *The Kingdom by the Sea*. He had approached from the east, and noted: 'up here, above

Weymouth Bay, there were holiday camps on the bluffs, looking more than ever like concentration camps ... On this sunny day, fully clothed people slept on deckchairs. They had scowling sunburned faces. I could hear them snoring from forty yards away.'

His mood improved, however, as he entered the town proper, leaving behind the imposing white art deco building of what was then a Pontin's holiday camp but would become the Riviera, now owned by that man Martyn Harrison, who had bought out Matt McGowan's hotel.

'Now it seemed downhill, across some cliffs, and down a gully to a sea-wall,' Theroux continued. 'I walked on top of the wall the last few miles into Weymouth. I liked Weymouth immediately. It was grand without being pompous. It had a real harbour. It was full of boats ... I liked the look of the houses, their elegance, and the smell of fish and beer among them. I walked around ... The weather was perfect. I thought: I could live here. That thought made me happy.'

Dorset was, too, a footballing backwater. As a player, it was hard to get spotted and I recall only two from my era in the late sixties and early seventies who went on to become professionals: Keith Walley, from my primary school, who played for Crystal Palace, and John 'Buster' Crabbe, from Westhaven School, who had a career mainly with Gillingham – in Kent, that is, not north Dorset. Later he would come back and manage Weymouth for a brief period when Matt McGowan was director of football. The board's sacking of Buster when Matt was on holiday had led to Matt's acrimonious retreat from the club.

As a kid, you supported supposedly more glamorous teams than your local one, or had a second, 'big' team. In the early sixties, I was a Burnley fan. Then Nottingham Forest for a season or two. Then Manchester City for their dashing side of 1968. And when I went to London University in the seventies, Fulham took my fancy.

Why does a young boy take a shine to a football club? I
didn't even know where Burnley was. In my case, I liked their
shirts of claret and blue. They gave the big city clubs a run
for their money, finishing runners-up in both League and
Cup in 1962 when I felt sorry for them. Forest were runners-
up, too, in 1967. Manchester City actually won the title; a
rare hiatus in my devotion to the unfashionable underdog.
I dumped them pretty quickly.

And Fulham? When I came to the capital, I had my pick.
But for a son of Dorset, steeped in Hardy's melancholy,
there was something exclusive, even lonely and deliciously
morose about standing on the Hammersmith End watching
the old Second Division while all your college mates went to
Arsenal, Tottenham or Chelsea.

Actually, none of them meant very much. You just had
teams when you were at school so that you could keep up
with other kids and their allegiances elsewhere. Only one
club has ever really meant anything to me: Weymouth FC.
The best banner I ever saw at a football match (along
with one at the Soviet Union v. Scotland match at the 1982
World Cup which proclaimed: 'Communism v. Alcoholism')
belonged to an Arsenal fan and read: 'One life, one love, one
club, one-nil'. It was how I felt about Weymouth, the Terras,
so nicknamed after their original colours of terracotta and
blue, now more the claret and blue of Burnley.

Even when I was at university and had all these capital
teams to choose from in an era when students could afford
actually to attend at least a couple of games a week (brilliant
during the power cuts of 1974 when they played in the afternoons and you could bunk off lectures to see games such as
Chelsea 3, Burnley 0), I would choose Weymouth every time
if they were in the London area. The most vivid memory
was a match at Hillingdon Borough: 4–1 down with eight
minutes to go, we somehow won 5–4.

I have always believed that it should be law that a father

has to take his son to watch their local club. My own son, Jack, came with me to watch St Albans City, where I now lived, in his pushchair. You always want a bit better for your son, though, and as he grew I took him to Tottenham Hotspur more often to spare him the non-League life. He liked going to St Albans, though; loved going to Weymouth. For that, among many other things, I was proud of him.

My own dad was a Geordie – from Northumberland, at least, so close enough – and we all know how Geordies feel about their football. He met Mum when he was in the navy and docked in nearby Portland Harbour, Mum's family having relocated to Weymouth from north London after the war. He cut a dash, she said, in his uniform at that dockside pub. They settled down in the town, Dad getting a job on the buses.

On the days when Dad wasn't playing in the Dorset League for nearby Chickerell (champions in 1963, me the mascot), he took me to Weymouth's old Recreation Ground. It seemed huge to me then. Night games were the best; kids are just captivated by them, as Jack, even now as a teenager, has always been. It is ever a joy to hear the excitement in his voice, see the thrill in his eyes. It reminds me of me.

The floodlights towered (bought from Portsmouth, promptly failing after twenty minutes of an inaugural game against them), their lamps dancing on the backwater; now more trendily called the inner harbour. When we moved to the Wessex, they went along too, standing obsolete and tall.

My pulse always raced as I got out of Dad's Ford Popular, our hot breaths steaming up the cold night air, along with the piping Oxo from the tea hut. They used to serve it in mugs in those days, trusted you to return them. The Gasworks End, the corrugated roofing amplifying the chanting, was home.

I never thought about it being non-League football in those days. It was just football. I never thought about the appeal of it, all its qualities, as I would do later in life.

As I aged, I loved this antidote to the Premiership and its glitz. You could turn up five minutes before kickoff if you wanted, still get in comfortably. Or you could arrive an hour before and have a drink in the bar, even stand there sympathizing with a player who had been dropped. If you were so inclined, you could give the chairman and the manager the benefit of your wisdom after the game. In between, you felt a part of it, part of something manageable. It was the human, affordable side of the game.

Then, I just loved the sights and the sounds and the smells. Never thought about how ordinary some of the football might have been in comparison with the top level. The players were high quality, heroes. I didn't even think about them just being part-timers, who had 'proper' jobs. One well-known local player once came in his overalls to paint the window frames at my primary school as part of his day job and I queued for his autograph.

But then, I was spoiled. In 1965, we won the Southern League Championship under Frank O'Farrell, who would go on to manage Torquay and Manchester United. The team's names still trip off the tongue – Clarke, Shepherd, Stocker, Hinchcliffe, Hobson, O'Farrell, Hannigan, Spratt, Jackson, Hutchinson, Camp – as easily as do Banks, Cohen, Wilson, Stiles, Charlton J., Moore (capt.), Ball, Hunt, Charlton R., Hurst and Peters from a year later.

In that touchstone year of 1966, we retained the title, this time under Stan Charlton, once of Arsenal and Leyton Orient. I thought it would always be like this. It would only be a matter of time before we were elected to the Football League, there being no automatic promotion at that time. I understood nothing of football politics, where the vote was really for League chairmen to keep each other in and non-League clubs out.

I thought our FA Cup pedigree would be taken into account. I had been brought up on tales of derring-do, of going to Manchester United in the third round in 1950, the game being at Maine Road as Old Trafford was still being rebuilt after the war. We lost 4–0 but were by no means disgraced. Our goalkeeper (and how did goalies ever wear those woolly polo necks?) was Bob Lucas, who was still at the club as president now in his late seventies, having been physio for years. It is not outrageous to describe him as 'The Nicest Man In The World'.

We always seemed to make the first round at least, drawing a host of League clubs. I witnessed many of the ties myself, home and away: Bournemouth, Bristol Rovers, Leyton Orient, Millwall, Northampton Town, Swindon. We beat a few of these huge clubs as well. First round day was always special. Crowds for League games would regularly top 2000 – even 5000 for derbies against our local rivals Yeovil Town, also known as the Green Slime – and rise up to 8000 for these even more special occasions. The Rec's record, in the days of little seating, was 12,512 in 1948 for a Cup tie against Yeovil.

They didn't come much more special than in 1974 when we drew 0–0 at Peterborough, then top of the old Third Division, before a 3–3 replay on a mudheap at home, the Posh twice equalizing in the last minute, of normal and extra time. No penalties in those days; we lost the third match at London Road 3–0 and had to endure that desolate late-night, long-distance and even longer-lasting journey home so contrasting to those optimistic trips going to the match.

But it all seemed worthwhile when we went to Cardiff City, then also riding high in the old Third Division, in 1981. We found ourselves two down in just half an hour but astonishingly fought back to win 3–2, one of the goals scored by Anniello Iannone, a window cleaner of Italian origin who became one of the club's legends, another by Mark Baber, whom I played against in primary school football.

The eighties were a good decade. The Alliance Premier

League, incorporating the best of the Northern and Southern Premier leagues, was formed; finally a step forward in the non-League game. That first season, we finished runners-up to Altrincham, a 3–2 defeat at their ground the championship decider.

No matter. It heralded an era of prosperity. Some famous names came and went: Graham Roberts, for example, sold to Tottenham for £35,000. Folklore has it at the club that the late Bill Nicholson, manager of Spurs' double-winning side of 1961, met a few Weymouth supporters on the station at Swindon as they travelled back from a game. Now a scout for Spurs, he asked them who the best player they had seen in non-League was. Soon the north London club were watching Roberts, buying him soon after. I bet Weymouth never had a sell-on clause or more payments when the defensive hard man went on to play for England.

The same was probably true of Andy Townsend, who went for £50,000 to Southampton, before joining Chelsea and Aston Villa. We had paid £13,000 – a fortune for a non-League club then – to prise him out of Welling United. I once saw the 20-year-old Townsend stand up to Millwall's fearsome midfield duo of Les Briley and Terry Hurlock in an FA Cup tie. Briley departed injured.

Shaun Teale raised a few more bob from Bournemouth before going on to Aston Villa and there were others: Tony Agana left for Watford for £20,000, Peter Guthrie, an outstanding goalkeeper, went to Tottenham Hotspur for £100,000.

I actually saw that deal done. As a founder-member of the London Supporters' Club – about half a dozen of us living around the capital – I was in the bar at an FA Trophy tie at Harrow Borough when Terry Venables and Irving Scholar, then Spurs' manager and chairman, were talking to the Weymouth chairman. I was a sub-editor on *The Guardian* at the time. It made a few paragraphs in the paper.

It was in the days when I didn't even know who was the Weymouth chairman or, to be honest, what he actually did. Didn't care. Like the majority of fans, the team was all I was interested in. Ah, for those happy, naive, carefree days . . .

Then there was Steve Claridge. I first met him at Wycombe Wanderers' sloping, old-town centre ground at Loakes Park before they moved to Adams Park at the end of an industrial estate on the edge of High Wycombe. He was a 19-year-old on loan from Bournemouth, fresh and freckle-faced, floppy haired and daft as a brush. He astounded me with his touch, willingness to work and his finishing in a 2–2 draw. In the bar afterwards I told him to sign for us, that he would attract more attention here than in Bournemouth's reserves. He smiled a Cheshire cat grin.

Weymouth paid £10,000 for him and he became a fans' favourite, staying three years. Typical of the way the club was being run at the time, however, no letter was ever sent out retaining him when his contract expired – the rule in those days – and he was allowed to leave on a free transfer, fetching up at Crystal Palace. He could, though, never oust Ian Wright or Mark Bright, then firing on all cylinders as a partnership, and soon left for Aldershot. Then Cambridge United, Luton, Birmingham City, Portsmouth, Leicester, Wolves and Millwall.

With all this money coming in, surely the club was in fine financial shape. The club also had a town centre social club that raised money seven nights a week, as well as a lottery that spanned the county, bringing in, it was said, more than £100,000 a year. This was a tidy sum in the eighties, enabling us to buy players like Andy Townsend and pay good wages. The club also owned seafront flats, which it used to attract players. The West Bromwich Albion and England legend Jeff Astle had been lured by the accommodation at the end of his career in the late seventies, window-cleaning for extra money.

There was also the stadium deal of the mid-1980s. Asda needed a site for a new supermarket and the Rec was earmarked. In return for giving up its ground, the club would be built a new £2 million one on the edge of town, the Wessex Stadium, and handed £1 million on top. It was 1987 and for the grand opening Manchester United came and played to an attendance of 5500. A strong United side that included Bryan Robson and Brian McClair was even beaten 1–0.

Now we would surely take off. We had watched as Wimbledon had won the Southern League championship and gone on to move up through the divisions to the First. They were elected to the League in 1977 on the back of some astonishing Cup performances, notably a win at Burnley and a draw at Leeds, and no chairman was able any longer to invoke the old pals' act faced with public affection for the Dons' efforts. It had to be us soon.

The first season at the Wessex saw a new system: promotion to and demotion from the Football League for one lucky and one unlucky club. Lincoln City had just been relegated from the Fourth Division and were the first visitors. They were comfortably dispatched 3–0 in front of a crowd of 3600. Indeed, the Terras went on to win their first five games to storm to the top of the table.

It was too good to be true. The pitch had been laid on the site of an underground spring and it burst. For several months the pitch was unplayable and a variety of grounds in the south-west had to be rented. In what Steve Claridge described as the most frightening night of his career, there was one notorious match at Bournemouth against Wealdstone when a brawl broke out. A certain Vinnie Jones was in the Wealdstone side.

Results tailed off and so did the team, finishing tenth.

Now it got serious. The money from the sale of the ground had been swallowed up. Players came and went. The stadium no longer yielded the same income as the old ground, with people only coming out there to drink profit-making drinks on match days, rather than using the old town-centre location every night. Relegation from the Alliance, precursor to the Conference, back to the Southern League inevitably followed.

The nineties was a dark decade, a good one to miss for someone whose jobs for *The Daily Telegraph*, *Independent on Sunday* and *The Observer* now took him round the world covering football. I always kept an eye out, made the odd visit, but relegation to a regional division of the Southern League, promotion, relegation back, promotion again was hard to keep track of. Managers and players arrived and departed in anonymity. We even gave Frank Worthington, of Leicester City and Elvis-impersonator fame, a few games in his early forties.

We had flown too close to the sun. Money had run out, ambition scaled down. From being one of the top ten non-League clubs in England, we had become so ordinary, so lifeless, so resigned to underachievement. So weary.

I was weary, too; weary of seeing other, smaller clubs outstripping us. Even clubs like Forest Green Rovers and Farnborough were in the Conference, surviving on gates of 600 or 700.

Now we we were forced to compete, and not on equal terms, with teams such as Bashley, Salisbury City and Dorchester. Dorchester's chocolate-box ground, designed to fit in with Prince Charles's vision of Olde Englande built at Poundbury, served football fans inadequately. Weymouth was East Berlin to Dorchester's West.

What made it all worse was Yeovil. Once our equals, it galled that they had left us behind. They had just won the Conference title, and reached the Football League. Before us. Now they were a thoroughly professional club and team, on and off the field. Their gates were regularly 6000, even 7000.

Yeovil was a town that had a population of around 40,000. Weymouth, the Isle of Portland and surrounding villages totalled more than 60,000 in these days of growth. Weymouth was a working town, a seaside resort that attracted up to 250,000 people in the summer when people came from miles around to witness its celebrated carnival. The success of Asda, purveyor to the proletariat, showed its blue-collar credentials. And working towns are football towns.

As I contemplate it all, I gaze around the car park again, freezing but not daring to turn on the car engine for warmth in case they hear in the boardroom and think I am doing a runner. I wonder what those two yachts are doing over there parked in the corner, why the Supporters' Club Portakabin has become so tatty. Think it would be nice to put up a big WFC sign on the side of the stand as proud statement of who we are.

I muse on Dad's warning, issued breathlessly as his emphysema is worsening, that these are men capable of making you look like a fool. My partner Vikki, wondering what is going on with what is supposed to be a formality, arrives thoughtfully to keep me company in the car park.

And then my mobile rings. Mr Archer informs me that the board of directors of Weymouth Football Club are ready to receive me again.

CHAPTER THREE

Dad

Dad was in his 'I told you so' mood when I got back to his house with Vikki. On the the way, we had taken in the offices of the *Dorset Echo*, just across the industrial estate from the Wessex, to speak to the sports editor Paul Baker. I had a feeling all hell might break loose the next day and I wanted to give my side of the story.

The board had turned me down. That is to say, they had rejected the rescue package. Not enough money, apparently. They – or rather the back of Steve McDonald's envelope – thought it was £100,000 up front rather than £30,000 now and the rest raised over a season. It showed their short-termism and current desperation. To heck with all the rest, the revitalisation of the club. They wanted money now.

They did offer me the position of vice-chairman, but did not want Matt McGowan back on the board after previous dust-ups with him. In other words, they wanted my ideas, my contacts, my sponsorship leads and the money that wasn't enough, but without conceding any power or responsibility to anyone else.

I was angry, particularly with the chairman Terry Bennett, and told them so. After Mick Archer had announced the board's terms to me, I could not hold my tongue. They were issuing terms to me? They had admitted, by telling of the debt in the local paper, they were floundering, had run out of ideas.

There was no way, I said, I was going to be Bennett's No. 2, thus being associated with this boorish figurehead. Neither, I added, would Steve Claridge pour money into a club being run this way. Nor would I want Tony Adams, with his immaculate reputation, involved. I got up and left. As I did, I told them I was going to the *Echo* as I felt that fans had a right to know what was going on at the club. Were I a journalist covering the meeting, I would have described myself as storming out.

Dad had warned me what to expect if I went swimming with sharks. 'They'll turn you over,' he had said. Not me, I believed. I was tougher and smarter than he or they thought. Besides, Higson had promised me the proposal would go through.

As I sat in the living room with Vikki and Dad, I noticed a tear fall from the corner of his eye. I went over and put an arm round his shoulder. 'You're more upset about this than I am, aren't you?' I said. 'Get off,' he said, any pain a private matter.

Hell did break loose the next day. The *Echo* printed my side of the proceedings accurately enough but, I later found out, Paul Baker had been summoned to the ground for the board's hastily constructed statement. The gist of it, not delivered until nearly 2 a.m., was Bennett's comment that Ridley's consortium 'was not to be trusted'. Why, I wondered, would they offer the post of vice-chairman to a man not to be trusted? They also reckoned that Claridge would come to the club for them in the future anyway. They could dream on.

The phone kept ringing. Claridge wondered what was going on. Tony Adams thought I was better off out of it. Darren Campbell, the Olympic sprinter who had once played for Weymouth for a season, was a contact and could not believe the board had voted against progress. He offered to help in any way he could.

My sister, Melanie, rang. Had I seen the website, she wondered? I did not even know what it was but now she introduced me to the dubious delights of the independent fans' forum, Terras Talk, on www.terrastalk.co.uk. The view of fans was mixed, but there was considerable support for me, so disillusioned with the club were many. Quite a few pointed out that no one could do any worse, surely, than the current bunch with the team fast heading for relegation.

Then there was Duncan Stewart, whom I had never met. He appeared to be some kind of self-appointed local spokesman who liked to think of himself as being close to the board. Every club has at least one, who will be recognizable to fans on the terraces and websites everywhere. I would later come to recoil from his foghorn voice. He wrote the most offensive, poisonous and untrue postings. Claridge and Adams were gamblers and drunks, he said. All Ridley's consortium lacked was a paedophile.

I was offended but not deterred, even then. But that night I could not sleep and did the only thing I knew. I got up at 2 a.m. and wrote down all my thoughts and feelings. By lunchtime, I had polished it into a piece for the *Echo* and they agreed to use it.

I wrote that Claridge and Adams had both told me to walk away. 'Forget them' – or another word beginning with f – was the gist of their response to the board turning down my offer. But Darren Campbell had told me to keep fighting, which was more in tune with my own stubborn thinking. 'And I so fight on,' I said. 'If the fans of Weymouth Football Club and people with the prosperity of the town at heart want me to, that is.'

I answered the scepticism on the website – said I understood it, given the way the club had run its affairs for so long. Some of it hurt. I defended Claridge, Adams and Matt McGowan, who now decided that he no longer wished to be involved, given the controversy. I promised them that I did not want, as some were suggesting, to make a killing from a new stadium development. But I was worried about the stadium, that we could go into it as a relegated club and it could become a millstone.

'Some people throw money at racehorses,' I said. 'I choose to put mine into my football club. This football club. Along the way, I expect some fun and a run for my money. I do not want to own the club, nor make a profit. I want to be part of a happy, harmonious group. Call me naive.

'But this is not just about money. Football is littered with clubs who have thrown money at a problem and still failed. This is also about bringing in a quality of personnel, of people with class, experience and expertise, so that this town can have a football team to be proud of and appropriate to a population this size.'

I added that since the story of my failed rescue package had broken – it was not a takeover, I insisted – a number of businessmen had contacted me offering help. It was true. I had had the offer of some financial support both locally and from a couple of exiled fans.

That night, a bitterly cold one, Dad and I walked into the Wessex for a hastily arranged friendly against Exeter City – the club needed the bar revenue from a crowd of about 150 – with our heads held high. Dave Higson even came to speak to me. Later on the website, Duncan Stewart accused us of not paying. We had been late, because Dad thought he could only manage the second half, and the turnstiles were closed. We could find no one to pay and the doors were open. The next day I sent a cheque to the club. Stewart claimed it was because he had 'outed' me. I was getting a flavour of some of the people and some of the problems around the club.

It certainly all kicked off a debate on the letters' page of the *Echo*. About two to one were in my favour; time for a change, new thinking and all that. One letter intrigued me. An old school colleague in Dorchester, Keith Miller, now vice-chairman of Dorchester Town, lent his considerable weight to preserving the status quo at Weymouth, backing the current board and rejecting me. I wondered why someone at our local rival did not want Weymouth moving forward and found an easy answer. His much smaller club needed us at their level for the revenue our supporters provided them from local derbies. He surely dreaded us outstripping them.

I returned to my home in St Albans and got on with my day job as a football writer for *The Observer*. On the Thursday, my phone rang. It was Dave Higson – could I get down to Weymouth the next day; the board had had a rethink and wanted to offer me the chairmanship. I could not, I said, I was busy with work but I would be down on the Monday.

The next day, he rang me again. They had had a rethink on the rethink. The offer of the chair was being withdrawn. They had forgotten they had a meeting with another potential investor the following week. My anger soon turned to amusement when I contemplated how the club was being run by such indecisive men. I began to realise that I couldn't work with them. I was sure that, panicked by my rescue attempt, they had gone out to seek an alternative in the face of a growing local opinion that my bid should have been accepted and were seeking to buy themselves time.

I told them that this changing their minds three times in a week was unacceptable to me. I said that unless they could tell me before 2 p.m. tomorrow – a Saturday when I was covering Southampton v. Bolton Wanderers – whether they wanted me or not, then I would withdraw. At 1 p.m. on Saturday, Higson rang to say they couldn't make a decision. Unknown to me, they then issued a statement to the local paper saying I was trying to 'bulldoze' them but the door was still open.

On the Sunday, I was getting ready to attend a dinner in honour of Tony Adams at the Savoy Hotel in London when my mobile rang. It was Geoff Butler, the Weymouth manager. He had heard the door was still open. What were my plans for him, should I come in as chairman? Everything would be under review, I told him, I could give him no reassurances. It was known that I liked the Tiverton Town manager Martyn Rogers, once a player at Weymouth and who had immeasurably improved the Devon club, taking them to Wembley for the FA Vase final. At times the conversation became heated, Butler haranguing me for my lack of knowledge of the game. I felt like saying that if he knew so much about it, why were Weymouth in the relegation zone?

It was time to close that door, for now. It – or rather this group of men – was upsetting me, Vikki and my Dad. Over the next few weeks, Steve McDonald resigned honourably from the board, having promoted my plan. The club was looking for a new investor and had spoken to a man once involved with Bournemouth when they went through a financial crisis before being taken over by a group which inherited a debt of £4 million to him.

The board also turned to Asda, such were the finances at the club, to try to get the £70,000 annual payment, for an agreement in principle to develop the ground and due at the end of the season, brought forward. They were even contemplating asking the developers acting as middlemen to invest and join the board. It reeked of desperation.

I was coming to Weymouth more often now. My mother had died a year earlier, suddenly, shockingly, in her sleep at the age of sixty-nine of peritonitis from a perforated ulcer that no one even knew she had. I had been stunned, along with my sister, but my father had taken on an altogether different personality. He had become subdued to the point

of depression, spending his days watching television, interrupted by a few evenings at the pub.

Back in 2002, I had taken him, along with Jack, to the
FA Cup final between Arsenal and Liverpool at Cardiff's
Millennium Stadium. This year, to try to cheer him up, I
now took him and Jack to the Carling Cup final between
Tottenham and Blackburn, Jack being a Spurs fan. Dad was
still worried about the prostate cancer returning but his
breathing had become a greater problem. I had to get
there very early to park the car in a multi-storey as close as
possible. He could walk no more than fifty yards before
having to rest.

Sad and lonely, Dad needed company. My sister came in
to see him every day and I resolved to come down to visit
him as often as I could. I wanted to get to know him better
now, anyway, and enjoy together the greater peace that we
both had in our lives.

Fiercely, stubbornly independent, he would always
insist on cooking, usually something from the freezer. We
would sit and watch TV together. *Trisha* in the morning,
Des and Mel at lunchtime, *Countdown* in the afternoon,
him enjoying his seven, even eight, letter words. It became a
safe, warm ritual in the bubble of his little two-bedroomed
modern house in the close. If there was a game on at the
Wessex in the evening, we would toddle off together. If
not, we would go up to his local and watch a match on the
television. We were pretty typical, I suppose. As many
fathers and sons do, we found it hard to express feelings
towards each other and one way was through the shared
experience of football.

There was a game one Tuesday night in early March,
against Ilkeston Town. With Dad also having a hospital
appointment on the Wednesday, it was a good chance to
visit. I phoned Higson, asked if I could meet with him to see
what the latest state of play at the club was.

Not good, judging by an appalling display of aerobatics against even lowlier Ilkeston; a brilliantly volleyed, out-of-context, late goal by one of our few decent players, the muscular striker Lee Phillips, rescuing a point. Meeting with Higson, along with Archer, at their factory on the industrial estate near the ground, he agreed it was time for a change. Archer nodded assent. The club was still losing around £2000 a week despite having cut the wage bill back to around £4000. Leave Terry Bennett to him, Higson added, he would work on him.

A week later, Higson rang. He had, he said, convinced Bennett that the Ridley plan was the only way forward. After all the acrimony and the struggle, it was done in a five-minute phone call. I was to become chairman of Weymouth Football Club.

I agreed, with only six weeks to go to the end of the season, that if relegation was to be avoided, the club should not be disrupted. Let Bennett, along with Butler, take the credit for keeping the club up. I still wanted rid of Butler, though, and I told Higson that I would be working on plans for next season.

With that in mind, I had lunch with Tony Adams. Yes, he said, he would act as a consultant, find some players, maybe come down to do some coaching sessions. I could not bring myself to ask for money from him. I put myself to the task of producing a glossy action plan document to show potential investors and sponsors.

I also met with Nigel Winship, a sharp young figure with his own information technology company, another lifelong fan, who had offered help when my first attempt to take over the club had failed. He believed in my aims, was willing to invest in a consortium and become financial director, and also introduced me to another friend and fan, Pete Daire, head of marketing at *Sky Sports* with responsibility for the sponsorship of the clubs in which Sky had an interest,

Newcastle, Leeds, Aston Villa and Manchester City, and a very bright young thing. The three of us worked on a sponsorship strategy for the next season.

A football agent friend also suggested to me that a good mate of his might be interested in sponsoring the club. It was none other than Ray Kelvin, the man behind the hugely successful Ted Baker menswear company. I duly met this eccentric and creative figure at the company's Camden Town headquarters and gave him a copy of the action plan. He was impressed by it all, he said, had often thought about getting into football. However, the meeting came to naught. It was typical of the response I was getting from some potential backers. I had no success to show them after all. All I had was hopes and dreams.

I did have more success with a television production company called Seek. I had worked with them on documentaries for Channel 4 about Tony Adams and Paul Gascoigne and they had gone to the BBC with an idea for a series about following people in the game for a season. The working title was 'Kicks' and they were interested in the Weymouth story.

Then, on a Tuesday in late March, I met with Martyn Rogers at Mick Archer's country house hotel near Dorchester. I wanted him as manager for next season, I said and offered him a package. He would be right for the club, I felt. A West Country man, he knew the whole scene in the south-west, could get players who were value for money. He was also Tiverton's commercial manager and we needed that, too. He would think about it.

Technically, I suppose, it was that process known in modern football as tapping-up – when someone from one club bypasses official channels and approaches another under contract somewhere else – even though I had no official position at the club yet and this was a private, informal meeting. But it happens all the time, is a part of the game. Perhaps the Tiverton chairman would do a similar thing were he looking for a new manager. Exploratory talks are commonplace. If both parties have some sort of agreement, then the official approach is made and terms discussed between clubs more fully then.

Later that night, Martyn and I both went to the Weymouth v. Bath City game, though in separate cars. He had a game coming up against us and wanted to check us out. Dad was feeling the cold and didn't fancy it. At half-time, Martyn and I did coincide for a drink. It seemed ridiculously clandestine not to talk to each other and, in a near empty bar because of a low crowd, it was duly noticed. Fortunately, we eked out a 2–0 win, one that would prove to be crucial in the relegation struggle.

The next day I was due to meet with a group of Weymouth businessmen, from builders to plumbers to electrical contractors, who had also read my article in the *Dorset Echo* and were interested in becoming involved. They knew how much the club meant to the town, how much it had gone backwards, and how much potential it had. Over coffee at a beachside café – it was a beautiful spring morning and I realized again how much I loved this town – they listened politely but none would commit. Again, the problem was hopes and dreams rather than the reality of any success. I had nothing to show them but my passion and commitment. It wasn't yet enough.

My sister told me I would meet plenty of people like that in Weymouth these days; men who gave the impression of money, talked about it, but were reluctant to put their hands in their pockets. Mel knew the local market inside out. She had worked in advertising at the *Echo* for twenty years.

After that, I was due to go back to St Albans but just couldn't. Dad's coughing and breathing were alarming me. He had an appointment with a consultant at the County Hospital in Dorchester the next day and I knew I had to be there with him. Hearing him inching his way up the stairs to bed that night was sad and disturbing.

He had been pale and gaunt for some time now, but only the next morning did I fully realize how thin he was. Once downstairs, he could not face the trip back up to wash, ready for his appointment. I washed him at the kitchen sink, horrified at the deep hollows that were his armpits as the flannel disappeared into the void.

By now I was really frightened, though did not want to show it as I could see the fear on his face as he gasped for breath and I did not wish to worsen things. I got him into the car with my sister's help and dropped them at the door of the hospital while I found somewhere to park the car.

It was meant to be a routine appointment but this was far from routine. I went to see the receptionist, told her that my father was in great distress with his breathing and needed urgent help. She took one look at him, contacted the consultant, and told me to get him round the corridor to the consultant's office where he would be seen immediately. This time, whether he liked it or not, he would not be walking, and I located a wheelchair.

It took the consultant two minutes to order an oxygen cylinder for him, about another three to arrange a bed on one of the wards. In between, he asked Dad about his smoking. With the denial of the addict, he told him it was about ten a day. 'And the rest,' I, a packet-a-day-at-least man, muttered.

Soon Dad was upstairs on a mixed ward. By now, my fear had turned to relief. I finally recognised how seriously ill he was, now knew that he was going to get some proper professional attention.

'When you are out of here,' I told him, 'we are going to get you a bungalow. How does that sound?' 'Bloody marvellous,' he said. 'I'm glad I won't have to go up those fucking stairs tonight. I'd have been in the shit.' I suddenly realised how Dad's language became worse when he was frightened.

Dad had never fully conveyed to me before the ordeal it had become. He was all right. He would manage. He pissed me off. Or rather, I was pissed off with myself for not intervening sooner, not noticing more. I had allowed his desire for independence to cloud my judgement.

We chose his meal for the evening, some breaded plaice. I watched him wince and yelp when they stuck a needle in his skinny wrist to take a blood sample and a tear, quickly fought back as he would want, came to my eye. Mel and I then headed back home to pick up a suitcase of pyjamas and toiletries for him. On his table, next to his favourite chair with its Homer Simpson groove, were a packet of cigarettes and a pouch of hand-rolling tobacco. I threw them away in disgust.

Dinner was being served when we returned. 'How's the plaice?' I asked. 'Like leather,' he replied in between the three morsels he could eat. 'Tough as arseholes.' It was always Dad's simile. Mean people were tight as arseholes, the men running the football club were daft as arseholes. It made me smile.

Mel and I also needed to eat, and good food was always a source of comfort. There was no escaping the football club, though. On the way out, we ran into Ian Hutchinson, a Weymouth midfield player and a porter at the hospital. He had a good left foot. A north-easterner, Hutch had stayed at the Russell Hotel when he first came to the town, Dad getting to know him while working there. I told him what we were doing here. 'It's not looking good,' I said. Hutch was one of the nice guys. He looked genuinely concerned.

I took Mel to the best restaurant in Dorchester, the Mock Turtle, and for a while our worries eased, our spirits lifted. When we returned to the ward, there was the momentary horror of an empty bed to confront. But he had only been moved to the High Dependency Unit.

Quickly we wound our way through corridors to a locked door, where you needed to ring a bell to gain entry. We explained who we were and were shown to his bedside. He was sleeping, stabilised we were told. Tubes and wires led from his body to machines, like old computer leads to a power point, to monitor heart and breathing. A small breathing mask covered his nose and mouth. This was a warm bubble of a room, containing only six beds, with attentive staff and specialist equipment. They had done a good job of creating a comforting and comfortable environment in what was potentially a frightening location.

The staff suggested we go home and sleep. I couldn't face Dad's house alone and opted for Mel's sofa but there was to be little sleep. And I was ashamed by some of the thoughts that raced through my head.

Some were harmless: better cancel Dad's milk and papers. Some, selfish, annoyed me: I won't be working on Saturday now, wonder if I can make it up to Worcester v. Weymouth? Some filled me with self-loathing: if Dad does die, I can sell his house and put the money into the football club. It's hard to sleep when a callous sentiment like that insinuates itself.

Given his breathing, his prostate cancer and his loss of weight, I always thought that he might go one winter. I didn't think it would be now, though. I want you to come to the football and sit in the directors' box for the first time in your life, Dad.

I went back to his house early in the morning to leave a note for the milkman before going back to the hospital. I checked his bedroom to see if there was anything else he might need and noticed an empty crisp packet by his bed. I was surprised that he ate crisps in bed. Picking it up, it felt as if it still had some in and I peered into the bag. It was half full of sputum and other glutinous contents of his lungs.

I choked back vomit as I carried it at arm's length to the bin.

Dad was awake when I got to the hospital. By now his skin was dry, his lips peeling and Mel rubbed moisturiser over his body and salve on his lips. He could take sips of tea only between gasps of oxygen from the face mask. Some ten years earlier he had had a mild stroke and been parked in a hospital bed, in the days when Weymouth had a proper hospital, opposite a man then in Dad's condition now. He recalled the time. 'I vowed I'd never get like that,' he said, forlornly.

We had a meeting in a private room with the consultant. You know how serious things are when there are boxes of tissues on every surface in the room. 'Basically, your father is dying,' he said, matter of fact. 'I know,' I said, pretending I had faced up to the prospect. Dad was coming to know it, too. That morning he had commanded me to stop smoking. 'I'm not going to die,' he had also insisted. By the early evening, it had turned to 'How long have I got?' I couldn't, wouldn't, answer. Nor would the consultant, to the first question relatives ask.

'I'm frightened,' he had said during the afternoon. It took me aback. I had sensed fear in my father at times but never heard him talk of it, never considered him to be unduly troubled by it. When you are a boy, it is you who is frightened. Your father is strong, physically and emotion-ally, and somehow the vision stays with you. Mine was stocky and powerful, a bull of a footballer, I thought, unlike this emaciated figure.

I went out of the hospital to have a cigarette. How could I do that, with Dad's lungs giving out? Something about a 'dark loyalty' to family behaviour, no matter how damag-ing, some psychologists will tell you. Mel told me later that he now said that he wanted to be cremated, so that his ashes could be placed at the top of Mum's grave. 'I don't want it dug up,' he told her.

Mel's husband, Simon, Weymouth through and through, whom Dad loved because he took care of his daughter, came to visit after his shift working for a local printing company. 'How are you, Bob?' 'Fucked,' said Dad. Hutch popped in at the end of his own shift. 'We'll win for you tomorrow, Bob,' he said. Dad smiled. He doubted it, I could see. 'Have a good game,' was all he could say.

He was tired, we were tired. 'Get some sleep, Dad,' I said. 'I don't want to go to sleep,' he said. 'I might not wake up.' As I left, a man in the reception area, recognizing me from my picture in the local paper, approached me. 'Got much of a chance at Worcester tomorrow, have we?' he enquired. There was no escaping this football club.

The next day, Saturday, was the longest day. I arrived to find Dad agitated, trying to get out of bed. He was disorientated but could no longer speak and was having hallucinations every few hours. I asked if there was anything they could give him. They suggested diamorphine to form a sedative, pain-killing cocktail with the oxygen through the mask and I agreed. Maybe it was more for me than him. I could not bear to see him so distressed nor hear him so in agony. As he struggled for breath, his lungs vibrated, his voicebox converting the noise to deep-throated coughs and groans. It was not watching him die that hurt so much. It was hearing him die. As a kid, I had seen my dad drunk. Now I would see him more naturally incapacitated. He gripped my hand in terror.

The day passed slowly, Dad no longer able to converse. Mel and I took turns to sit with him. The machines and drips, amid the warmth of the unit, were mesmeric. My heart sank when the pulse reading went over 100, or below 90. Did it mean anything? I watched the drip of glucose descend millimetre by millimetre.

At one point, they put a bigger face mask on him, to try to get more oxygen into him, but he rebelled, ripped it off. He was claustrophobic, terrified by the way it covered his face. His refusal to take it was to be another nail in his coffin.

Then, he caught me making notes: observations about him and me, lists of 'things to do' at Weymouth. 'Writing a story are you?' he somehow managed to ask.

Except for Dad becoming agitated every few hours for ten minutes or so, the somnolence was interrupted only by the landing outside of an air ambulance, by the football results flashing up on a TV screen in the corner. 'Weymouth lost 3–1 at Worcester, Dad,' I said. 'We're in real trouble now. I'll sort them out for you.'

The staff now told me he was likely to be stable overnight so I made a dash home to St Albans to get fresh clothes and a night's sleep in my own bed. Between bouts of tears on the drive home came anger at not having insisted on that bungalow after Mum had died; at not going with him to his GP a year ago to tell him how serious it was getting; at allowing him to shop, cook and clean, when he should have had more help, not least from me; at having agreed to the diamorphine that seemed to be giving him such bad side effects. Now he was in a virtual coma. At least when he was agitated, trying to get out of the bed, trying to rip out the drips, he was alive.

My phone rang at 4.30 a.m. and I stubbed my toe painfully as I rushed downstairs to answer it. It was indeed the hospital. Dad had taken a turn for the worse. I dressed in a daze, drove the 140 miles west with the dawn rising in my rear-view mirror, fearing I had broken a toe as the pain stabbed each time I pressed hard on the accelerator.

When I got there he was gone from the High Dependency Unit and a chill went through me for an instant. Yet again, he had just been moved to another ward. I couldn't work out whether this was because he was getting better or because he was a hopeless case and someone with a chance of survival needed his bed.

When I found the ward, he was stable but still having the vivid hallucinations every few hours. The nurse had been very worried, but then I told them I wanted to be there whenever *It*, whenever anything, happened. I needed to see the consultant, I said. I had questions. I would have to do with a locum, it being Sunday, and I would have to wait several hours.

Dad was on an ordinary ward again, opposite a kindly old lady called Florrie, whose Dorset burr told the nurses that she didn't want to be any trouble. Next to him was an old gent, soon to be visited by his family, the Foghorns from Upper Class in the Marsh. The teenaged kids – 'I so do not like hospitals,' they whispered to each other – told loudly, in those unembarrassed voices that speak with the self-certainty of the moneyed, of trips to Mexico and Tanzania and discussed with him the outcome of the Boat Race.

'What time's kickoff?' he asked of that afternoon's rugby match between England and Ireland. Mel looked at me and smiled. 'About every four hours with our Dad,' she said.

Finally the locum came. Dad had about five hours to live, said the young man, looking about the same age as the policemen these days. I was numb. I wanted him to die with what was left of his dignity and as pain-free as possible, I said. Was there somewhere more private than this ward? They would see what they could do.

A few hours later, he was moved to an anteroom behind the nurses' station. It was stark, with blue lino on the floor and a TV suspended from the ceiling, but at least it was private. Now there was just one tube, just one hole in his arm, for the diamorphine to go into. No longer were there any monitors for his heart or breathing.

I sat at his bedside and gazed on this, to me, once powerful man now in a coma. They had removed his dentures (he had had them since his twenties, in the days when they removed teeth simply for convenience) and his cheeks were concave. His legs were as thin as corner flags and I could see under a sheet, the straight-line outlines of his bones. There was little flesh on them any more. There was blood in the urine bag attached to the side of the bed. His left eye was badly bloodshot. Now when the hallucinations hit him, he barely had the strength to raise his body in protest.

I craned over him at times, listening for the slightest change in his breathing, wondering if that faint snoring was a death rattle. (I had never known what that was, until watching my Uncle George die. For an hour before his last breath, a deep, unnerving, rasping sound emerged continually from his throat.)

In the evening, Simon, a burly man's man but with the sensitive, emotional side that often gets hidden under a working-class cloak, came to say goodbye to Dad. Mel and I expected to be doing the same at any minute. But he clung on. He was not going gently into that long goodnight. I sent Mel home for some rest and soon began to wish I hadn't.

For it was to be the longest, loneliest, most painful night of my life.

At about 1 a.m., Dad discovered a reserve of strength and, hallucinating again, lifted himself from his bed, mumbling and grumbling, his eyes wide open to offer a window to the terrors playing out in his mind. He strained to lift himself out of bed and I found myself pinning him down. It was easy, given his frail state, but deeply offensive to me. In an annoyed moment, I had once done that to Jack as a toddler, desperate for him to go to sleep. I felt ashamed, anew, that the thought of smothering him with a pillow, to give him a peaceful end, crossed my mind. Fleetingly, for a moment, I think I understood mercy killing.

No longer able to bear it, I went to the nursing station and begged them for help. They took over and, exhausted, I fell asleep for two hours on a small sofa in the corridor.

Mel returned early in the morning and I went outside for

a cigarette and to make some calls. I told my ex-wife, Jo, an experienced nurse, now a health visitor, what was happening. She wondered why they were no longer giving him glucose. Lack of any sustenance could be the cause of his distress, she suggested. Diamorphine might also be causing the hallucinations. I phoned Vikki. She told me she was coming down from London to be there. Dad had always liked Vikki.

I felt better, the more so when I returned to find four nurses bathing Dad, changing sheets and installing a bed with metal railings on the sides so that he could not clamber or fall out. They had responded to my throwing of the toys out of the pram. He was now calmer and as Mel and I sat with him peace descended for a while, disturbed only by, of all things, a long brush scraping at the window. When I looked out, a window cleaner was reaching up.

I was still angry, though, and met with the consultant. Why were we told two days ago that Dad had only hours to live? I felt that my father was being allowed simply to fade away, and in discomfort. I thought that he should have nourishment and that the medication was wrong. The consultant pointed out to me that medicine was not a precise science, more a combination of art, with its intuition, and science, and a time of death should not have been given out.

I was pleased that I had spoken my feelings, not been intimidated by medics, and it seemed to pay off. The consultant said they would give him a saline drip and change the medication. He could haemorrhage, they said, but they would see if he might rally. It was a risk worth taking. He had one last chance.

I went to Mel's for a bath, and had a meal with Vikki at the best restaurant in Weymouth, Perry's on the quayside, before returning for another night's vigil, taken in two-hour shifts alternating with Mel, times when I could talk to him, about me and him, about life, about football. I had heard that people in comas can hear everything. I told him I loved him. All was calmer, the drip and new medication soothing. I dozed.

I no longer felt so alone. Vikki helped Mel in brightening up the room with flowers and family photographs. We even managed a roast lunch in the canteen. Vikki was wearing a Weymouth FC sweatshirt for warmth and a woman sitting opposite noticed us.

'Are you that man?' she asked. Indeed, I was the man trying to take over Weymouth Football Club. 'Something needs to be done there,' she said. She and her daughter had helped other supporters paint one of the bars there, she said, and received not much thanks for it. 'In fact, the chairman said he preferred it the way it was.' There was no escaping this football club.

I even managed to catch up with what was happening in the world. The ITN correspondent Terry Lloyd – I had encountered him on a couple of journalistic jobs, nice man – had been killed in Iraq. I was also shocked by American soldiers, brought up on PlayStation games, were whooping it up atop a tank having won a battle. Most important on the news agenda, it seemed, was a blister on David Beckham's foot that was troubling him ahead of the crucial England v. Turkey World Cup qualifier the next night. Ten p.m. brought the news that Weymouth had lost 3–0 at Martyn Rogers's Tiverton. I might well be taking over a relegated club.

With Dad now stabilised, we entertained hopes over the next twenty-four hours that he might even pull out of this somehow. It was but denial, the first stage of grief.

Now Dad's breathing was shallow but he looked com-fortable as England played Turkey on the TV. England scored, and I told him the good news. 'Do you think he's getting better?' Mel asked. I smiled. 'No I don't,' I whispered, mindful that he might hear. Half an hour later

I stood up to check him, holding my hand across his mouth.

There was no warmth, no breath. He was dead.

'I think he's gone,' I said. Mel, Vikki and I exchanged silent looks, checking each other's reaction. There was none but a thousand thoughts raced between brains, behind uncertain faces. England scored again. I now had a bigger reason to remember the night of Wayne Rooney's debut for England on 2 April 2003. Mel and I kissed Dad on the forehead. His skin was now smooth and he smelt fragrant. The old joke was true: this was the best he had looked for ages. I went to fetch a nurse, who came to confirm his death.

After spending seven days and nights in this place, we were out of there quickly, with almost unseemly haste. In a side room, a nurse told us about the procedure now, but little sank in. All of a sudden I was back at his house, in the spare bedroom, unable to sleep, hearing every noise. Why do floorboards only creak at night?

Gallows humour takes over sometimes, as a deflection from the worst of the pain. Mel relayed how she had told her youngest son, Lee, of the time Grandad died. 'So he missed England's second goal, then?' came the reply. Mel phoned the undertaker. 'We've lost Dad,' she said. 'Have you looked in the Royal Oak?' I said flippantly in the background.

A few days later I returned to the hospital to pick up his things. His watch, his toiletries, his little suitcase containing the pyjamas that were never needed. It felt a sad little collection.

The funeral was a dignified, even uplifting, occasion, certainly for me. Dad's twin sisters, Margaret and Mary, and their husbands, Brian and Ian, travelled down from Northumberland. Uncle Hugh, Dad's half-brother and the last remaining of the five sons, was ill himself and unable to leave County Durham.

The Weymouth club captain, John Waldock, also from

the north-east, agreed to read the Dylan Thomas poem 'Death Shall Have No Dominion', and Hutch and another Terras stalwart who knew my dad, Mark Robinson – called Curly, as footballers coin nicknames, because he had straight hair – also attended. Afterwards, I asked the driver of the hearse to pass by the football ground on the way to the crematorium. Dave Higson had arranged for the club flag to be flown at half mast.

Because I am embarrassed by vicars who fumble over their eulogies of people they often do not know, I gave the address myself. It felt cleansing, healing, having spent ten days feeling the numbness of an orphan – funny, how that concept is difficult to associate with middle age.

I told of Dad's life and his love for football, both playing and watching, and how he had done his duty by giving it to me. I caught a tearful Jack's eyes as I said it. I was grateful for my dad and my son. I was sorry, I said to a sizeable crowd gathered at the church, that Dad would not get to see the better times that were around the corner for the football club. I hoped.

PART TWO

Love is all you need?

People will come. They'll arrive at your door as innocent as children, longing for the past ... For it is money they have and peace they lack ... They will sit where they sat when they were children and cheered their heroes. They'll watch the game and it will be as if they dipped themselves in magic waters. The memories will be thick and they will have to brush them from their faces. People will come. This field, this game, is part of our past. It reminds us of all that was once good and could be again. People will most definitely come.

James Earl Jones as Terence Mann,
Field of Dreams

CHAPTER FOUR

April shower

Knowing that I was going to be chairman and watching the team struggle through that spring, relegation threatening and unable to intervene, was agony. At least that's what the fan in me felt, the fan who went to Dave Higson one morning at Park Engineering and offered to pay the £300 wages of a new player for the rest of the season if it would help to get someone decent in.

But with my new head of chairman-in-waiting on, I could not help musing privately that it might be no bad thing if we were relegated. Is this what they think higher up the scale, when they ponder the increased costs of promotion, the decreased costs of relegation, when it comes to players' wages?

Many of those clubs have taken the easy option and gone into administration and it crossed my mind with Weymouth. It would mean that any new money coming in could go into the club and revitalise it, rather than pay off the mistakes of the previous regime. It would be dishonourable, however. Local businesses should be paid for the services they had rendered the club. In addition, welshing would be to lose what little was left of the goodwill from people we would need to woo anew.

I also thought fleetingly that if we were to go down, it would mean that we could hire a cheaper manager, have no need to increase the wage bill. We would be in a regional division of the Southern League and probably be challenging for the title anyway. And I knew Weymouth fans would turn out for a team at the top, no matter the level. They had in 1997, when the team took the Western Division title by winning their last fifteen games, with gates climbing to as high as 2800.

People, younger fans mainly, still saw it as a huge, memorable achievement, pointing to securing promotion at Baldock Town (for goodness sake) as a high point, even though it was akin to, say, Sheffield United once having won the old Fourth Division. It reminded me of a wonderful introduction written at the time by a colleague at *The Guardian*, Matthew Engel.

'Seeing Sheffield United in the Fourth Division,' he said, 'is a bit like seeing an old friend in charge of the prison library. "That's all very nice for you, but how on earth did you get here in the first place?" '

No, relegation was too grim to contemplate. Besides, non-League football – actually, I now disliked that term for its patronizing connotations, and these days preferred the FA's new description the 'National Game' – was being restructured the following season.

The Conference, the league below the Football League, had grown in stature down the years with a buoyancy to surpass many down-at-heel clubs in what was now League Two. It would have regional divisions, North and South, below it. To have a reasonable chance of being in the new league, you needed to be in the Premier Division of the Southern League and finish in their top thirteen, or else try to go up through a series of ugly play-offs.

Not that even finishing between fourteenth and seventeenth would be a foregone conclusion, from what I was seeing this spring as we slipped into the bottom four relegation places. Between fingers over my eyes, I watched us eke out a crucial 2–1 win over Welling, the winner scored by a lanky centre forward that Geoff Butler had brought in – not good enough but valuable today – called Michael Jackson. Thriller, indeed.

A 1–0 win at Hednesford, Lee Phillips scoring, was then priceless. The same player scored again in a dreadful 1–1 draw at Bath City on Easter Monday, when I stood on the terraces with Jack. It was still touch and go, but finally, on the penultimate Saturday of the season we reached safety, thanks as much to the failings of others as a 1–1 draw at home to Hastings United.

Now Terry Bennett could stand down with some honour and three days before the final match of the season, at Crawley Town, I was elected chairman at a board meeting, this time without rancour and within minutes. I asked Peter Shaw, in a bridge-building exercise, to become vice-chair, which appeared to flatter him. Bennett, the fish-and-chip man clearly battered by the pressure of the season, would take a couple of months' leave from the club, it was agreed. All knew I was angry with him for his lack of competence and leadership. He had awarded Geoff Butler an extension to his contract even though he knew I was coming in as chairman. Later, the *Echo* reporter covering the club, Matt Pitman, informed me that Bennett had told him, 'That's for fucking Ian Ridley' when approached for a comment about the new deal.

That night, I wondered what I had done, about the commitment I had taken on and where life was taking me. Then a fan posted a message on the website, citing the Dorset motto: 'Who's Afear'd?' It made me smile, gave me renewed purpose.

My mind was all over the place after the events of the week and a two-day whirl of local media interviews. It was strange being on the other side of the fence, but I did know how to give them a headline with a decent quote.

Driving down to Crawley on that first Saturday in May, I suddenly feared I had left the iron in my flat plugged in, having pressed a clean shirt to attend a Weymouth match in suit and tie for the first time in my life. I had to ring my daughter, Alex, in between her maid of honour's duties at my ex-wife's wedding, which was coincidentally that day (I was pleased for her: new beginnings all round), to go round to my flat to check. I had, indeed, left it on and it was red hot.

I had told Geoff Butler the day before that I would not interfere with picking the side but wanted three young local reserve team players, Nathan Walker, Scott Dennis and John Lamb, to make the trip for the experience and to send a message that young, home-grown players could make it with the club. Reluctantly, he agreed. I also asked for five minutes with the team at 1.30 p.m. to outline the future.

By 2.15 p.m., we were still one player short, the veteran midfield player Danny Bailey. He had had the shortest journey to Sussex, from London, but still could not make it on time. It was symptomatic of the lack of professionalism at the club. I finally spoke to them about all being given a chance, if they wanted it, to come with this club as we shot for the Conference and the Football League, in a new stadium, over the next five years. We were on the verge of exciting times, I said.

Clearly inspired by the new chairman, they were a shambles from start to finish and subsided to a 5–0 defeat that could even have been worse. Walker and Lamb played part of the game as substitutes and didn't do badly. We had finished two points clear of relegation, in seventeenth place. 'I wasn't too unhappy,' said Butler. 'I wanted you to see what needs to be done.' I, on the other hand, was unhappy and I didn't like a manager who wasn't after a five-goal thrashing.

In the car park afterwards, I approached Duncan Stewart, now I had put a face to the poison on the website, to try to see if there was common ground, to explain my views about the club. He shouted me down, wouldn't hear me, a large aperture between a moustache and beard firing off a volley. What was he so worried about? What was his interest in seeing a club so down-at-heel? I had my theories. He had liked to think, like some other diehard fans, that he was part of something exclusive, close to the movers and shakers at the club. Now he wouldn't be, for I would not have, nor knew of, such alliances and allegiances. Now there would be more fans – I hoped – at the Wessex and he would just be one of the many, his voice less significant.

We had one more game before the summer break, a testimonial the following Wednesday against the arch-enemies Yeovil Town. It was for our long-serving legend of a striker David Laws, a burly and battling goalscorer, another brought down from the north-east by a previous manager, Graham Carr, and a wonderful servant. Having just won the Conference and been promoted to the League, Yeovil were now our role models, as I wrote in the programme, much as it pained me to do so.

We were awful. I had paid Steve Claridge £250 myself for him to turn out in a Weymouth shirt for Lawsy but despite his quality, laying on a deserving goal for the legend, we were outclassed and lost 5–1. Claridge told me later he was shocked by the standard and the lack of guidance from management.

I wanted to sack Butler after the game (later I heard from Tony Adams that another mutual friend, his former Arsenal colleague Paul Merson, had said to him that he didn't think I'd be much good as a chairman because I was too easy-going to sack anyone) and I consulted the rest of the board. None dissented but they asked me to do it with sensitivity.

As I walked to Butler's tiny office under the stand with him afterwards, I had butterflies in my stomach. All personal feelings aside, I was convinced I was doing the right thing, however, and had chosen this moment so that he had the whole summer to find a new job and, tonight, the chance to say goodbye in person to everyone he knew at the club.

He wasn't too shocked, had seen it coming. It is why, as a shrewd old pro, I suspected he had persuaded Bennett to give him another year's contract in that interim period before I took over. Both, I believe, wanted to make my life as difficult as possible. I said I would give him a reference and we would negotiate a pay-off in due course. I sensed his contempt for me: 'a misguided amateur', he once called me on the phone. But if professionalism was what Butler was about, give me amateurism.

As I left the ground late that night, Gaye, partner of the kit man Pete Dennis, approached me. She was angry and in tears. 'Why have you done this? Geoff was a good manager and a nice man,' she said. I agreed with her on neither count but said only: 'I hope you'll come to see why it had to be done and where we are going now.'

I suddenly felt very callous and very lonely. Even lonelier now that I didn't have my dad to go home to and talk to about football. There was much to do and he wouldn't be here to see it done. I began to realize that a summer break was for others in the game.

Where to start? Apart from paying off some debt and looking in depth at the tangled finances of the club, finding a manager was the obvious priority. The day after I had sacked Butler, my phone suddenly started ringing with applicants on the line. The grapevine works quickly. It was another Southern League manager, who, he told me, had received a text message from Butler the previous night saying simply: 'Sacked'. I would bear him in mind.

I phoned Martyn Rogers again. He ummed and aahed. I liked him not only because of what he had done with the team at Tiverton but also because he was adept at commercial management, operating on a full-time basis. It was what I wanted for Weymouth. I knew it would be a big decision for him, as he would have to move his family across the border from Devon to Dorset, but it was a bigger, better-paid job and I thought that he would jump at it. Given any encouragement, I would approach his chairman for permission to discuss terms. But encouragement was not exactly forthcoming and it concerned me.

There were others. Faxes came into the club, from a former Everton player who had managed in non-League circles in the north-west, from another who had kicked about the West Country for years. I had my eye on another manager and went to watch the FA Trophy final at Villa Park between Burscough, an overachieving village club in Lancashire, and Tamworth. Shaun Teale, once of Weymouth's, Bournemouth's and Aston Villa's defence, had, remarkably, led little Burscough as player/manager to a major achievement at this level.

And, against the odds with Tamworth having just been promoted to the Conference, after winning Weymouth's league by some distance, Burscough won it. Shaun, at the age of thirty-nine, gave a towering display in their back four. I spoke to him afterwards and arranged to meet at a hotel near the Aston Villa training ground later in the week. Yes, he would be interested. He had gone as far as he could at Burscough on limited resources.

Shaun brought his wife to the interview; I brought a copy of the local paper's property supplement to show them as a signal of my seriousness. They loved Weymouth, they said, and would happily move back. One of their children had been born there during Shaun's time as a player with the club. We would get the bonus of him still playing, and still playing well. Perhaps I would ring his chairman.

I also met Kevin Hodges, Dorset-born, long-serving player and then manager at Plymouth Argyle, now an FA regional representative in Bristol. He wanted to get back in the game. I liked his ideas and his dignified manner. I reported back to the board that a shortlist was taking shape.

I spoke to Tony Adams and Steve Claridge as well. It was too much to hope that either would take the position, Tony as his first job in management. However, he would come down to do some coaching and fundraising, he said. Steve had just had a good season with Millwall and was currently in the middle of negotiating a new contract with them. He would not give up his professional career just yet, though now thirty-seven. Shaun Teale would be a good man, he said.

There were many other things that needed to be done. First, to get some money into the club. The overdraft had been running at around £100,000 at the end of the season, on a limit from our bankers of £60,000. The club's debts had been consolidated into one amount with the bank and totalled, on top, around £150,000. We were paying it off, including the interest, at around £2000 a month. Also, there were pressing creditors of another £50,000. In addition, the loans book showed that directors were owed about another £40,000.

It made the total debts some £340,000, not a healthy position. Still, the board wouldn't have entertained me coming in if it had been healthy. Bad as it sounded – and it did, given that income from gates, sponsorship, merchandising and bar takings was painfully thin – it was not in the league of some clubs even at our level. Worcester City's annual accounts would reveal them to be more than £750,000 in the red, and they were a club similar to ourselves in stature and ambition. I felt it was manageable.

Besides, we had just received the £70,000 from the developers, Trent, on behalf of Asda, which brought it down to £270,000 and, crucially, the overdraft to £30,000, enabling us to operate reasonably freely. Now it was time to pay off those creditors and get in the money I had been promised.

As a fan, I had rarely, if ever, been interested in the finances of the football club I supported. I was mainly interested in the team, grew weary of the directors telling us what a difficult position the club was in. I suspect it is the same with every fan up and down the country. They are interested in who the club might sign, how it might do in the next game, the next season.

Now I had to take a crash course and it was fascinating. I quickly realised that the club was undercapitalised. The ground was listed on the balance sheet as being worth £2.2 million, but the twelve acres we owned were certainly worth much more than that. There were, however, only 1.2 million shares in the club, at 50p each, valuing the club at £600,000. It was something that would need to be addressed in the future, I noted, with the club vulnerable to a predator. For now, there were more pressing matters.

Only around 400,000 of the shares had been taken up and I wanted to get that up to at least 600,000 over the next season, to bring in £100,000 of new investment. I duly put in my own initial investment, which I was able to increase to £15,000 for 30,000 shares. It meant I owned around 7.5 per cent of the club. In my first proposal to the club, I had wanted existing board members to put in another £10,000 each but they had refused.

Matt McGowan, after his rejection by the gang of four on the board, was no longer willing to be involved and would sadly not be investing his £10,000, so I was now forced into casting the net wider for investment and new board members. Fortunately, I had found others who believed in my vision of the club.

Steve was still willing to loan the club £10,000 – though it would take a while for me to get it out of him, as I expected – but Nigel Winship was enthusiastic and willing to put in £5000 to start with. Overdraft now down to £10,000.

I had been covering a match at Portsmouth and got talking to their manager, Harry Redknapp, who had been reading about the events along the south coast at Weymouth. He knew a bloke, he said – and Harry always knew a bloke – who was a Terras fanatic and had pots of money, having just sold his company. Kept offering him tickets for Pompey but the bloke just wanted to stand on the terraces at Weymouth. He gave me a number.

I phoned Andrew Brown at his home in Bournemouth and invited him to the club to talk. He drove into the car park in a top-of-the-range Jaguar but was quiet and unassuming, calm and dignified, just the sort of man I wanted on board. He quickly said yes and surprised me by immediately agreeing to buy 50,000 shares.

Then there was Charlie Lesser, a friend of mine and Tony Adams, who owned his own successful coffee trading company in London. Charming and honourable, like Andrew at a good age in his mid-forties with experience but energy and ideas still, he offered to buy 20,000 shares just to help me out as an old mate. He accepted a seat on the board but would not be able to make it along very often, he said.

Now the overdraft was wiped out and we were actually £25,000 in credit. One morning – I got into my regular routine of spending mornings early in the week in the boardroom on my own working on admin and finances – the company secretary Sarah Redford, who I was quickly coming to see as the club's rock, with her genial and efficient manner, came up with the latest financial figures. 'I don't think the current account has been in the black since I came to work here,' she said.

I felt like a cross between Yul Brynner's character, Chris, in *The Magnificent Seven*, recruiting for the hopeless task of defending a Mexican village against bandits, and the George Peppard figure in *The A Team*. I love it when a plan comes

together. As well as directors, I also took on a new physiotherapist, Roger Hoare, well qualified and recommended
by Bob Lucas and that would do for me. We had had too
many injuries and long absences the previous season – funny
how players take longer to come back in a failing team –
and although it would cost more, at around £175 a week, it
seemed an expense worth bearing.

Being in funds, of course, wouldn't last long, even though
these were the joyful summer days of not having players'
wages to pay. Football clubs always manage to leak money,
no matter what, as I was about to find out.

Now it was time to pay some dues. Bills had gone
embarrassingly ignored for much of the season. The coach
company who transported the team to away matches,
Bluebird, were owed around £15,000; a local businessman,
Micky Jones, around £20,000 for his work in replacing
corrugated roofs covering the terraces from a couple of years
back. Sherrens, who printed the match day programme, were
down to the tune of £6000.

I visited each personally, trying to get goodwill back.
They appreciated it, particularly Micky, a powerful local
businessman, and we reminisced about my dad, who had
worked for his building firm for a while as site foreman
erecting houses near the football ground. Micky said he
would help me if I needed it. He owned a field at the back
of the club. If we wanted to flatten it, the players could use
it for training, he said.

It was a pleasant interlude, but at the end of it, I was back
to reality. We had gone from £25,000 in credit to £16,000
overdrawn again, with only one more source of summer
income. A local guy with bags of enthusiasm, Brian White,
had decided to bring speedway back to the town. I had gone
as a teenager to watch years ago but it had ceased business.
Now he wanted to put a track around our training ground,
build up some terracing and run six meetings as a pilot. The

previous board had reluctantly agreed but I wanted to encourage him, not only because he deserved to succeed in bringing more professional sport to the town, but also because we could do with the money. With rent and bar takings, we stood to make around £2000 a meeting.

It was time to take stock in the club, of staff and expenditure. There was much I discovered that astounded me. We were locked into leasing photocopiers and washing machines for the club kit on five-year agreements that meant we would end up paying about three times what they were worth. Now they were often breaking down. It would have been cheaper, and more practical, to have bought some outright but then the club seemed to have been operating on short-term deals rather than long-term planning.

The club lottery was also a tangled money pit. Formerly, the club had thrived on its Dorset Goldliner scheme. Once there were 10,000 members and more around the county paying £1 a week; quite some income for a non-League club, even allowing for a prize fund of around 50 per cent. These days, the National Lottery took many people's quids. There were more charities than ever. Why should people give it to a football club? It was losing, in fact, around £6000 a year.

Even more worryingly, I was contacted by the council's safety officer. The club had been allowed to stage games at the end of last season only because crowds were so low, he said. Technically, we should not have had a safety certificate. The bases of the antiquated, 130-foot high flood-lights were unsound. Emergency exits needed clearing of overgrown weeds. The roof of the main stand had holes in it. The internal electrical wiring of the whole ground was unsafe. It was quite a list and he expected the work to be done by the start of July if we were to be allowed to stage pre-season friendlies, let alone league games.

On top of all this, the club's fixtures secretary, Pete Saxby, came to me one day.

'You're hoping for crowds of over 1000,' he said.

'Yes,' I replied.

'How are you going to get them all in?'

'How do you mean?'

'You do know that three of the turnstiles aren't working? They are rusted or locked in.'

I didn't know. And I didn't know how any of this was going to work or get done. It was daunting. What had I taken on? One task at a time, I supposed. My first month at the club had revealed the problems. I had another month to find the solutions.

There was also the problem of getting the pitch, which was bare and rutted, in a decent condition, and painting the rusting metalwork around the ground. Around fifty seats in the main stand were broken. Then there were six floodlight bulbs that needed replacing, at a cost of around £250 each, plus the cost of a specialist company coming to fit them. The club shop also was in need of a refit. It had developed more into a programme den and we needed to be selling merchandise this season. I wanted the whole dilapidated place, which stank of decline, to be safe and look spruce but we had little time.

What was that about football people enjoying the summer? I once interviewed the then Liverpool manager Roy Evans. 'Love the summer,' he said. 'You can't lose a game.' Right now, I envied managers and players.

I had already discovered in the space of a few weeks, the ups and downs of a football club – and this was without even having played a game. It was not so much a rollercoaster as Nemesis.

I was also discovering what a small town this could be. One morning at 7 a.m., I dropped Vikki at the station so she should get a train to London. By 9 a.m., two people had phoned me saying they had seen me there.

Meeting followed meeting followed meeting with all sorts

of firms who might sponsor us as I chased leads and contacts. There was Comet, Somerfield, Asda, First Bus, our regional transport company. But everything was a hard sell. When I wasn't driving between my home in St Albans and Weymouth, I was off interviewing managers in Bristol or Birmingham, phoning board members. The club, after all its struggles in recent years, its false dawns, had prompted a lot of scepticism. It would not be turned around easily.

Stuck in all the concerns, I was in need of a lift. The club was in need of one. We really had to get a manager in place, to make a statement of intent. When in doubt, get back to the priority of football.

CHAPTER FIVE

Love and Claridge

I phoned Steve Claridge and told him that I thought Shaun Teale was going to be the man. 'Fair enough,' he said. 'He'll be decent.' There was a pause. 'Unless you want it,' I said.

I was trying it on, really. I knew that Steve was out of contract at Millwall but that he had been trying to negotiate a new one with the chairman Theo Paphitis. Despite his veteran status, Steve showed no signs of slowing up – partly because he had never been that quick anyway – and thought he was worth more than the £3000 a week they were offering him, having already been on £4000. He was still as fit as a butcher's dog and still had his touch.

'No, not really,' he said. 'I'm not ready to give up my professional career yet.' If not Millwall, he reckoned that several others in the Championship might take him on over the summer. There was still a big call for the kind of striker who could keep possession, bring others into the game, and chip in his fair share of goals. Besides, he added, he was getting work as a pundit with Radio Five Live and Sky Sports and to step down would be to lose the profile that brought him that work.

'But I do want to go into management soon,' he said.

There was something in his voice, particularly the last comment, that suggested the idea was not as far-fetched as I thought. I put the phone down and considered it.

I had known Steve for nearly twenty years. Back in the mid-eighties, as a 19-year-old, he was in Bournemouth's reserves, unable to break regularly into the then manager Harry Redknapp's first team. When I saw him play on loan for Weymouth at Wycombe, he showed a great first touch, held the ball up neatly, linked the play, created and scored. Afterwards in the bar, I told him he would be better off signing for Weymouth, getting himself noticed as had players like Graham Roberts and Andy Townsend, and would progress in the game more readily. It might be one step back to take two forwards.

Weymouth signed him for £10,000 and he became a fans' favourite with his all-action style, socks round his ankles, legs and arms pumping. In those days, before Jean-Marc Bosman took the football authorities to European Court of Justice and secured the end of a restraint-of-trade clause, which changed the face of the game, players could be retained even though out of contract. Without the letter informing him, though, Steve was free to move and Crystal Palace snapped him up on a free transfer. In that market at that time, it was an omission that cost at least £25,000. From Palace, unable to get past Ian Wright and Mark Bright into their first team, he moved on to Aldershot.

He then became one of the game's great travellers and characters, taking in Cambridge United twice, Luton, Birmingham City, Portsmouth before reaching the Premiership with Leicester City, famously scoring the goal at Wembley in the play-off final against Crystal Palace that took them into the Premiership. The next season he scored the winner against Middlesbrough to bring them the Worthington Cup.

From there it was a brief unhappy spell at Wolverhampton Wanderers and finally – we thought – a return to the club he grew up supporting, Portsmouth, where he also had a brief spell as player-manager after the sacking of Alan Ball. When Milan Mandaric, hastily, relieved Steve of his duties, he could no longer stay on as a player and ended up at Millwall. There, as with everywhere he had been, he was the fans' player of the year. More important for his career, a succession of managers down the years had recognized his quality.

I had caught up with him again during his Birmingham City years and we became firm friends. I liked his honesty. Through it all, he had been seen as a bit of a madcap, who got himself into scrapes and wasted his money on gambling. We documented it all in collaborating on his autobiography, *Tales from the Boot Camps*. It was not an easy task, given his flibbertigibbet lifestyle, but it was always rewarding.

Like that succession of managers, I realized that sticking with him brought its rewards, not least in bringing colour to my life. And I knew a much shrewder, smarter man than the folklore of the game told. With his shirt-out, socks-down appearance, many a defender had underestimated him. Now he was a good judge of a player, an interesting tactician, knew the game inside out. In his media work, his co-commentaries struck the right balance between humour and analysis.

He was a wilier figure than the image suggested. With every signing-on fee he had received from a club, he had bought a house or a flat, both to stop himself gambling it away and to build up a nest egg. He now had an impressive property portfolio.

I left it for a few days, got on with other of the myriad jobs around the club. The 'old' board had supplied us with their budget for the previous season but it was sketchy, and did not contain several costs that were emerging, the hidden costs of running a football club. You had, for example, to pay for entry to certain competitions and for ground grading inspections. We needed something more detailed. I met with Nigel Winship, who had also been working for Barclays Bank as well as having his own company, and we met to work on proper figures for the new season.

We looked at income, thought we could increase it by recruiting more sponsors and, of course, getting more fans in through the gate. We reckoned we could pay a new full-time manager £600 a week, around £30,000 a year, and wanted to give him a playing budget of £6500 a week, up by around 50 per cent. A coach in football can make the most of some limited players for a while, but we had to have a fighting chance.

It would not be the highest wage bill in the league by any means – we heard stories of the money being spent at Newport County and Havant and Waterlooville – but it would probably put us in the top six and should give us a chance of competing.

To achieve those figures we would need to bring in sponsorship of around £100,000 a season and average gates of 1000. It was a tall order but could be done, I believed. With new directors' investment, we thought we could break even on the season, if not in trading terms, as the buying of shares did not count in the profit and loss, then certainly in the cash flow.

Then one night Steve phoned. He had been thinking about it, he said. Come and see me. I phoned Nigel Winship. We worked out, in case Steve was serious, the most we could go to. It was a package of £1000 a week basic – we were getting a manager and a striker, after all, who could score twenty goals a season and create that many more for others.

After that, it would be all about bonuses. If the club earned more, then so could he. If we did get more than 1000 through the gates, it would be down to him and he should get a percentage, along with win bonuses. The package added up to around £75,000 a year. It was a huge sum for our level but I figured he would pay for himself, such would be the increased revenue he would bring. It would be a three-year contract.

I knew it was peanuts to him, however, that he could

double it at another club just as a player. Swindon Town were hovering in the background. All I could do was offer him the chance to be in at the start of something exciting. I knew he relished a challenge, liked to go where the fans were passionate, and I could assure him of that. He would be the pivotal figure of the club, its touchstone, the one who galvanized the town. I hoped that would appeal to him.

Intrigued, hopeful but without expectation, I made the familiar drive to his house a few miles off the M27 between Southampton and Portsmouth, down an unmade road to his father's market garden, next to which they had built a house, named by his dad 'Wembley Heights'. It was Steve's bolthole, his sanctuary and resting place far away from his itinerant lifestyle and the strains of football.

As usual, he was walking round the house in stockinged feet – insisted visitors took their shoes off, too – and wore his uniform of tracksuit trousers and sweatshirt, today's emblazoned with the crest of Millwall. As I outlined the deal to him he lay, as usual, on a sofa. To outsiders he might have seemed lazy, but even in this summer period of footballers' holidays, he was running and going to the gym every day and knew the value of rest. It was quite simply professional.

I had printed the details of the contract and handed him a copy. I half-expected him simply to toss it aside. Instead, he studied it intently. He wanted more on his basic salary. I said no, but I would agree to expenses, for his mobile phone and petrol when he went scouting, provided he got receipts. He wanted more bonuses, for goals, wins and attendances. He mentioned figures, I halved them, and we compromised. We both agreed that the better he did, the more revenue would come in, through gates and sponsorship and maybe even prize money, and that as the main attraction he should get a share of that.

I was less sure about £20,000 a year as a 'loyalty'

payment. It was standard with managers at a higher level, though unusual at ours. I told him that we could not pay it in the first year but would begin in the second, as by then, I thought, we would be making money.

On top, there was a £25,000 bonus for promotion, which I was happier to accommodate. If we did go up, it would mean that we would share in Conference deals, including TV money from Sky, and would be in a much stronger position.

Steve also wanted a five-year contract. I had no problems with that. I saw him staying, building a team to take us into the Conference within two years, stabilizing then having a go for the Football League when the new stadium was built. Then, we would have the windfall amount on top, some £1.5 million, and in common with the previous board, I believed most of it should go in trust to provide a future income for the club. The board could also decide then whether the squad might go full time and whether we should invest and push for the League. If he achieved that, Steve could move on to a bigger club with our blessing. Besides, if anyone did come in for him over those five years, then the club would be guaranteed a sizeable sum in compensation.

I was surprised that he was taking this so seriously. His willingness to negotiate showed that he wanted the job. What about his media work? he wondered. I had anticipated the question. I said that he could continue. We needed him to take training on Tuesdays and Thursdays and be available for certain community functions. I thought it would even be good for the club, since being billed as Weymouth manager would help spread the word and raise attendances. I had also, I told him, phoned people at Radio Five Live and Sky Sports and they had no problem with him being a Southern League manager. It was what he had to say, rather than whom he was attached to, that interested them.

He was quiet, which was unusual. I knew I had him. The

rest was detail. After three hours we had a deal. We spent another hour talking about the potential of the club, the squad he would inherit. A decent nucleus, I said, but needing a lot of work. I saw him, I added, as a potential Martin O'Neill, the inspirational manager he had played under at Leicester, who started at Wycombe, took them into the League from the Conference before attracting the attention of bigger clubs. He seemed to like that thought. I wanted agreement here and now, I said. What I didn't say was that I wanted it done before he saw the pitch, the ground and the remnants of a squad that had finished seventeenth.

When I left, I could not wait to tell all the directors that I thought we had a new manager. I reached Dave Higson in the Canary Islands. All the board seemed pleased, too, but I detected some reservations in the voices of the old guard. They were used to men like Geoff Butler, before him a disastrous appointment by the name of Des Bulpin, and unused to thinking so radically and ambitiously.

That night I slept only fitfully, partly out of excitement, partly out of worry at what I had done. Now we needed gates of 1200, now we needed sponsorship of £100,000 if we were to break even. I tried to take solace in Goethe's words: 'Be bold and mighty forces will come to your aid.'

The phone rang at midnight. 'Go through the squad again with me and tell me who's any good,' said Steve.

And he phoned again early the next morning. A £5000 signing-on fee would seal it. We did have the money now, or at least plenty of capacity on our overdraft, but it wasn't in the budget. I couldn't let it break the deal, however. This was too big, too important to the future of the club.

I had worked out by now how to defer some of the costs of his bonuses, by taking out some 'insurance'. This mid-summer we were 16–1 to win the title and I contacted Angus Loughran, a fellow journalist and racing commentator who knew the betting market inside out. I would give him £2000 of my own and Park Engineering would chip in with another £1000. It would bring us odds of 10–1 – that amount of money at our level inevitably reduced the starting price – and would cover it all. Proper insurance, my enquiries told me, was prohibitive.

A journalist's instinct is always to want to tell someone, but the club needed a big announcement as a signal of intent to put us on the map. I kept it quiet until I could organize a press conference for the following week.

I felt I owed it to those managers on the shortlist to tell them they hadn't got the job. It was not a nice task but they took it well enough, appreciated being told person to person rather than reading about it. I have always found that with football people. They expect rejection, have grown used to it down the years, as an occupational hazard. All they ask for is honesty. Shaun Teale sounded particularly disappointed, which was understandable as he knew he was close to the job.

I met again with Nigel Winship, updated the budget. I didn't hear from Steve over the weekend and began to worry he might have had second thoughts. Then he rang on the Monday. He wanted his medical insurance paid.

Now it was time to organize the press conference. I phoned the *Echo* and the *Western Gazette* first, then the four local TV stations, two in Southampton, two in Plymouth. I phoned the Press Association, knowing that to be the best way to alert the national papers, and told them the new manager would be 'a nationally known figure'. Within an hour that phrase was running as a strapline across the bottom of *Sky Sports News*.

I got a call from *News at Ten*. Knowing my friendship with Tony Adams, was it going to be him, they asked? I couldn't tell a lie, even it if would have been nice to have a crew along. No, it wasn't, I said. I wanted as much interest as possible but couldn't mislead anyone.

As the day of the announcement arrived I wasn't quite sure how we had managed to keep it so quiet. Actually we hadn't. Steve had let it slip the night before to an old free-lance contact of his, who promptly filed it for the *Western Daily Press* in Bristol. I was annoyed because I wanted the *Echo* to have it first that lunchtime.

We attracted a crowd, Steve arriving ten minutes before, which gave him less time with the directors to be questioned about his vision for the team and the club than I would have wanted. 'I hope you are going to sort out the throw-ins,' said Peter Shaw, my new vice-chairman. 'We kept giving the ball away last season.' I looked at Steve a little embarrassed. I knew as a professional, he would not take kindly to such a footling interfering question.

Though the board stood proudly in the background at the press conference, I could sense they were a bit miffed at not getting long enough with Steve. I said if they held on, we would have more time later. These were men used to managers doing their bidding and it was clear Steve was more confident, more his own man and less easily ordered, than they were used to. I knew him to be a free spirit, and that he would operate best if given his head. It did not mean, though, that I would let him get away with things when the interests of the club came first. He knew that, too, because he knew how protective of the club I felt.

The media commitments took a while. As a veteran of such events, I knew that we should have a gathering of all for a statement and some questions, then do one-on-one interviews for radio, then television, then daily press, then Sundays, then local, to give them an angle to throw forward. At two hours, it was tiring but really exciting. Steve was exceptional, knowing what everybody wanted. He was more anxious about the state of the pitch.

I told the throng that if Arsene Wenger and Sir Alex Ferguson had both applied for the job, I would still have given it to Steve. And I meant it. Steve was just the sort of figure that the club and the town could rally behind. He also knew the game at every level and could recruit accordingly, at the right price. Ferguson and Wenger wouldn't have been able to. It was, I said, the most significant signing in the club's 113-year history.

Afterwards we met with Dave Kiteley, our quiet and likeable reserve team manager, and Gary Borthwick. Gary had been working with the Under 16s but I had always admired him as a combative midfield player with the club back in the eighties and liked his immediate acceptance of the changes being made at the club. I wanted Steve to bring him into the system. They got on well.

'I'm going to get you some decent money,' Steve told Dave and Gary. My eyebrows lifted. Having Steve Claridge at the club was like that horrible moment in the back of a taxi when you see the meter clicking up more quickly than you anticipated. But Gary was also a painter and decorator. I reckoned in return I could get him and his men to paint the ground, get it looking spick and span.

We toured the ground, which didn't take long. Steve could not understand why the home dressing room was at the end of a draughty corridor and the bigger away one next to the physiotherapist's room, which had an adjoining door. He wanted them swapped. He also wanted them decorated, and new 'slipper' baths put in, as well as non-slip lino laid in the home dressing room. I agreed. Just as the quality of a training ground can attract players at the highest level – it is, after all, their place of work – a proper dressing room could make the difference between a player signing or not. It was a necessary cost of being more professional. I didn't realise that the cost would be £3500, though.

We got some great coverage. 'IT'S CLARIDGE' proclaimed the *Echo* and all the TV stations carried features. *The Non-League Paper* the following Sunday even ran a centre spread, showing postcards of Weymouth and wishing Steve well. They added that the town was in for a hell of a ride.

The reaction of the players was positive and they could now see the ambition in the club. One of them, our stalwart defender Simon Browne, went into the *Echo* to give voice to the feelings of optimism around the dressing room.

We were on our way. We had created a stir and now it was time to turn that into revenue, funds for the coming season, by capitalizing on the publicity and the euphoria. There would be potential sponsors to contact, and now it would be easier to get meetings with them, and fans' forum nights at the club to host. I was also due to meet with the BBC about filming the documentary following our season. This would make it easier to sell.

We might even shift some season tickets now to get some revenue in. That night, Steve rang. He wanted two free season tickets, one for his dad and one for a mate.

CHAPTER SIX

Summer of discontent

One Monday morning in June I met with two producers from the BBC at their White City offices in west London. Seek TV were pitching their idea for a series about following footballers and clubs, from top to bottom of the English game, for the season and wanted me to be the consultant.

It would, I reckoned, be a good way of getting them to follow Weymouth and get a 'facility' fee. In return, they would get access to every level of the club. I also thought the idea of being on television might help us sell the club to sponsors. I knew that reality television could make you look a fool, but if it brought money into the club, I personally would look as foolish as they liked, as long as they did not make the club look silly.

They were more interested now that we had Claridge on board. The story of a Southern League club going through a transition would serve as a nice counterpoint to the bling of people such as Kieron Dyer and David James, and the professional clubs like Manchester City and Ipswich Town, that they would be following. And it would bring us £15,000. It was encouraging.

I drove, in a good mood, down to Weymouth, for a series of meetings: with the property development company brokering the deal between the club and Asda for a new stadium; with Nigel Beckett, the Supporters' Club representative on the board, about revamping the club shop; and for a fans' forum with Steve that night.

Steve rang. He wanted to make sure he was going to get his win bonus, even if he was injured and couldn't play. I wondered why. He said he would still be coaching and managing the team and, as a player too, should share in it. It was hard to argue against.

I also met with Mick Archer and Dave Higson at Park Engineering to update them on everything. They were not happy, having felt snubbed by Steve the previous week at the press conference. It was clear they were used to being more influential with the manager and now they were feeling less and less involved.

I tried to reassure them, that it was a busy time and sometimes I was in meetings, dashing around, trying to get things moving again after years of stagnation, choosing my words carefully so as not to denigrate their efforts. They, after all, were the two men most responsible for putting money in to keep the club afloat. They deserved respect. But they had also given me the go-ahead to do what I believed needed to be done at the club.

They were concerned, too, about the costs. They could cover losses, they said, when the figures were lower. Now they worried about Steve's package, the potential wage bill, and the costs of refurbishing the ground.

I understood but what, I asked them, was the alternative? To continue the way we were, with a low wage bill, falling attendances and sponsorship? Perhaps relegation? I outlined once more the strategy of investing. With the new directors' money, more sponsorship and other fund-raising ideas, like the TV series, and a sporting dinner that I planned to put on, and by perhaps negotiating a better deal with Asda, and increased gates, we could break even, in cash terms, over the season. There might be a small loss, but the first year of any new business was going to face that. Once we had refurbished the ground, that was a cost that would not be repeated next summer, when we might also try to put on a pop concert to raise money.

I was not sure if they were reassured. They said they backed me but it did not sound wholly convincing, though Higson appeared the more understanding. I certainly felt that the wind had been taken from my sails.

That night, more than 300 fans crammed into our narrow, two-bar Wessex Lounge for the forum with me and Steve, Higson an observer. I outlined, as honestly as I could, the vision for the season and the next five years, the stadium development, Steve's role, the costs.

Understandably, they really wanted to hear Steve, though. 'We're going to give it a right good go,' he told them. 'If we fail, it won't be for want of enthusiasm and trying. This club has been down on its uppers for too long. We may have been in the gutter but we can dream. Don't you want to live the dream?' It brought the house down and the phrase 'Live the Dream' would stick.

All the while, Vikki was typing into a laptop, précising our words for consumption on the club website. The next day, when reprinted in the *Echo*, they would stir local controversy. I had said that it was our turn to get the Boxing Day derby against Dorchester Town and if we didn't, our fans, who provided them with around £20,000 of income a season – about a third of their gate receipts – should boycott the game. It was meant to be ironic but some failed to see the joke.

I also announced a new appointment to the club. After much persuasion, my sister Mel had agreed to leave the *Echo* and become our commercial manager, part-time at twenty-five hours, though she and I both knew she would give more to it than that. I worried about accusations of nepotism but there seemed none. Mel was very popular in the town, a lively character who knew the place, its mentality and its people, inside out. She was on first-name terms with all the owners of businesses. I know of no one better. Certainly for what we could pay her. And, unlike the previous manager in his dual role, she was not on commission.

After two hours of questions and answers and satisfied that we had really begun a new era, we repaired to Perry's for a well-deserved steak, Steve spurning all their 'fancy' sauces and ordering double vegetables. A man approached us as he was leaving. 'Good luck to the both of you,' he said. 'I'm an Arsenal fan really but I'll come to watch a few games.' I thanked him. It was a gratifying moment.

It had been a long day, full of ups and downs, highs and lows. Football, I was finding out, was like that. You experienced as many triumphs and disasters in a day as in a month in most other walks of life. Many, many more days like this would follow over the next month even before pre-season training began.

The next day, for example, there was a meeting with Bob Mowlem, the new club secretary, who had been appointed by the old board. He seemed a good choice. Broad of accent, tall and upright, he was diligent and fully supportive of what we were seeking to do with the club and I immediately liked him. I was sure I knew him from somewhere.

It was followed by a photoshoot for the local paper with the producer and star of the pantomime at Weymouth Pavilion the following Christmas. He was John Forgeham, for many years in *Crossroads*, now the chairman, Frank Lazlett, in *Footballers' Wives*. He was a nice guy and we had much in common, vowed to stay in touch. We roped in a couple of glamorous players' partners for the event.

Then it was a meeting with Steve Dadd, a sort of Mr Fixit round the club, nominally the press officer under the previous regime, a role I now embraced, and a painter and decorator by trade. 'Get Dadd to do it,' it read on the side of his van. He feared I wanted him out of the club after he had been critical of me on a fans' website. In fact, I wanted him to organize a few things, like an open-top bus for Carnival Day and the refurbishing of the dressing rooms. He was relieved and agreed.

It was one of the things about the club. We could not afford many full-time employees, in fact could not afford many part-time, but there remained a group of people, however much it had dwindled over the last few years, willing to volunteer to help the club. It was touching. All they needed was kick-starting. An appeal in the local paper for more brought a variety of responses. 'I want one of they jobs,' a local character said when he came to see me. 'I wanna stop they kids sitting on the fences during the game.'

That night, on my way back to Hertfordshire, I also met with Nigel Winship to go over the budget one more time. At his house in Ringwood, we crunched some numbers, based on the board's figures from last season, and came up with one to present to them. They then pointed out, somewhat gleefully I thought, that we had missed the VAT, even though it was not on their balance sheet of the previous season.

It was a surprise to discover that clubs had to pay VAT at 17.5 per cent on gate receipts. Imagine that all over the country, I thought; think of the money the Exchequer is taking from football. Manchester United alone must pay millions. No wonder so many small clubs get in trouble with the taxman.

Back to the drawing board. We could claim some VAT back here and there but now the target in sponsorship had to be at least £100,000 for the season. Could we do it?

I had already met with all sorts of companies who might sponsor us, chased leads and contacts. I was trying hard with New Look, the national chain of women's clothes retailers who had their headquarters in Weymouth, and I could never understand why they were not more involved in the club. There was Somerfield, Asda, First Bus, our regional company. The club, after all its struggles in recent years, its false dawns, had prompted much scepticism. It would not be turned around easily.

I dashed up to London for a meeting with Pete Daire at Sky Sports Marketing for his input into our sponsorship packages; and arranged with him a sponsors' night at the club which he could attend. It was followed by a dinner with a man from Comet who was interested in football and might just invest. In the end he didn't, but you had to put in the legwork, just in case.

Steve rang. He wanted to know if I had sorted out the medical insurance. Not yet, I told him. There are rather a lot of priorities.

And so it went on. There were meetings with the kit suppliers, to make sure they could handle the increased numbers of replica shirts I expected us to sell; with the local council, to introduce myself and try to get them onside about the new stadium; with the local college, to talk about setting up an academy. The bank also had to be kept abreast of the financial position as we began to go into the red again amid our new investment in getting the ground up to scratch. There were always interviews to be done for local press or radio.

What with letters from fans and people trying to sell us things – I was more interested in it being the other way around and Mel being on board was certainly improving that very quickly – the paperwork built up. I had files for everything. In fact, I had more files that Jim Rockford.

I rented a house in the town. Commuting between St Albans and Weymouth, I could no longer live at Dad's, couldn't bear it, and I could not keep sleeping on Mel's sofa. It was comfortable enough, but her husband Simon got up at 6 a.m. to go to work and was worried about disturbing me. The new house was a decent place, with a view of the sea; I had decided that if you were going to live on the coast you ought to be able to see it. I could never quite work out why Mum and Dad used to go months, perhaps even a year, without going anywhere near the seafront.

It was in my new location that I came across a former Weymouth chairman. Once a solicitor in the town, Paul Cocks was now running the Oasis Café at the end of the beach road out of town. I had been at school with him, him in the year above, and I had not had much contact, though I had noted his period in charge of the club. He was another who had written a letter to the *Echo* about me and I was not best pleased. I mentioned it to him while having a sandwich with Vikki at the Oasis and an argument developed about the football club, and his running of it. He said I should have read the letter more carefully, that he was not against me taking over. And then he stormed off, me trying to apologize.

The house had four bedrooms, which meant that we could put up players. It would not come cheap though. With bills and council tax, it was going to cost me another £1000 a month. There was no way the club could pay. Even that didn't come easy. I had seen one house, agreed on it, only for the owners to decide that they didn't want to rent it after all.

It all got too much one Monday morning in July, the start of a new season just a few weeks away. I was greeted at the club by two huge bills. We had had to employ a specialist company from the Midlands to shin up the floodlights, fix the bulbs and test for safety, paying the hotel costs of two men. It totalled £3500, about the same as for the de luxe lino in the home dressing room and the referee's room. And we hadn't even done the corridor or the away dressing room. The war chest had run out and we were still a fortnight away from pre-season friendlies and income.

I toured the dressing rooms. The work to install new baths and paint the walls had been left half-finished and no one was about. Work had still not started on the refurbishment of the club shop. Steve Dadd also phoned me. First Bus would not let us have an open-top bus for Carnival Day, unless we paid them £750.

In addition, the main pitch still had huge bare patches, quite apart from the worn-out goalmouths. The club did not employ a groundsman, preferring a company from Exeter who used their local employees, mainly a young apprentice, Jimmy, overseen by a supervisor who visited now and then. They had assured me it would be a flat, green surface ready for the start of the season. The adjacent training ground, which had been unusable for a year, was a cowfield and work had not even started on that.

Steve came down that day, bringing with him his new assistant. Neil McNab, once a top player with Tottenham Hotspur and Manchester City, had been sacked as manager of Exeter City the previous season amid a financial crisis at the club. Living near Steve in Portsmouth, he was now at a loose end until taking up a coaching job in America in August and had agreed to help out with our pre-season training. As I took him and Steve over the pitch and up to the training ground, I was deeply embarrassed by the state of the club to which I was introducing two professionals used to so much better.

Actually, I was furious. I could not believe that the board had allowed the club to deteriorate into such a state. I was upset that they appeared to enjoy the privileges of directorship – boardroom hospitality, seats in the box – without having discharged the responsibilities of care and maintenance.

I was angry, too, at the apparent *mañana* culture where nothing was getting done. I was used to living around London and operating in newspapers, where you had an idea and acted on it. Now it was wait until the last possible moment. I had been away too long. The coast, with its easy living, can make you lazy and complacent. I was no longer full of its ways. In such a mood of pique, I was not about to see that they might have it right and I might have it wrong. Either way, it was clearly one of the reasons why the football club had stagnated for so long.

It was time to throw the toys out of the pram. I rang the ground supervisor Clive, who was working on another contract somewhere else in the town, and summoned him to tell him that this needed to be sorted, or else we would be reviewing the contract, which had a year to run. It was another of those deals that looked superficially cheap to the board but ended up expensive. I also rang his boss, in Exeter, to tell him the same.

I contacted First Bus to say that we needed help and that if we did not get it, we would not be well disposed to the company in the future. It was an idle threat. Right now, we needed people more than they needed us. They were mostly fed up with this football club and its promises – of money, of profile – that never materialized.

I also phoned Steve Dadd to tell him that the dressing rooms needed sorting out and quickly. I rang Nigel Beckett. I wanted the design for the club shop done very soon and the work started ready for the new season. We needed to sell merchandise. It was hard, though. These were volunteers and you could not come down hard on people who were giving their time and effort for nothing.

Claridge rang. His dad knew a bloke who did turf cheap. They would be coming down next week with a van load to lay in the goalmouths. At last, he was ringing me wanting to help, rather than wanting something.

A line from *Shakespeare in Love*, penned beautifully by Tom Stoppard, went through my mind. 'How does a play come together?' says the stage manager character played by Geoffrey Rush. 'I don't know, it's magic.' And I hoped it was true of football as well as the theatre.

All the while, I was being followed by a camera crew on the first day of what would become a regular pursuit. They had what they wanted for now: plenty of conflict and a portrait of a club in a mess. The camera lingered on piles of rubbish and rubble. It made us look tinpot but for now I didn't mind. I was determined to turn this thing around and people needed to see what the job involved.

They didn't follow me into the shops in the town centre as I bought beds and linen for the new house. As I came out of one shop, a middle-aged man and his wife recognized me.

'You're that chairman fellow, aren't you?' he said.

'Yes,' I replied.

'God bless you. Thanks for what you are doing for the club.'

'Thank you,' I said. 'I hope you'll come and see us play.'

'We will,' he said.

I am a mug for a compliment. After the day I had had, it was lovely to hear; suddenly all this unpaid hassle seemed worthwhile again. But then, what else could there be in life, except for a passion for something you believed in, something that had been such a part of the fabric of your life?

For a while it was more than the fabric, it was the whole nine yards of material of my life. I was getting used to the minor disasters, such as finding out that the padlocks on the front gate weren't working and that the club was being left unlocked late at night, and enjoying the minor triumphs.

Dave and Mick sent a couple of big, strong boys down from Park Engineering to unblock the rusted turnstiles. The two big yachts I wondered about in the car park finally disappeared. Dave Higson had agreed to let a mate keep them there for a while. I went back to Micky Jones about the roof of the stand. Yes, he said, he had some material to patch it up if we could get someone to fix it. I phoned the local fire brigade. Up they went on their extended ladder as part of a 'training exercise' to cover the offending holes that leaked water, all but two they could not reach, anyway.

Then there were the little gestures, such as that of Pete Saxby. Pete, the fixtures secretary, was a mother hen of a figure, always clucking, always fussing. There always seemed to be a problem that needed sorting. I thought we ought to offer him a token sum for his work, said we couldn't afford to pay him more than £25 a week. 'Don't want paying,' he said. 'I would rather a young player got a contract.'

Not so others. The word was getting round that Weymouth had new investment, and some wanted a piece of the action. Staff at the club, having tightened belts for years, were not surprisingly after pay rises. Gordon Hollins, the part-time bar manager, was a case in point, Trevor Marsh, the maintenance man, another.

We managed a little and Gordon proved to be worth it, fixing up a meeting with a man from an alternative brewery who not only undercut the current drinks supplier but also, at my insistence, agreed to pay for the refurbishment of the smaller lounge.

I was concerned, I told Gordon, that we were not making enough profit from the bar, that we needed to tighten up. He told me, in return, that we were giving away too much drink. The directors felt that it was a perk of the job to get beer at 50p a pint, he said. I told him that would be stopping. Everyone paid full price for their drinks.

The July friendly matches loomed. So much to do, so little time . . . There had been a *cause célèbre* locally when the previous board, in a mean-spirited act, had withdrawn season tickets for ex-players who had reached 500 appearances. There were club legends like Tony Hobson, Bob Forrest and Anniello Iannone, who had been badly treated, I believed. Simply solved. I reinstated them. I also asked 'Anni' to come back as a matchday host. However, he wasn't a gladhander, he said.

Mel, warming to her task, was now starting to sell more

advertising hoardings around the ground and we met with a local sign-maker's, Spint Signs, saying that we would give them all the new business if they would make us for free a big new fixtures board to replace the tatty one now standing at the entrance to the car park. That and a big WFC sign on the side of the stand would make an immediate statement. The owner Neil Smith was so grateful and impressed that he bought £4000 worth of shares on top. It was working . . .

Then again, other meetings were less pleasurable. The former chairman Terry Bennett came in, wanting to return as an active board member. I said I would think about it. My father having to read the derogatory comments Bennett had made about me in the winter still cut deep. Now he was being too nice to me. It didn't square.

I met with the local independent radio station, Wessex FM. I had an idea that we could get Claridge to do radio ads on the day before home matches. It would end with the tag line: 'Jurassic Coast Soccer – It's Epic!' Corny but catchy.

I didn't want to pay, though. We would bill Wessex as our media partners, putting them on the cover of the pro-gramme, and giving them a free advertising board and ad in the programme. I was becoming familiar with the world of contra deals. The ads, though, were pricier than I thought. We would end up paying.

I had better luck with the *Dorset Echo*, whom we also proposed billing as media partners. After a long day at the club, a little down at what I thought had been slow progress over the summer but was, in reality, quite a turnaround already, their sports editor Paul Baker rang me to say that the marketing department had agreed a sponsorship of £2500. They had already started to print our fixture posters again, via a helpful fan who worked there, Kevin Frampton. I had seen them in pub and chip shop windows as a kid and wanted to start the tradition again. I didn't think I'd end up being one of the people who delivered them.

It so often happened. Just when you were beginning to wonder if you were getting anywhere, along came something to lift the spirits. It was a seductive process.

I had been trying to do a deal with a local supermarket, Somerfield, who were opening a clothes section at a store at Littlemoor, an area of town where my sister lived. In return for promoting them, through publicity in the local press and around the ground and in the matchday programme, I wanted them to supply us with pasta and chicken meals for the team coach and new suits for the players. It was proving a tough request. Locally, they had little budget.

They rang me, though, wanting Steve Claridge to come and open the revamped store. We set a date. I asked them for £300 to do it, eked it out of their head office. I thought we could give Steve £100 and keep £200 for the club. A few days before, Steve phoned to say he couldn't make it. He was up in court that day on a motoring offence. He had been speeding again and stood to lose his licence.

Instead, they settled for Steve's first signing, Scott Partridge. Scott was out of contract at Rushden and Diamonds and his arrival was my introduction to the world of the football agent.

On a blazing hot day that July, Scott turned up at the Wessex Stadium with Clive Whitehead, the Professional Footballers' Association representative in the south-west. Clive was a decent man, who was still in the *Guinness Book of Records* for the longest professional contract ever awarded in the English game – a staggering eleven years with Bristol City in the eighties. They went bust and he was sold to West Bromwich Albion as they cut their losses.

He struck a hard bargain, but not a fierce one. I was staggered that Steve was willing to pay Scott £550 a week, which seemed like a fortune at our level. I told Steve that if he wanted him, it had to be within the £6500 limit. He said he wanted quality rather than quantity, that it would indeed, when the squad was finalized, total no more than that.

That night was the first one back in training and Scott joined in wearing borrowed kit. At a local school, Budmouth, they did a running session, which Steve led from start to finish, running the legs off players much younger than himself. It was good to be out in the fresh air, watching them, and I suddenly felt excited.

After all the trials, tribulations and setbacks over the summer, this was what we were here for: to see a group of players representing the club. We had a good turnout. Many out of contract wanted to come back. I thought that by using his knowledge of recruiting and adding to a nucleus that included about seven decent players, Steve would have a good enough squad to finish in the top six.

After consulting his wife – players' partners actually having a lot of say in a football club – Scott became the first recruit and duly came with me to Somerfield for the standard silly pictures with a football in the aisles. We had to downgrade the fee to £250 and I gave Scott £50 out of my own pocket.

Now I could see headway. I had sought to prioritize my time into three areas: the squad, the sponsorship and the new stadium development. But there would always be some things to distract me; there was so much to do at this club, so many hearts and minds to win over.

Like the row about chips. Yes, chips. Whenever I had taken my son to a game, he often wanted a bag of chips and so did many others. They used to cook them in the tea bars around the ground but no more because volunteers found it too much of a greasy chore and I got letters of complaint. I contacted the Supporters' Club. The word I was getting back was they were not keen. In fact, someone on the committee who worked in the main tea bar said it would be 'over his dead body'.

I made mistakes. Working in the office with Sarah Redford was Roger Mutch, a former policeman who helped out answering the phones and administering the club's loss-making lottery. Since Roger was only administering it, rather than actually bringing in revenue, I decided that we could not afford to keep him on. Telling him was harder than sacking Geoff Butler. Roger, after all, was a fan of the club and had done nothing wrong.

Within days, though, I realised that Sarah could not cope alone in the office. I rang Roger to apologize and ask him to come back. After his initial understandable anger, he agreed to work three days a week.

We needed to get more revenue in. I had not chased hard for a shirt sponsor as our directors Dave Higson and Mick Archer at Park Engineering had said that they would do it for one more year. I believed we were worth £30,000 a year but it was more than they were used to, having had last season's for nothing, in return for underwriting certain of the club's debts. I told them that they had already had good value from the media coverage of Steve's arrival, their name emblazoned everywhere, and it would be a good season for them finally to get their higher-profile rewards. They agreed.

Steve had also brought a mate, Terry Clarke, on board with his shopfitting company in the Solent area to sponsor the stadium for £15,000, so he was beginning to pay his own way already. We had the media partners in the *Dorset Echo* and Wessex FM. With Pete Daire, we had also worked out Gold, Silver and Bronze packages, worth £10,000, £5000 and £1500. In return, companies would get publicity, access to Steve Claridge and match sponsorship.

It was a tough nut, though. This was more than companies in Weymouth were used to paying and for what? We had Claridge now but it was still a leap of faith.

We held a sponsors' night, made a presentation. One forthright local businessman told me that we were going about things the wrong way, that the people in the room didn't have money. I thanked him for his input but didn't agree. One company, another engineering firm of the sort which abounded on the nearby Granby Industrial Estate, did say they would put in £3000, which was a bonus.

An old acquaintance had just returned to the town. With her husband and son, Richard and Max, Georgina Grayson had just opened a new, upmarket nightclub on the seafront called Banus. They were a progressive new business too, she said, and would help us out, though having refurbished this year funds were limited and they might do more next year. She gave Steve and me gold membership cards. The evening had not been wasted.

A few days later, Mel got a call in the commercial office from one of my three cousins, Kim, Colin and Keith, who now ran the sheet-metal business set up by their father, Ticker, my mother's brother. They would take a silver package, they said. It was a generous gesture and really cheered our spirits. Now we were getting somewhere. Mel was really delivering.

Nigel and I went to the board with a revised budget based on the VAT figures and the sponsorship of £100,000 that was materializing, with Mel also doing well with matchday sponsorship packages. The new figures, I added, were based on gates of 1200. Peter Shaw doubted it would all happen but nevertheless proposed the budget be accepted. I sensed yet more scepticism from the old guard.

I met with Trent, the development company who were liaising between us and Asda, in the shape of two sharp-suited, well-spoken men in their thirties down from London, Alistair Jespersen and Toby Atkinson. We sized each other up. I was suspicious. I had been horrified to come across some paperwork which detailed how the club's board, when in dire financial straits back in March before they invited me back in, had been offering to sell the freehold of the stadium to Trent for £300,000 then lease it straight back. Fortunately, no agreement had been reached and we still owned the land.

Terry Bennett had been leading the negotiations on behalf of the club, Asda offening £1.5 million and a new stadium. It was nowhere near enough for the acreage we owned, I believed. Nor was the proposed stadium adequate. I did not want a repeat of the mistakes of the hastily conceived Wessex.

The specification for the ground was sketchy, written on one side of a sheet of A4, and contained such generalities as: 'plenty of storage space'. The capacity of 6000 was also less than we had already. Though crowds of 650 rattled around in the current Wessex, the ambition had to be to plan for success, rather than failure.

I told Trent that we would prefer to engage our own architects and specialist stadium builders, and receive a lump sum instead. I believed we could get a better stadium and more money in the bank on top. The negotiations would be long and hard. But we needed to be tough. This was a deal that would determine the future of the club.

In the meantime, Trent were preparing various studies – retail, traffic and environmental impact – for West Dorset District Council ahead of a decision the following February whether or not to include this in their ten-year plan for the area. I agreed I would lobby and continue to publicize our case locally, and met with a local councillor, Ian Gardener, a Weymouth fan, and our local MP, Jim Knight, whose majority was among the lowest in the country at 153, Dorset South having gone Labour for the very first time in 2001. Both were onside.

It was funny. I had come into all this because I loved football, loved the game. For most of the summer, it had been about anything but football. At least on the July day that the 2003/4 fixtures came out it felt more real. In

advance, you receive a questionnaire from the league asking
for your 'pair', the local club you are nearest to, so that you
can be at home one week, them the next. It is a bit like MPs
pairing up in the Commons if either can't make a vote. The
questionnaire also asks for special requests on certain dates.
We had requested Dorchester at home on Boxing Day.

And so I scouted for the Dorchester games first. Yes:
home on Boxing Day, away on New Year's Day. Quite some
holiday period. We would go to Hednesford on opening
day, had Newport County as our first home game on the
Tuesday. You always look for the last day, too, dreaming of
three points for the league title . . . At least we were at home,
to Grantham.

The team building I could leave to Steve with confidence.
He was more impressed with the squad, once he had cleared
out some deadwood, than I expected him to be. In the right
fullback Steve Tully, a lively character, pacy going forward,
and the striker Lee Phillips, whom Steve immediately
thought he could get £50,000 for from a League club, he
had two diamonds, he said. He was surprised to find them
at this level.

He also recruited Lee Philpott, whom I remembered from
Steve's days at Cambridge United as a tricky left-winger.
When Cambridge, astonishingly, had narrowly failed to
gain promotion to the Premiership in their first season, Lee
went to Leicester City where he would meet up with Steve
again. He had just finished an injury-plagued season with
Hull City but, even at thirty-three, would add quality to our
midfield, now playing in the centre of it. He lived up near
Doncaster but would travel down for training and matches
in plenty of time and stay over at my house.

In also came Martin Barlow, a crafty little midfield player
from Telford United, and Lee Russell, a rugged defender
who had been with Steve at Portsmouth. It was taking
shape. The only real disappointment was that Alex Browne,

central defender and club legend having played more than 500 games, was out of contract when I arrived at the club and was seeking a new one. I said that the new manager when he was appointed would have to make that sort of decision, but Alex did not want to wait for me to appoint one and instead he decamped to our local rivals, Dorchester Town. He clearly remained a Terra, though. I offered him a season ticket as a member of the 500 club and he gratefully accepted it.

In the meantime, I was still trying to do my job and covered the Open golf at Sandwich and Wimbledon fortnight. A holiday was out of the question, though I was spending all my spare time at the seaside. My daughter Alex and son Jack, now seventeen and thirteen, came down for a while as their holiday with Dad. Alex insisted I put 10p in a jar every time I mentioned the W word, to be saved for a treat. I think I clandestinely went out and bought twenty cigarettes, or several hundred, with the kitty in the end.

After all the meetings, the plotting and the planning, it was a relief finally to play football. We had inherited a lame pre-season programme and it was too late to improve it. David Pleat at Tottenham told me that these things needed to be arranged the previous November. Gérard Houllier said he would bring Liverpool down the following pre-season.

The first game, at home to Barnet of the Conference, was a huge disappointment. The game was decent enough, a 1–1 draw, and it was nice that their manager Martin Allen complimented us on our setup. This despite being banished to the stands by a Dorset referee, Janie Frampton, for foul language. There were other foul-ups. We had forgotten to do anything about ordering sandwiches. Mel, bless her, nipped down to Asda during the game and bought some herself.

What concerned me most was the attendance: just over 500. Perhaps Peter Shaw was right to be sceptical about the crowd figures. Despite Steve's presence, maybe this town had lost its appetite for football.

It continued through other, badly scheduled, home games. We drew only a few hundred for Stevenage Borough on a Friday night, a mere 150-odd for a game the next day against Chasetown, a small West Midlands League club.

Watching the games, I found myself worrying about the match balls going out of the ground. But not for reasons of bad shooting. I made sure Pete Saxby had got someone to retrieve them. They cost a few bob.

The team was playing well, though. I had sought a friendly with Aldershot in May but they had declined. When they heard Steve was to be our new manager they contacted us again, though, and offered us a game at their Recreation Ground, Steve having been a firm favourite there as a player years ago.

They had just been promoted to the Conference as Ryman League champions, and attracted good crowds. Indeed, they would cram in nearly 4000 a couple of weeks later when their opening league game, against Accrington Stanley, was televised live on Sky. They were a terrific little club on the up, models for us.

But with Steve playing his first game with his first-choice XI starting, we outplayed them to win 2–0. As I sat in the directors' box, he winked as he left at the end. He knew, he said in the car afterwards, that we would now be all right, would do well. His only real concern was Scott Partridge. Steve and Lee Phillips were shaping up to be the first-choice pairing in attack and though we needed backup, Scott would be an expensive substitute.

We still needed something in midfield. Someone at Aldershot that night told me that Paul Buckle, who was having a good game in their midfield, lived in Honiton, about an hour's drive west of Weymouth, about three hours from Aldershot. Now thirty-one, he was in his last year with the Shots. He would be a good player for us next year, I thought, and mentioned as much to the Aldershot chairman Karl Prentice, a shrewd man and a chairman I admired.

The next day Karl phoned me, saying they might be able to 'do something with Paul'. I phoned Steve and within a couple of days 'Bucks' was a Weymouth player. He was taking a pay cut of £100 a week to join us but the travelling would suit him. Besides, he said, Aldershot had promised him more money and it was proving a difficult negotiation. He didn't want to play hard ball. He preferred to go to a club where he was wanted, where he could be in at the start of something.

Steve was also in the process of acquiring Luke Nightingale, with whom he had played up front at Portsmouth. I remembered the two combining for a goal against Leeds United in an FA Cup tie a couple of years earlier. Luke was out of contract and having trouble finding another League club and so Steve would be able to get him for a cheap wage. The squad was growing more impressive each week but with four strikers now, how would we keep everyone happy?

That was for later. Now Steve had made seven new signings, all for reasonable wages and still a few hundred pounds within the budget I had set him. That would be taken up by the bonus system we had agreed: £30 a point if top of the table, £25 if top six and £20 if top half. I believed in incentives. If we were achieving those results, we would surely be bringing in income.

After Aldershot, I knew we could compete even though we gave patchy performances with mix-and-match teams against the likes of Winchester City and Harrow Borough. Still I had concerns. We were still a long way from being professional. We had taken chicken and pasta meals for the players to Winchester but the microwave on the coach was broken. I wondered if anything would ever work properly at the club.

With attendances poor for the home friendlies, we were not bringing in as much money as I had hoped. I had agreed to lift morale after gloomy years for the players, to pay 25 per cent of wages for pre-season. What with that and the bonus system, I wondered anew if this was going to work. The sponsorship money from Park was still outstanding, and other deals Mel had agreed would not pay out until later in the season. Attendances would be the bedrock of the new strategy.

Ten days before the league season began with an away match at Hednesford Town, I drove up to Leicester for a meeting with a man from Asda's commercial department, trying to persuade him to put in some sponsorship since we were now negotiating a new stadium with them. It would prove another long, fruitless journey since they were worried about the sign it would send to other clubs who had an Asda in their town.

Before I got there, though, my mobile rang to interrupt my worrying about whether the club shop would be refitted in time, whether the replica shirts were on the way and whether we would get the green light to play league games from the following week's safety inspection.

It was Sarah from the club and she had some bad news.

CHAPTER SEVEN

All right on the night

The letter of resignation said that the four – Terry Bennett, Dave Higson, Mick Archer and Peter Shaw – believed that I had outlined my plan for the club and it was only right that I should be allowed to see it through. They were stepping aside to let me get on with it.

The subtext was clear. They did not believe it was going to work and did not wish to be associated with it when it went belly up, as they were sure it would. Shaw went on local radio to elaborate: the costs were now too high and were based on unrealistic attendance figures.

This was the man who had proposed the acceptance of the budget in the board meeting. This was the vice-chairman of the club saying, in effect, that he no longer believed in the club's ability to attract fans. It was an insult to Steve Claridge, I felt, but also to the supporters and their capacity for backing the club, turning out in numbers. I thought of something Gérard Houllier had told me: you cannot build a cathedral with doubters.

I had mixed feelings. Driving up the M1, I was stunned at first, then angry that they should do this ten days before the season started. Then again, I was relieved. These, Higson apart, were not open-minded nor progressive thinkers and I would no longer have to answer to them, suffer their negative remarks in board meetings. I rang Shaw. He was dismissive, but I expected little else. It would not be long until he wrote to me demanding back the money he had loaned the club, a few thousand pounds.

Soon Paul Baker from the *Echo* was on the phone to me. People were worried, he said, about the costs at the club this summer, that it was unsustainable, that Claridge was on a fortune. I wondered which people they were, but then I knew that Paul was close to the Park Engineering duo. I gave him an interview. 'This is an investment, not a gamble,' I said. What had been the alternative? The club was going bust anyway under the previous board.

I had to get to work quickly. I drove back down to Weymouth to see Matt McGowan, spent a couple of hours in his kitchen drinking coffee, smoking and chewing the fat with him. OK, he said reluctantly. He would come on the board, as vice-chairman. But he would not be putting money in. That was fine, I said, I needed more his experience and wisdom.

I thought of two other people. Tristan Murless had been at that beach café meeting few months earlier. By all accounts he was a bit of a jack the lad about the town, still boyish at forty, and reminded me a little of the ducking-and-diving James Beck character in *Dad's Army*, Private Walker. Tristan had his own electrical business and, as a member of the Round Table, helped with the organization of Weymouth Carnival. I approached him, too, and he agreed. He would help run the bars, do the electrical work around the ground, he said. He was owed a lot of money by a man called Martyn Harrison – the man who had bought the hotel from Matt McGowan – and would buy shares in the near future.

A month earlier, I had been in our club bankers in the town with Nigel Winship, changing the signatures on the club accounts. A burly figure in jeans and sweatshirt, aged around thirty, approached me. His name was Jamie Lyones, he said, and he had his own scaffolding company in the town. 'I think what you are doing at the club is fantastic,' he added. 'Anything I can do to help, just let me know.'

Now I rang him, invited him to meet me at the club. He seemed an engaging, enthusiastic character. He had been asked to join the board before, he said, but always felt that Terry Bennett was just trying to get money out of him. What he really wanted to do was play an active role at the club. He was a 'doer', he said, had various business interests, including an Internet company that sold sex toys. He could, he said, sell anything. I thought we had better keep that quiet, but his attitude was just what was needed. The previous directors were resistant, notably Peter Shaw, to doing any more work for the club.

I hoped Jamie would be able to invest some money as the season went on and he said he would. In the meantime, I wanted people like him and Tristan prepared to get their hands dirty. They set about freshening up the stadium with gusto. I soon called them the Chuckle Brothers. To you, to me.

One night just a couple of weeks before the start of the season, they came with me to a Supporters' Club committee meeting, for which the agenda was money and chips. The committee had been the backbone of the club, raising more than £20,000 the previous season. They ran the tea bars around the ground, the club shop, and organised fundraisers such as car boot sales.

Now I wanted them to raise £30,000; feasible since I thought that we would sell more merchandise. I think the committee was taken aback, but we on the board were working hard for nothing and I expected them to as well. They were also reluctant to cook chips, they said, but would give it a go. I said that we would also be bringing in a burger van, splitting profits 50–50. It helped having Tristan and

Jamie as backup. Later I heard that Jamie was being dubbed 'the chairman's muscle'. It made me smile.

There were casualties. The Supporters' Club treasurer Lloyd Starkey resigned, and another supporter, Richard Woods, thought we were denigrating their efforts and quit. I assured him that I respected him and them greatly, though, and he returned.

Out of adversity had come strength. We now had a completely new board, except for the supporters' representative Nigel Beckett, and I felt we were on the march.

Money was starting to come in. I sold a sponsorship package to my employers at *The Observer* and Vikki, a sports writer with *The Sun*, got them to buy one too, a rare occurrence as they normally only back major concerns, such as England, rarely individual clubs. In addition, *The People*, with whom Steve had a column, also took out a deal. It was gratifying. Unfortunately, some offers had to be turned down. A circus wanted to hire our car park to put up a big top but it coincided with a match.

The problem was that as fast as the money came in, it went out. No sooner had you received good news from a sponsor you had been wooing than a bill would come in. The Conference wanted £1750 for our application to join the new setup of North and South Divisions under the existing National League, for the following season.

Steve rang. For our opening game at Hednesford, he wanted the players to stay in a hotel on the Friday night. I was reluctant. He said the players would pay a third of the cost, leaving the club to pay about £600. It would show we were professional, he said, give the players a lift. Steve believed implicitly in preparation. I decided to back him, especially since he was still beneath the wage limit of £6500 a week, but said we would review it match by match.

Some things I paid for myself, staple things in the life of a chairman. There was a golf day for our club captain John Waldock and £50 to sponsor a hole was the least I could do as part of the testimonial for a player, and person, I admired. The PA box had been leaking and damaging the stereo equipment to play CDs before games, so I bought a new one for a couple of hundred quid.

At last the season began, not a moment too soon after all the effort and agony of the summer. But I would not be there and it felt odd, awful. Most people would have relished a ticket for Arsenal on the opening day of the season, my work taking me to Highbury, but instead my heart was in Hednesford, a former mining town in Staffordshire, to the north of Birmingham. A mere five months ago, we had been battling against relegation with them, crashing 4–0 at home. Surely, after all we had been through since then, we would fare better than that. Hopes were high, as are those of every football fan in the country on the eve of a new season.

Not a match has been lost, optimism is in every step. It is like going away on holiday and coming back thinking that there might be some life-changing mail on the doormat. That new manager, those new signings he made in the summer are going to make all the difference. The travails of last season are forgotten. This year, we are going to challenge for that title.

The Hednesford programme was full of references to Claridge and Ridley. It was taking me a while to get used to being written about, instead of the one doing the writing. I was described as the new owner of Weymouth. I wished. One columnist took me to task for having written the previous year in *The Observer* that Farnborough Town had disdained the spirit of the FA Cup by switching their tie against Arsenal to Highbury just to make money. Good. Someone had been reading. I confess, though, that the prospect of a windfall now, in my new persona, was tempting, even if I hoped the purist in me would have wanted our town to have a wonderful day at home.

'Weymouth still face problems with four long-serving directors resigning and ex-manager Geoff Butler's insistence that he will take legal proceedings against Ridley over his dismissal,' the programme also noted. It was true; but Geoff was blustering. He didn't want to go to court. All he wanted was a settlement of that extra year on his contract he had persuaded Terry Bennett to grant him as a way of sticking two fingers up to me. We would get round to it.

We were, Hednesford said, among the bookmakers' favourites now, with the appointment of Claridge an 'inspired' move. Actually, it was because of one sizeable bet on us.

We apparently looked anything but favourites, and inspiration was lacking. A stalwart supporter Tim Davis, who was the club's unpaid and remarkably dedicated football-in-the-community officer, was texting me updates. The feeling of being on the receiving end of them has become one of the modern sources of pleasure and pain for a fan. When it beep-beeps, you pause. Is it a goal for them? Or us?

It was tense, hard to concentrate on Arsenal. I had butterflies in my stomach and each text message prompted a missed heartbeat, a deep breath, before I could open it. Beep-beep. Penalty to them. Beep-beep. Jason Matthews saves. Beep-beep. Goal disallowed. Lee Phillips header two feet over the line. Beep-beep. Full-time 0–0.

In my heart, I had hoped for a convincing win to serve notice that the club was back among the big guns of this league. I thought in Claridge and Phillips we would surely have goals. I also thought a win would help boost the gate in advance of our first home game against Newport County on Tuesday night. As it was, we had merely matched last season's away result against the Pitmen. Would fans think nothing much had changed?

Still, draw away, win at home; the stuff of champions.

Point gained, and all that. Hadn't lost on opening day. I hoped I wasn't the only one who believed it.

Steve certainly did. As soon as I had finished my match report at Arsenal, I phoned him. It was decent enough, he said, we had battered them and deserved to win. Like me he was disappointed. I didn't want him to hear my disappointment. It was important he believed it to be a good result.

Self-doubt assailed me again, though. I had been dreaming when I imagined that we might storm the league. We clearly weren't that good yet. Eight of the games on opening day were drawn, the other three being settled by the odd goal. This was going to be a tight league.

I drove down to Weymouth on the Monday ready for another couple of days of meetings and admin ahead of our match against Newport. Did we have enough stewards and turnstile operators? Were the terraces clean? Would fans really see a difference? Did they care? What they really cared about was a winning team and we didn't have one yet. So would they even come?

I turned up at the ground ridiculously early for the 7.45 p.m. kickoff, couldn't sit around any longer. On the way, I bought some claret and blue flowers, went to Dad's grave and laid them. I was sponsoring the game in his memory and was thinking about him constantly, wishing he could have been here. Then again, if it was a damp squib, I wouldn't have wanted him to witness the humiliation. Vikki and I got out of the car at the new board advertising fixtures and sponsors at the entrance to the car park. A passing fan kindly took a photo of us in front of Dad's name.

I was astonished to find workmen still grouting and tiling the dressing rooms at 5 p.m., lines still being painted in the car park. A new batch of advertising hoardings, Mel still selling madly, arrived at the ground at 5.30 ready to be fixed around the perimeter wall. We carried them out and put them in position.

I went up to the PA box to check that all the music was in place for the new era. I thought about 'Things Can Only Get Better' but it sounded too New Labour. I wanted 'Welcome Home' by Peters and Lee, for Steve. It was cheesy, but got the message across. I was trying to convey to the announcer, Pete Pavey, the timings for 'Right Here, Right Now' by Fatboy Slim mixing into Bruce Springsteen's 'Born to Run' as the teams ran out. Pete, another club stalwart of the sort who were doing a sterling job this night, was more used to putting on a record and announcing the teams. He looked at me as if I was nuts.

I went upstairs to find that the sponsors' lounge had not been cleaned. Vikki got the vacuum cleaner out and we set to work. 'I must be mad,' she said. 'I don't even do this at home.' The next time we looked up, it was around 6.30 and the Newport directors were arriving. I looked out of the window, down on to the car park. It was filling up. Was it going to work . . .?

I couldn't stay still. Went down to the dressing rooms to see Steve, say hello to the players. Checked we had enough bar staff in. Saw that Sarah Redford and Pete Saxby in the office were coping. Went to the club shop, to see how we were selling. Looked great now. Nigel Beckett had done a great job, with Kevin Mutch, son of Roger, who works for New Look and who had cadged some proper shop fittings and cabinets out of them. Outside to check on programme sales. All done with a cheery face to mask the jitters. The club needed a smile.

Then back upstairs to greet and speak with the Newport directors. Thankfully, in our club president Bob Lucas we had the perfect gentleman to see that everyone was well taken care of. A preoccupied and nervous chairman had been overlooking his duties. The next time I looked at my watch, it was 7.15 p.m.

I looked out of the window with trepidation but I couldn't

believe what I saw. The car park was full. There were queues at the turnstiles. I just had to go outside. As I walked through the bars, the place was heaving. All hands to the pumps, quite literally, and Tristan and Jamie needed another pair. Downstairs, just watching the players warming up, must have been 400 people. There were times last year when we wondered whether we would get that many to a game. There must be more than 1000 here, musn't there? Now all it needed was a winning team.

The first half hour I was as tense and nervous as I had ever been at football. As a watching journalist, you are detached. As a fan, I got wound up, but nothing like this. Now, I lived every kick but without the fan's right to shout and scream. I was going to have to start coming to games with more than just twenty cigarettes. I had smoked three already.

Then we got a free kick, about twenty yards out, just to the right of their goal. Ian Hutchinson stepped up to it. From my new vantage point high in the stand in the directors' box I could see its left-footed flight perfectly. Up it went over the Newport wall, down it came under their crossbar for the first goal of the new era. It was the most wonderful goal I had ever seen Weymouth score. Good old, dear old, Hutch.

Wouldn't you know it. Straight from the restart Newport launched the ball into our half, cockup in defence, 1–1. Dad would have liked that.

Back and forth the ball went in the second half. We could have lost it as they created chances and the heart sank. Then we won it and the spirit soared. The ball dropped into their penalty area and Lee Phillips popped up with a low volley steered into their net. The Wessex went wild. I could not resist standing up, arms aloft

It is funny that you go to a game for entertainment, for your money's worth, but as a devoted fan you would happily settle for getting short-changed when your team is winning. I wished the referee could have blown for full-time there and then. Instead there were fifteen minutes of agony before we could explode again. For most it was in joy. For me it was relief that this night had worked.

I hugged Vikki and a tear came to my eye. No matter what the future held, we would always have this night, when it all came together, when it all worked.

In the end, the crowd totalled 1453. Peter Shaw was not one of them. This had been a wing-and-a-prayer business all summer, based on a belief that this was a football town, and that people would turn out to watch if you gave them proper facilities and something worth watching. I felt humbled.

Steve was delighted, though he said we hadn't played as well as we had done at Hednesford. It would do for me. Four points from two games; do that for the remaining forty games and we would get the championship, I reckoned. I was sure that eighty-four points would win it.

It was nearly midnight before I got away. I wanted to go round to thank everyone, from Sarah to as many of the volunteers as I could find, for helping to launch the dream. Actually, I was reluctant to leave the place, knowing that I would barely sleep with the excitement. They know bigger nights than this at Manchester United, Chelsea and Arsenal, even at Yeovil, but I doubt they have ever felt as proud and as elated as I did that night.

I got up at 7 a.m. to write the 'Chairman's Chat' column for the programme for Saturday's home match against Nuneaton Borough and, still on a natural high, I got carried away. 'It was an emotional night for me,' I wrote. 'The sight of so many people and the sound of the buzz around the ground really made all the hard work done by so many people here over the summer worthwhile.

'I also sponsored the game in memory of my late father. I would have loved for him to have seen it all but I know that he would have been proud of everyone that night and he was there in spirit. And what spirit everyone showed, fans and team alike.

'But, to quote Winston Churchill: "This is not the end, this is not even the beginning of the end. But it is the end of the beginning." '

The day after the Newport game was Carnival Day, probably the biggest day in the town's year. More than 250,000 flocked in for the sideshows, rides and, highlight of the day, the procession that snaked from the Pavilion Theatre car park at one end of the beach to the Lodmoor Country Park at the other, a journey of no more than a mile and half but which took an hour and a half, so many 'floats' were there.

At 3 p.m., I went over to the ground ready to help the volunteers decorate the open-top bus that, after several weeks of hassle, I had finally managed to obtain from the bus company. It was due to arrive at 4 p.m. At 4.30, I got through to the manager. He was sorry, etc. It arrived finally at nearly five and it was a mad dash down to the Pavilion.

It was hard work but I had persuaded Steve to stay down for the day and take part as the ambassador for the club. We judged one of the categories of float together, when he wasn't on his mobile, that was. As the evening turned cold, he managed to stay upstairs at the front of the bus, but this wasn't his thing. We shook our fists in mock horror at a few young lads wearing Yeovil Town shirts. He acknowledged the cheers of a few on holiday wearing Birmingham and Leicester City shirts.

I was a bit taken aback in the car park at the theatre when I got chatting to Micky Jones, thanking him for supplying the material to patch up the stand roof. 'I can't help you any more,' he said. 'Not while you've got Jamie Lyones on the board. We've got history. And he owes me money.'

I had had my first taste of small-town rivalries. It would not be the last.

The next day took me to the west coast of France to meet up with Tony Adams, who was on a sponsored long-distance cycle ride to raise funds for his Sporting Chance charity, which helped sportsmen and women suffering from addictive illnesses. I was writing an article for *Observer Sport Magazine*, then going on to Paris to the World Athletics Championships to record Jonathan Edwards's retirement from triple-jumping. I also wanted to ask Tony to come and do a fundraising dinner for me at Weymouth.

All the while, I was on the phone to the club, checking on things. On the Saturday, we were playing Nuneaton Borough, the pre-season favourites to win the championship, having just been relegated from the Conference. It was an epic struggle, text messages informed me, Steve bundling home a goal for a 1–1 draw after Nuneaton had taken an early lead. I had hoped for a winning message to be sent, but at least Steve had scored his first goal and we were still unbeaten.

What disappointed me more was the attendance. At 1379 – which we would have been delighted with before the season had started – it was almost 100 down on opening night. I had hoped we would have got 1500 after winning our opening game at home. Still, it was the highest in the country at our level during this holiday season and only beaten by four in the Conference.

Then someone told me that the *Echo* the night before had carried an interview with Steve previewing the game, saying that he was feeling an injury and might not be playing. When I heard, I told him not to do that again, that we needed people to think he might be playing to maximize the gate. It wouldn't exactly be a lie. Steve was so fit that he recovered quickly and, anyway, often played while hurting, as he did against Nuneaton. I felt like Lew Grade: you're killing me at the box office.

Steve, as he is prone to if people are trying to control him, did not take kindly to being told what to say and what not to say. I pointed out that if the gate went down, so did his bonus. At this point, he very quickly grasped what I was saying.

I was back in time to travel down to Devon to see us play Tiverton Town on the August Bank Holiday Monday. It was a reunion, both for Steve and me, with Martyn Rogers. I feared the worst; a player or manager you have tried to get can often do damage against you. Besides, we rarely took anything way from Tiverton, and had been beaten 3–0 towards the end of the previous season when our relegation fears were at their most pressing.

Something else increased my sense of trepidation about the day. During the week I had received an anonymous letter at the club. It detailed allegations about Jamie Lyones, saying that he had made some enemies in local business dealings, owed money and had threatened people. It alarmed me.

The only fair thing was to show it to Jamie. I also needed to gauge his response and hear his version of events. We sat in Tivvy's little stand an hour before kick-off and he digested it. 'It's all bollocks,' he said. 'OK,' I replied, 'I will take your word for it and will back you.' He had been an asset so far and I could only speak as I found, rather than believe someone anonymous who may have had an axe to grind.

It looked as if it would be a long, fruitless day. We fell a goal behind, then lost Lee Phillips to injury, bringing Scott Partridge on. I was already starting to worry a little that Scott, even so early, was becoming a peripheral figure.

But Scott immediately took to it and helped create an equaliser just before half-time for John Lamb, the young left-winger Steve had promoted from the reserves. John was a frail figure – a manager of a McDonald's franchise in the town, he had clearly not been sampling enough of his employer's product – and I was delighted he was getting his chance. That was one good thing about Steve. He had brought in some quality, expensive at our level, in the likes of Lee Philpott and Scott Partridge but was also making the most of the resources already at the club.

The tension of watching the game from the directors' seats was too much for me. I still wasn't used to sitting and keeping my cool. So for the second half, I made my way on to the terraces to stand with Jack and watch the game there, keeping my distance from the main bulk of fans but able to move about. It was bizarre hearing 'Ridley, Ridley, give us a wave' from fans twenty-five yards away. It was always a joy to have Jack at my side but now a bit embarrassing.

It was a tense duel in the sun but with about a quarter of an hour left, Steve got to the byline expertly and cut the ball back for John Lamb to lash into the net, no more that ten yards away from me. That was another thing I liked about non-League football – how close you could get to the action.

We held on for a 2–1 win and from being nineteenth after the goalless draw on opening day – mainly due to the alphabetically unfortunate W at the start of our name – we were now fourth in the table. We were in great shape and spirits. Steve sent me a text as I drove home. 'I don't feel I am getting enough love from you,' it said. I smiled and rang him back. 'But you're getting enough money,' I said.

More points, and bonus money, followed on the Saturday when we won 2–1 at Hinckley, who had won their first two home games. Steve netted his second of the season and Scotty, in place of the injured Lee, got his first for the club late on. Now we were second, with eleven points from five games. Above the average of two points a game.

With Bath City at home on the Tuesday, it was all looking rosy. Except that you find out pretty quickly as a chairman that every silver lining has a cloud.

CHAPTER EIGHT

The numbers game

As a fan, it was an exciting week to contemplate. After Bath on the Tuesday, we had another home game against Merthyr Tydfil on the Saturday. Six points from those two – and neither of those clubs had started the season well, languishing already in the bottom half – and we would be top of the league.

I was no longer just a fan, however. We could not afford a chief executive but clearly needed someone to oversee, pull it all together, from playing matters to admin. Sarah and Roger in the office could take care of a lot, Mel was selling away merrily, but it needed a hand on the tiller. And being best when busy, I enjoyed dipping in and out of every facet of the club. Even if I did fret. But then I had accepted myself as a worrier, as someone who used it as motivation. What was that adage about if you wanted something done, ask a busy person?

It was, though, coming together, and on the surface all was going swimmingly. Tristan and Jamie were working wonders around the stadium, getting it cleaner and more inviting, as well as keeping on the ground contractor's case and making the bars more efficient. Volunteers like Steve Dadd and Nigel Beckett were motivated anew. All could see the green shoots of recovery in these balmy days of August.

Underneath, we were still paddling furiously, issues ever

to be dealt with. The women's team wanted to play all their games on the stadium pitch, but it was difficult enough with the reserves and the passing game Steve had implemented needed a good surface. We couldn't afford to let it get in the same state as last season. So we worked out a compromise of up to four games, their big ones. They were duly miffed.

There were programme notes to be written – and now the programme, with the editor James Murphy on form, looked glossier and more literate – interviews with local papers and radio stations. There were letters to answer, fans who had made complaints, about things like the public address system being too loud, to be contacted. I felt it needed the personal touch. I had also been trying to ensure that a bus service on matchdays from the town centre was running properly. I met with the contracted head groundsman, Clive, to tell him how unhappy I was that the training ground was still not being worked on.

I needed, too, to have a word with the maintenance man Trevor. There was discarded chewing gum blocking the urinals. He would need a pair of rubber gloves. The *Football Diaries* crew was now following me frequently, to the point I often forgot they were there but even they drew the line at filming this. I was trying to point them in the direction of club 'characters' but they kept coming back to me and Steve.

Success and sadness still arrived on a daily basis. There would be joy at Mel selling another sponsorship package, regret that Neil McNab, Steve's excellent coach, had set his heart on taking his family to America to take up a coaching position and would not be persuaded to stick with us.

Most important, there were meetings about money. I had still not settled with Geoff Butler for the final year of his contract. And we were still working on the budget for the season, fine tuning on a weekly basis, now that we had some early figures.

First, football being the priority – because from its success came every income stream – I needed to meet with Steve, to see what we had learned from the first five games of the season. I went to his house and we decided to go on to watch nearby Havant and Waterlooville play, to scout players and future opposition, with both them and their opponents Dover Athletic also in our league.

The ground is in a grim area of Havant, a town near Portsmouth. I had never been able to work out how they attract such a decent brand of player on gates of around 400. Now I was finding out how the finances at this level, probably many higher up, too, worked. Quite simply, directors put in money, on a monthly or annual basis, to keep the losses manageable.

We watched as Havant took a two-goal lead, then Steve wanted a cup of tea at half-time, so we made our way to the boardroom. At Weymouth, we extended hospitality to scouts and club officials. The problem, I was about to realize, was that Weymouth as a club had never really got on with Havant. I recalled that a few years ago I had been in the boardroom at the Wessex when the former Manchester United and England player Neil Webb was manager and Matt McGowan was on the board. Weymouth had just beaten Havant 5–0 and Matt took great, gloating delight in adding that scoreline to the list when the other results were read out, to the displeasure of the Havant directors. Bad blood had apparently existed ever since. Such are the rivalries in football based on.

At the entrance to the Havant boardroom, the chairman Derek Pope stopped us. Steve would not be allowed in wearing those jeans, he said. Actually they were black and perfectly presentable. We went into the bar instead, but I could not resist informing Mr Pope, a prickly, rough-edged man of the sort I was coming to meet in non-League football, that in pre-season we had accorded a Havant representative full hospitality for a friendly he had come to watch, even though he was informally dressed. Mr Pope told me not to come into his boardroom uninvited. I would remember this. We left early, cheered that Dover had scored twice to force a draw.

The next day, the day of our game against Bath City, Geoff Butler arrived at the Wessex Stadium for his 10.30 a.m. appointment. I had been receiving letters from a solicitor at the Professional Footballers' Association threatening court action but I knew that Geoff would not want that, given an earlier case he had brought against Salisbury City as well as everything coming out about him and the club in court.

He claimed he was owed £16,000 – at £200 a week for 12 months, plus £112 a week in expenses and back commission for sponsorship he had arranged. I was unwilling to pay more than £8000. Why, I wondered, should we be paying expenses that he would not be incurring? He had been talking to Dave Higson and Mick Archer at Park Engineering and they wanted it sorted, telling me that they had left money in the club to pay it. But it was money they were lending, as the loans book that Sarah kept in the safe in her office showed. They were not donating it. The club was still ultimately footing the bill. And I was still annoyed that Terry Bennett had given him this contract when he knew that I would be coming in as chairman.

Geoff pointed out that he would have been due the expenses if he had stayed. But he wasn't staying, I said. That wasn't the point, he countered. And so it went on. I was beginning to understand that football worked on 'expenses'. Some people seemed to see them as a way of getting cash in hand.

After three hours, we settled on 10K. He thought he had got a result, I thought the club had got one. Sarah faxed the settlement to the PFA. I later came to learn that payoffs up to that figure are non-taxable. He was always going to settle for that. Another lesson learned about the crazy world inside football. He walked away with a cheque and I didn't expect to hear from him again. I certainly wouldn't be saying anything other to the press than the joint statement of mutual content that the matter had been settled.

The money factored in, Nigel Winship and I met yet again that day to go over the figures. They were becoming an obsession. As someone once said about money: it's like sex; you think of nothing else if you don't have it, other things if you do.

The gate receipts from the Newport and Nuneaton home games were in. Yes, it looked as if we could realistically expect to average 1200 through the gate. We had also received a mess of bills, which ought to give an indication of real, rather than projected costs. I had always been responsible with my own household accounts, tried to pay them off within the deadline. Now the gas, electric and water rates on a bigger scale were tedious chores.

Football accounts ought to be simple enough. You work out your gate money and your sponsorship income, then deduct all the expenses, then decide what you can afford to pay the players. For a financially successful club like Manchester United, paying out 50 per cent of your income in wages represented good husbandry. Few clubs did it, however.

Many were paying out money they weren't getting in. If directors or a financial benefactor were prepared to pay the deficit each year, fair enough. Jack Walker had done it at Blackburn Rovers, then decided that the club must pay its own way once he had provided the initial impetus. As a result, on gates of 20,000, Blackburn no longer competed as once they had done when they realized Walker's dream of winning the championship of England.

Often, after relegation when income falls, clubs can be stuck with average players on long contracts. And then you are paying them more than you can afford. That, though, is the going rate. Players who don't get it with you – and the best players are the ones everyone with any ambition wants – will get it elsewhere. Football is a game of skill and judgement off the field as well, about finding the right players at the right prices. Not even Sir Alex Ferguson, Arsene Wenger and José Mourinho – even Roman Abramovich – always get it right, however.

I had always stressed that this season would be a season of investment, of speculating to accumulate, a loss leader. The town and club needed new impetus and it was going to cost. After this season, when we no longer had to fork out to get the stadium up to scratch again to the tune of around £50,000, I hoped to leave a legacy of a club working within its means. I hoped, within two years, to have done the club a service by both taking it to a level appropriate to its status and fan-base but always making it subsequently break even each season. I saw too many chairmen thinking they were doing everybody a favour by chasing overexpensive short-term success then leaving them with huge debts when they had had enough of the struggle and the criticism.

Nigel and I sat down and looked at the figures that were now a reality rather than the speculation of the summer. The Nuneaton game had grossed £7217.50 through the gate, not quite the multi-million pound operation of Old Trafford but more than double what they had been taking per game at Weymouth last season. After deductions of £262 for expenses – referee, turnstile operators and the like – plus VAT of £1074.95, we were left with £5880.55. The net figure for the Newport game was £6400.

On top, we took around £1500 through the bars per game, and as someone who didn't drink, there was some irony in hoping others did. Mind you, I always thought a quid for a small Coca-Cola was a bit steep. There was also around £500 for programmes. Along with £850 for matchday sponsorship, it meant about £9000 coming in per game.

With the shirt and stadium sponsorship, it was around £10,500 a match.

All that was fine. The trouble was, you also had expenses. There was water, gas and electricity at around £1000 a month. There were the phones, another £150 a month, though Jamie was working on a deal to try to get the cost down. The washing machines and photocopiers we leased were costing around another £100 a week. As well, there was the inherited debt. We were paying interest of £1680 a month and around £400 a month to service the overdraft.

Above all, there were wages. The admin staff wages, for Sarah, Mel, Roger and Trevor, along with small payments to helpers such as Bob Mowlem, were manageable enough at around £1000 a week, but the players were the key. We had given Steve the budget of £6500 a week, rising to around £7500 a week with bonuses. And with him earning an average of £1500 a week, it meant we would be losing around £2000 a week over the season.

Nigel's detailed figures showed that the trading loss on the season would be around £150,000. It sounded a huge, worrying sum after the £80,000 lost last season, but our aim was to break even in cash-flow terms, so that the club did not add to the current £300,000 debt. With £100,000 having come in from directors already, and with Jamie and Tristan having promised to put in more, we were duly, gratifyingly, on course to break even in real terms.

Perhaps we would even make a profit if gates continued to rise and we got promoted, taking into account the prize money. Then there was still the chance of an FA Cup run . . . No, best not to get carried away.

It meant, though, that I could sit down to watch that night's game against Bath City in reasonable spirits. It was actually a pleasure when matches kicked off. No, actually that wasn't true. It was respite, and a reminder that this was the real business of a football club. I always remember Paul

Gascoigne saying that the ninety minutes of a match was the only time, and the field the only place, where he felt truly free. But it was all right for players, they didn't have to look around the stands and wonder what the gate revenue might be, what were the bar takings, how many programmes we had sold.

It was another good crowd – 1567 as Pete Saxby would come to tell me late in the second half; it was the only time during the game that I liked to be interrupted – but we needed three points to keep them coming.

It looked like we would comfortably get them. We were 2–0 up in half an hour, Steve scoring again, along with Steve Tully from the penalty spot. Then Steve was the victim of a scything tackle from behind. It signalled what could happen at this level. I had warned him in the summer about some of the physical stuff in this league but he was not worried, said he had had it all his career. This was something else, though. Now we were seeing no-marks looking to make a name for themselves by making marks on the legendary, socks-down shins of Steve Claridge. He seemed to take it better than I did. In his *People* column the previous week, he told good-humouredly of a centre half at Hinckley who had spent the game kicking him, then told him afterwards he was a legend.

Steve became a passenger for the last ten minutes of the half and Bath gained some momentum. It was turned into tangible product when our young central defender Mark Kenway, another whom Steve had promoted from the reserves, got himself sent off just before half-time for striking one of their players off the ball and Bath reduced the gap to 2–1 from the penalty spot. It was barely believable when, in the second half, our ten men found themselves 3–2 down with ten minutes left. Finally, Steve wriggled around in the box to win a penalty and Tully converted for a fortunate draw.

Afterwards I was was furious with Kenway and told Steve so. I wanted him fined two weeks' wages but Steve said that he was distraught and he should forfeit just one. I reluctantly agreed, not wishing to be too Draconian too soon, or to disturb morale further than the incident and result had done. It had been thrilling stuff – and Steve had promised fans they were in for entertainment, if nothing else, this season – but I knew that fans came to watch winning teams, for the all the talk of thrills.

The saving grace for me was no win bonus and the best crowd of the season so far. And though we would not ascend to the top of the table, I could go away to Italy, where I was covering Italy v. Wales in a World Cup qualifier, in Milan, in good heart.

And so, five days later, I sat in a pizzeria by the magnificent Duomo on a Saturday afternoon with Vikki, waiting for those agonizing text messages. Mel informed me that we were 1–0 up. Then 2–0 up. Life was good. I was surrounded by Welshmen and couldn't resist enquiring if any of them were from Merthyr.

None was, but they wanted to know how Swansea City were doing at Yeovil. A quick couple of texts later and I was able to tell them they had already lost 2–0. My own smugness was soon interrupted, however, when the next beep-beep told me that Merthyr had halved the deficit against us. My appetite for the pizza was disappearing.

Around half an hour later, I was getting twitchier. The game must be over by now. I was about to board the metro for the San Siro when I got the beep-beep. I opened the text expecting to read 'won 2–1'. Instead it was '2–2. Last-minute equaliser.' Merthyr most foul.

I felt sick and in a daze. As I walked from metro station to stadium, some Welsh fans around me were singing 'always look on the bright side of life'. I couldn't help smiling. 'It's only a game of soccer,' said one Italian to a Welshman. 'Oh no it's not,' he replied. And that's how, right now, I felt too.

Steve rang just as I was going into the stadium and I asked him to ring back in ten minutes. He didn't. Typical. So I rang him. He needed, he said, a new centre back and a new striker. The centre back I could understand. We had Jamie Impey, tall and imposing when at his best, frequently injured and I did wonder if Mark Kenway, though a talented footballer, was going to be strong enough for this level. Steve had also, due to injuries, been forced into playing Lee Russell, more naturally a central defender, at left back.

But a striker? What was wrong with Scott Partridge? Steve found him difficult to play with in the absence of Lee Phillips, he said. He had missed chances, wasn't working hard enough to ease the pressure on the defence, flitted in and out of games. I felt that having given Scott three years on good money, we should give him a chance. He had, after all, grabbed the winner at Hinckley the week before.

I put the phone down and surveyed the beauty of the San Siro as it filled up. A member of the Welsh press corps approached me. 'Hi, Ian. My name is Anthony Hughes and I am the secretary of Merthyr Tydfil Football Club,' he said. I could only smile. 'I have two words for you and one of them is off,' I said. He smiled in return.

For the second time in a week, we had conceded a two-goal lead and slipped to fourth in the table, with Nuneaton Borough and Worcester City setting a fast pace. In fact, I wouldn't have trusted the team to walk a dog, so bad were they becoming at holding leads. But we were still unbeaten, third in the table, and I was trying to stay positive, as my programme notes always told fans to do.

Always look on the bright side of life, I thought, as I was herded by the *carabinieri* with a now silent knot of Welsh fans, their team having lost 4–0, down into the metro after the game. We had sneaked the win in added time at

Hinckley the week before. Couldn't really complain. And no win bonuses to pay this week, which was just as well as the crowd figure had fallen to 1123.

The mood of the club was sombre when I got back on the Monday, a board meeting to look forward to. I was also taken aback to find new furniture in the Wessex Lounge, the club's main bar, which made it look like a gothic night-club. Tristan and Jamie had been doing deals, and reckoned that for £1800 it was worth it. I was less convinced, and neither was it in the budget, but I had to back their enthusiasm.

Charlie Lesser had also offered to pay off the club's debt to the bank, the club repaying him instead at 1 per cent less interest. It was tempting but we decided that it might look as if a director was receiving remuneration, which was strictly prohibited by the club's articles and memoranda.

We were doing well enough financially, though, Sarah reported. The overdraft was down to £28,000 and there was £27,000 in an account we had set up for directors' investment so that it did not all get swallowed up in paying off the debts of the past but could instead be used for team building or essential costs, like kit. It was a pleasure to double Sarah's matchday bonus to £20. Crowds, after all, had doubled and so had her workload.

Games were now coming thick and fast. In fact, the first six weeks saw teams play eleven games, which was more than a quarter of the league season. The idea in the non-League game was that after a summer without income, clubs needed as much as they could get as soon as possible. I understood why.

On the Tuesday we went to Chippenham Town, who had been the surprise packet the previous season, finishing fifth and even being in with a shout of the title at one point. Again we were 2−0 up, thanks to two beautiful curling shots by Steve, and again we conceded. This time I was not so nervous though, and Luke Nightingale sealed the win late on with his first goal for the club.

The display of passing football made me really proud, with Paul Buckle and Lee Philpott particularly impressive. Afterwards Steve Dadd approached me to say that a home fan in the gents had been talking about what a good side we were. 'That's my team you're talking about,' said Steve, delighted at the turnaround this season.

I poked my head around the Chippenham dressing-room door as I was leaving, to say cheerio to Tommy Saunders, the manager who had applied for the vacant Weymouth job in the summer. 'I wouldn't mind your centre forward,' he said. 'You couldn't afford him,' I said with a smile. That Friday I read in the *Western Gazette* that, according to Tommy, I had told him that Claridge was on as much as his entire squad. That sounded like Tommy, all right. He had applied for the Weymouth job, he told me in the summer, out of frustration that he could get no extra money out of his board when they were going for the title and had tailed away. I could now understand both sides of the argument.

Steve was on fire and bagged another brace on the Saturday at home to Cambridge City on a beautiful sunny day to give us a 2–1 win. I had taken the day off from my work to be there, because all the club's teams, from under 8s upwards, had assembled for their team pictures and I wanted to talk to them about the new Weymouth. I took the microphone, told them what Tony Adams had once been told as a kid at Arsenal: 'Remember who you are, what you are, and who you represent.'

With the crowd back up to 1454 and us up to second, only two sets of win bonuses clouded the horizon. But what stuck in my mind that day was a tackle by Lee Russell. There were ten minutes left and we were clinging on to our lead when Lee brought down one of the Cambridge

forwards, through on goal, and was fortunate to escape
with a yellow card.

The journalist in me said that had I been covering
the game, I would have demanded a red and written how
disgraceful was the challenge. Now, I was just grateful that
we had clung on to the lead. Come the end of season, it
could be an important moment that had saved two crucial
points. My standards were slipping. Now I was beginning to
understand a little better that self-centred approach of those
within the game. Professionalism, and not Corinthianism,
too. The tackle had not been vicious or malicious. Lee was
just doing a job for his team and his club. Mind you, had
it been on Claridge I would have been furious.

I tried not to show too much emotion in the directors'
box. Personally, I had always admired the sangfroid of
Liverpool directors whenever I had sat in the adjacent press
box at Anfield and observed them. I tried to be the same
myself, treating triumph and disaster as equal imposters,
behaving with dignity. Even I was impressed, though, by the
equanimity and magnanimity of the Cambridge contingent
faced with such an incident. I am not sure how I would
have reacted. I hoped I wouldn't find out.

The next Tuesday took us over the Severn Bridge to
Newport, a curious return since we had played them, also
in the league, only a month earlier. Such were the vagaries
of the Southern League fixtures, worked out, word had
it, by a bloke on holiday with a pencil rather than any
computer.

Newport had been a famous old League club years
ago, respresenting Wales in some stirring European ties, but
fell into the Conference at the same time as Weymouth
went into decline. Their plight worsened, however, beyond
our mere relegation. They even went out of business and
lost their ground, reforming in the humble Hellenic League
and playing at borrowed pitches over the border in England

before returning to the new athletics stadium, named Spytty Park, in the town.

Like us, they fancied themselves as a potentially big club with a big fan base. They also, as a consequence, had their fair element of the, shall we say, overenthusiastic fringe. Now managed by the former Arsenal and Crystal Palace midfield player Peter Nicholas, somewhat grander of girth than in his playing days, they were also aiming for promotion. They would be up for it against us. Nicholas, somewhat ungraciously, had told me how fortunate we had been to win the first encounter.

It was a tight, scrappy affair, on a bumpy pitch. I have always detested grounds with athletics tracks around them, which dissipate the atmosphere. At Spytty, such terracing as there is behind the goals is at least forty yards away from the pitch at one end, a high jump run-up also separating pitch from spectator. Not that anyone stands at that end.

Only one comedy moment lightened the mood. Our full back Simon Browne sustained a hamstring injury and the stretcher was called for. They were one man light, however, and the mascot, Spytty the Dog, lent a hand. Or a paw. Except that he dropped the stretcher and Simon went sprawling.

Actually, Simon inadvertently began a racial row as a result. Fans on the website wondered how he was. He went on himself to say he was fine but that the Welsh idiot who had dropped him had not helped. On came Newport fans – and these modern phenomena of Internet chat rooms and forums have become an often abusive cross-fertilization – to complain. Back went ours to say they had been called English twats.

I emailed Simon to tell him that it might be best if he didn't contribute to the forum. I didn't, I said. I thought it best to let fans have their independent voice, not to bite on anything, and use the press or programme notes to comment.

It finished as a 1–1 draw, Luke Nightingale grabbing the goal, and we were grateful to get out with our unbeaten record, and second place in the table, intact. Four points off Newport – the same against every team and we would surely be champions. No, stop that again. First things first, don't count chickens, and all the other footballing clichés. You just couldn't help your mind wandering off now and then, though.

It positively flew into the stratosphere three days later when we won 2–0 at Weston-super-Mare, this time with Steve, feeling the effects of ten games in five weeks, leaving himself on the bench for the first time and John Waldock and Lee Philpott scoring. It was reassuring to see that we could win a game without Steve, not that he would see it that way.

Now we hit the top of the table, with twenty-three points from eleven games, and Steve didn't even feel we had hit our stride yet. All was well in the world and even the fans on the stretch of terracing at the Wessex known locally as the Barbara Windsor Stand, or the Babs – because it contained the oldest knockers – seemed relatively pleased.

It was a wonderful feeling and, on the Sunday morning, I just stared at the standings. Vikki's team Sheffield United were also top of what I would always call the Second Division and she cut both tables out of the papers and pinned them up in my kitchen.

I knew this chairman thing couldn't be that difficult.

CHAPTER NINE

The Cup that costs

For non-league clubs, FA Cup runs are the most memorable achievements, lingering long in club history. Even now at Weymouth, people still talk of the time back in 1950 when we went to Manchester United and lost 4–0. Or of 1981, when we won 3–2 at Cardiff City after being two down. I know, because I was there. No, at the second one.

For a club and its players, Cup runs provide a fresh focus beyond the weekly plying of the trade. The butchers, bakers and candlestickmakers step out of the pages of their local papers into the national press for a while.

Cup runs also offer a potential financial windfall that can reinvigorate clubs. In recent seasons, Farnborough Town and Exeter City had seen their debts wiped out by plum draws, against Arsenal and Manchester United respectively. Fans may dream of days out at Highbury and Old Trafford, as I had always done. Chairmen dream of cheques arriving with postmarks from London N5 or Manchester M16, as I now did.

But for every dream come true, there were scores unfulfilled and costly. Too many clubs budgeted for a run, even if not one to the later stages of the competition. Then, when it didn't happen, they were faced with a choice: cut back on the playing budget and either sell or shed players, or go on as you were and just rack up a bigger loss in the annual accounts.

Actually, selling or shedding players was not that easy in mid-season. The transfer market shrinks the lower you go. These days, you pick up players out of contract or on free transfers from clubs desperate to get them off the wage bill and those deals are done in the closed season. With players' contracts set in stone, a club has to honour them; unless it goes bust, that is. Racking up a bigger loss in the annual accounts it was, then.

I was determined that we wouldn't get into that. Our budget showed no Cup prize money or gate receipts. They would be bonuses if they arrived. Once, we had held the record – even above celebrated Cup giant-killers and local rivals Yeovil Town – for the most number of appearances by a non-League club in the first round but it had long been surpassed. A Weymouth chairman would have been a fool to have banked on a windfall these days. So poor had our record been over the past twenty years that we now found ourselves starting out in the second round of qualifying, even before the end of September. For Premiership clubs, the Cup did not start for almost another four months, for Football League clubs, another six weeks.

At this stage, Cup runs yielded little in the way of revenue. Unlike the league, where home clubs keep their own takings, in the FA Cup they are shared 50–50 at this stage, to help the smaller clubs. Later, they are divided up 40–40 with the remaining 20 per cent going to the FA itself, for prize money and administration. We could be drawn away to a very small club where the attendance was only a couple of hundred, mostly our fans. At least you got your coach paid for, though if the crowd really was tiny, expenses could outweigh takings, which meant that both clubs had to share the loss.

Prize money, though, was tantalizing. It had been one of

the FA's major achievements during Adam Crozier's time as chief executive. In an attempt to revitalize an ailing competition, they had signed a lucrative TV deal with the BBC and now there was a substantial prize fund. The winners would get £2 million, the beaten finalists £1 million. We could not fantasize about such things but even at our qualifying stage the winners would receive £7500. If we made the first round, that would bring in £20,000.

On top of the money, I dearly wanted us to have a run, to be in with those League clubs in the first round proper. There was more of a chairman about me these days but I was never going to lose my inner fan that easily. It would be good to get in some extra cash perhaps to pay off some debt or finance some signings after Christmas to strengthen a title push. But above all that, I wanted our name to be known nationally again. I was sure, with the contacts in television that both Steve and I had, that if we could get to the first round, could get a League club at home, we would have a good case for persuading either Sky or the BBC to make us their live game. We both had contacts in the sports departments there. As well as another carrot of £20,000 for reaching the second round, there could be at least £50,000 for a live match.

We got a bad draw, though. Newport County away. We had already had two tough games against them and we knew we would be in for a third. On the morning of the game, I rang Steve to wish him luck. He was clearly touched. 'Piss off. You're only worried about the money,' he said.

There seemed nothing to be worried about early on, text messages informed me. Goals by Steve and Ian Hutchinson put us a comfortable 2–0 ahead. Then it all came home to roost. All the cracks that Steve had papered over well so far this season were suddenly exposed as we conceded three second-half goals and fell to our first defeat of the season.

Our limited, stretched squad had finally snapped. I couldn't pretend I wasn't upset when I spoke to Steve later on my way home from the Chelsea match that I was covering. However, I did understand. We hadn't been playing that well, were fortunate to be top of the table. It was the league that mattered. And all the other clichés.

It was to herald a cruel, horrible October. There is a bit of a tradition within the game that being selected for the manager of the month award is a curse and bad results will inevitably follow the good that won it. Steve had won it for September. Fortunately for him, Cup results do not count and in the league we had taken twelve points from six unbeaten games. Now we would pay, both for the award and the Cup defeat.

No, you don't actually budget for Cup runs, but what it means is that you are then left with blank weekends, league games not scheduled in the early stages because too many clubs from your own competition are still left in the Cup. It means a big impact on cash flow. The books may balance at the end of the season, but there can be fallow months when the overdraft mounts. In addition, you can budget all you like, project income and expenditure in a given month, but unless sponsors and creditors pay up at the right time, you are knackered, with a hole in the accounts.

The problem at Weymouth was that we had become good payers. No longer did we put off the coach bill, the cost of printing the programmes, until the end of the season. I preferred, as with my own credit card bill, to pay them off each month and have everything in order rather than get hit at a time, at the end of the season, when you are most vulnerable. Actually, that wasn't the problem. It was more that companies who owed us money were not quite so diligent. In business, a thirty-day payment code usually operates. Not always, though.

At a board meeting, Jamie Lyones suggested that we get in

a 'factoring' company. He used one in his own businesses, he said. The company chased your debtors for you and took a percentage, threatened legal action if they didn't cough up. I couldn't see it working for us. We who had delayed payments these past few seasons suddenly getting heavy with local companies? It would look hypocritical and I was sure they would get round to it. Even Park Engineering, who were behind with their shirt sponsorship payment.

Actually, Jamie was starting to concern me. At his suggestion, we had hired a local security firm to keep vigil at certain entrances to the ground and the main stand, taking the £1 transfer fee, something that had been done voluntarily by the women's team but who were prey to being ignored. Too many people had been sneaking in for free. This on top of a problem with season tickets. This year's had been printed the same colour as last year's and some people were getting in with the old ones, thumb hiding the date. We reckoned we were now saving around £400 a game but some fans did not like the look of nightclub bouncers around the place. I asked the company to make them wear blazers and ties, rather than black bomber jackets. I didn't want Max and Paddy from Peter Kay's *Phoenix Nights* on the front door.

In addition, Steve Dadd wrote a jolly enough little column in the programme detailing fans' trips to away games. They were often quite funny. In one, he made a reference to a large obstruction on the road on the way to a game, closer inspection revealing it to be Jamie in his car. Jamie took exception to the reference.

Thus, one day Steve Dadd came to me saying that Jamie had collared him at the ground, saying that it was disrespectful and never to write something like it again. I apologized to Steve, sought out Jamie and told him that I thought he had overreacted. It was just a bit of fun, I said. He reckoned that it had undermined his authority as a director. He said I should back him; I thought he should loosen up.

I began to worry about Jamie's motives for joining the board. Had he done so in an attempt to raise his credibility locally? He did not like to be joked about in any way. He should have been in my shoes sometimes. You just have to learn to take it, most of it being affectionate anyway. Also, amusing as it was, this 'chairman's muscle' stuff did bother me a little. I didn't think I had need of any, even if I am not the most intimidating of physical specimens.

Then one night in a minor local competition, the Two Counties Cup, on nearby Portland, Jamie spent the whole game telling me that this would not look good in the eyes of fans as the team, a mixture of youth and reserves, was losing 3–1. I told him not to worry so much, that we were still unbeaten in the league and that was what counted.

It was an early indication of how mood turns so quickly in football in general, and Weymouth in particular. Negativity about the football club had become a way of life and two defeats, no matter how peripheral, invoked deep gloom. I tried to take the positive tack: we were fortunate to have as many people still caring about the fortunes of the club.

One thing Jamie could be thanked for, along with his willingness to do the jobs around the ground that no one else would, was his suggestion that we take on Tim Davis, our football-in-the-community officer, full time. Tim, a placid, gangling figure of a man – but with that Dorset melancholy about him – who was never seen in anything other than a club shell suit and a baseball cap, was utterly devoted to the club and had been giving all his spare time for free.

Though he would now cost us another wage, we figured that he could also oversee the lottery and revamp our scratch card operation, going out into newsagents and companies.

It worked, to the point that the lottery and cards began to make about £400 a month – by having cut prize money as well – rather than losing that sum. There was a disappointment. I had wanted all the junior team managers to sell scratch cards to parents on a commission basis, that commission then going into their team's funds. They would not, however.

Tim also established a system for small companies as community partners, where they would get an advert, at the ground and in the programme, and two season tickets for £500 a year. It brought swift dividends and we ended up with fifty-two of them. 'I want you to get back my salary,' Tim said. It was typical of the can-do attitude that was prevailing, with everyone pulling in the same direction despite the financial restraints.

And there were some. Due to that away draw in the FA Cup, we were without home revenue for nearly a month. And when we did get back to playing at the Wessex, we suffered a big setback, losing our first league game 1–0 to Stafford Rangers, dropping us to second in the table. I arrived at the club that night for a quiz evening after covering a game at Portsmouth to find a pall of gloom over the place. It was the chairman's job that night yet again to be cheerful. I felt like Alfred E. Newman out of those old *Mad* comics – what me worry?

After that, we had no Saturday game scheduled for another fortnight, and no home game for three weeks because of being out of the Cup. And so, to bring in a bit of income, we fixed up another Two Counties game, against Dorchester Town, who were also out of the Cup. There was a bit of bargaining involved. They wanted to play at home, so did we. We convinced them that the gate would be higher at our place and that we could share it. They agreed. At least this way we got to keep the bar takings.

We also needed a new centre half, with Steve telling me

that he was spending hours on the phone in the week after the Stafford defeat to try to sign one. 'They keep you on the phone for ages these days, The Samaritans,' I said. 'Have they got a holding system as well?' He was not much in the mood for jokes at the moment.

I was speaking a couple of times a week to Gérard Houllier at Liverpool and he always used to ask how things were going at Weymouth. I mentioned our defensive frailty and he recommended a French centre back. Damien Perimelle had been at the youth academy at Rouen and was now playing for a lower-division club, Paris FC, until he could get something better fixed up.

We made the arrangements for him to travel over and I went to pick him up at Southampton airport, driving him straight to training on a Thursday night, the *Football Diaries* crew in tow and capturing my rusty French. Tristan Murless was going to put Damien up in the self-contained apartment annexe he had had built in his back garden. After training, Steve and I took him to Perry's and bought him a steak. I could hear him talking on his mobile to his family in France, telling them how beautiful the harbour was.

In front of a crowd of 704, he did well enough on the Saturday afternoon, revealing himself a footballing defender rather than the brick outhouse who would head and kick everything away – occasionally the ball as well if required – that Steve really wanted. We lost the game 3–2, Dorchester celebrating at the end rather more enthusiastically than the occasion demanded, but they had put one over the old enemy in the season's first skirmish between the clubs.

As I made my way through the bar afterwards I heard a voice calling my name. There, sitting with the Dorchester manager Mark Morris, was Keith Miller, that old school colleague. He hadn't liked me then, I hadn't liked him, not just because of the Dorchester–Weymouth divide even in those days but because he was, I felt, not the most sincere of people.

I half expected him to introduce me to Morris but instead he offered his hand and I shook it instinctively. 'Congratulations on what you are doing here at Weymouth,' he said. 'It needed someone to get hold of it.'

Now, I should have been gracious and thanked him, but I instantly recalled his letter to the *Echo* back in the winter when – then the Dorchester vice-chairman but now no longer a director – he congratulated the previous board on having rejected my offer in favour of, he said, stability and longer-term progress.

'That's not what you said back in January in that letter to the *Echo*,' I said. And I walked away. I was still not totally in tune with this duty of being nice to people I had no respect for.

Worse was to follow in the boardroom. I had got Damien up to meet the other directors and he asked to speak to me privately. He liked the town and the club, he said, and had enjoyed the game. But he was worried about being part time and bored during the days, with only two nights training a week. He wanted to go home, he said.

We had wanted him to stay and play another Two Counties game in midweek against Bridport but there was no point in keeping him on if he had doubts. I got on the phone, booked another air ticket with my credit card. The club shouldn't have to pay for my mistake. Tristan duly took him to Southampton airport the next day. Damien's stay, and hopefully signing, was supposed to be a nice sequence for the TV documentary but it ended up on the cutting-room floor.

We beat Bridport 7–0 to halt a run of four defeats, though only two had been of any consequence, and when we rescued a point at Worcester with a 2–2 draw on the Saturday – for once it was the opposition squandering a two-goal lead, not us – it looked like we were back on track.

Then came Havant and Waterlooville at home.

Given the relationship between the clubs, it was not a night I was looking forward to. I was, though, determined to be dignified and to treat their directors with respect. It did not get off to a good start, however. When I saw their chairman drinking in our public bar, I went up and invited him to the boardroom. 'No, I'm happier here,' he said. 'I don't like you and I don't like your club.' I just left it, and him, saying only that I was sorry he felt that way. Sometimes you don't know whether you dislike yourself more for speaking out or not speaking out. I had learned a lesson from the Keith Miller incident but didn't feel any better for holding my tongue this time.

It got worse. Havant were up for this game and flew into every tackle. They pinched a goal and held on to it. We had lost our second home league match in succession, our third important game in a row. And the crowd was only 803, more than 500 down on the Stafford game. Some said it was Champions League on the telly, some the foul night, but even so, this was going back towards the dark times. While most in our league, particularly Havant, would kill for an attendance like that, to us it was a real setback.

One of the things about visiting teams coming to Weymouth is that they also bring a horde of directors and guests with them, often more than for a home match. Given some of the hovels we were visiting, our stadium, though in need of upgrading, was a positive paradise. Havant had a party of about a dozen, more than they seemed to have at home.

I was doing my best to be stoic at us falling to fourth in the table, doing my best to be civil and entertain these folk, when Jamie Lyones came rushing in. 'The Havant players are kicking in the dressing-room door,' he said.

'You'd better come and look.' Max, or was it Paddy, had reported trouble to him.

When I went down, I could hear shouting and banging coming from the away dressing room. It was nothing really unusual for a winning team. I knocked on the door and their assistant manager, Micky Jenkins, a decent, milder sort of man than normally associated with their club, came out. There was no problem, he said. I did not want to go into their dressing room to inspect it.

I accepted it and went upstairs. One of their directors asked me what the problem had been and I told him that a security man had reported damage to our dressing room. 'It's always the same here,' he said huffily.

I asked him what he meant and he harked back to incidents years ago, then to the one involving Steve and me in September. 'I knew we wouldn't get out of here without some problem. Look mate, just send us the bill,' he added. I disliked his aggressive attitude and I calmly asked him and his other directors to leave.

It had been a sour night all round. I was annoyed that Jamie had probably overreacted again but kept that to myself, still wanting to back my people. When I later went to look at the dressing room, there was the usual mess but no real damage. I was annoyed with myself, too. Their director had been wrong; I wanted it to pass off without acrimony, to show that we at Weymouth knew how to behave and treat people, even if they had offended us. Instead, I had been drawn into a row that made me look like a bad loser.

I began to understand how rows did break out in football. For years, I had been writing columns on spats in tunnels – and tonight apparently security had also had to break up a potential punch-up between a few players in ours at the end of the game – and verbal fisticuffs by club officials. I had urged them in print to grow up.

Now I understood more how they happened, how feuds simmered and resentments were fostered. An Arsenal player throwing a pizza at Sir Alex Ferguson in a contretemps at the end of a game produced great copy and amused the nation, but I now recognized the raw emotions involved. And grasped how childish this passionate, heat-of-the-moment game could make you look and feel.

I had wanted to show that there was a different, inclusive and gracious, way of running a football club, of being a chairman. I had let my standards slip. To make amends, I agreed to an old sparring partner coming to work within the club. Our public address announcer Pete Pavey, who had a lovely, lilting Dorset burr, was finding it too much to keep up with team news, scores from elsewhere and his reports for Wessex FM as well as play music and keep the fans entertained. We needed someone alongside him to do the music.

Matt McGowan approached me to bat on behalf of Duncan Stewart, previously that most vociferous of my critics. Matt and he were old friends, spent their mornings in a coffee shop by the harbour putting the world to rights. And Duncan could certainly put it to rights. Everyone else was to blame.

He was actually working as a DJ and was rather good. And so I agreed for three reasons: 1. Because he would probably make a good job of it. 2. Because I wanted to show magnanimity. 3. If you have a critic, I figured, it was better to have him inside the tent urinating out, rather than outside the tent urinating in.

I was going through a period of self-doubt and sleepless nights. The takings had been poor for the Havant game. It was also noticeable that if you lost a game, fewer people stayed behind and spent money in the bar. Our cash flow was bad and it was hard to tell the bank that it would all add up at the end of the season when the attendance for our last home game was 400 short of the break-even figure.

To any club, money becomes less troublesome when you are winning, less of an anxiety; not just because the club makes more of it but also because the mood of the place lifts and you agonize less. Lose a couple of games and the problem seems overwhelming. I recalled what Ken Merrett, the secretary of Manchester United, once told me. Lose a game, and you get letters complaining about the stand roof leaking or the meat pies being cold. Win a game and all you get are letters wanting tickets.

At dark times like this, everyone within the club needed to look at themselves, though clearly too many in the game, comfortable in their contracts, do not. It was incumbent on me, as chairman, to look most closely at myself.

What was I doing wrong? Was I saying the wrong things, making bad decisions? Was my body language wrong? What with the finances, and many talks and meetings about the stadium development, had I taken my eye off the ball and neglected our core business, which was, quite simply, football?

I never wanted to bother Steve with my problems, as he had enough of his own. Besides, if he saw I was down, it would probably transmit itself to him and thus the team. I had to be the positive face of the club in public, do my worrying and problem-solving in private.

I just had to tell Steve about what had gone on backstage with the Havant game, though. As usual, he cut through all my self-analysis with his own ready-made pearls of wisdom. 'Wouldn't worry about it, mate,' he said. 'They're a bunch of arseholes.'

CHAPTER TEN

Turning of the tide

The darkest time, they say, is just before the dawn. I clung to that belief.

I had sensed within the club a loss of impetus after the first flush of enthusiasm. It is obvious and easy enough to trot out that football clubs are results-driven, but I had paid lip-service to it. I had not grasped deeply enough that clubs and supporters live week to week, game to game. It was because I had the long-term picture in my head, the five-year plan and vision, and a few bad results were not going to deflect from it. In Weymouth, the short-termism began to concern me.

Matt McGowan, for instance, began to question the fitness of the team and whether they were training enough. I found this hard to accept, knowing how demanding Steve was, how fit he himself was. After all, one opposition manager, quoted in the *Echo*, had described us a few weeks earlier as 'superfit'. It was more, I believed, that a punishing first few months of the season with a stretched squad had taken its toll and we needed to freshen it up.

I did fear, though, that any lack of confidence from within the boardroom might undermine Steve. I had always wanted him to become a director but Matt had pointed out that, under club rules, a paid employee could not sit on the board and so I had to give way, not that Steve was particularly concerned. He was not the sort to sit and discuss blocked toilets in a smoky room for hours on end.

I also had a fleeting concern when Mark McGhee was sacked as Millwall manager that Steve might be tempted to apply for the job, with him being mentioned as a popular choice among the London club's fans. I didn't like asking him and he said I didn't even need to ask. He was happy at Weymouth, he told me. He knew he had a chairman who could see through a couple of home defeats and keep the bigger picture in view, would not give in to the braying of the minority.

We were still incredibly fortunate to have him, I believed. That autumn, he was featured on *Superstars*, on BBC1, in a series of sporting challenges that had been filmed in the summer at La Manga in Spain. He did remarkably well, rare for a footballer up against track and field athletes, and reached the final.

'To be honest, I'm a rubbish person,' Steve told an interviewer. 'I know that. I'm useless at everything in life except sport. Playing sport is what I do and gives me a bit of self-respect and esteem. Otherwise, I'd be a real loser. I've always been able to turn my hand to anything sporting, especially anything that involves some hand-to-eye co-ordination. I'm a competitive bugger as well. I can probably be a pain in the arse but I mean no harm.'

I also liked what the host Johnny Vaughan had to say about him: 'Steve Claridge is my very favourite type of footballer. In fact, he's one of my very favourite people. He drinks voraciously from the cup of life, burns the candle at both ends and still has energy to spare. Does the man never sleep?'

Steve's words, his deeds, cheered me, and I only hoped that everyone else in Weymouth realized just how good for the club he was. What also cheered me at the time was arriving at the club one morning to be confronted with the most astonishing, touching gesture.

The mail had increased with a few bad results and I worked my way through it, replying. One I read was barely believable. The fan, a Mr A. Chubb, was really impressed with the way the club had made such quick progress, did not want us to fail for lack of funds. He enclosed a cheque for £9500 to buy shares. At a time when cash flow was so poor, it was a godsend. I wrote back to thank him, to invite him to the club. He didn't want a fuss, he replied. It was humbling and heartwarming.

It was also welcome relief amid being bogged down with meetings, with developers, staff, the board, knotty little issues always to be sorted out. Jamie was unhappy with the bar manager, Gordon, and wanted to bring in his own people. I thought we should persevere with Gordon for a while as his workload had increased and we needed to encourage him. Gordon would soon resign because of disputes with Jamie, however, and Jamie thus got his way, though none of his managers who came over the winter stayed too long. The bars did, however, seem to be doing better and so Jamie, again, got my backing.

And I had meetings with the local theatre, the Pavilion. I was trying to do a deal to get them to give out tickets for our games in return for us promoting the Christmas pantomime and letting us have their ballroom for nothing. I wanted the Supporters' Club to put on a dance to bring fans, players and staff closer together on a jolly night in contrast to the gloom the club had known for a while.

There had been the Annual General Meeting, too. Among the thirty shareholders who attended was Dave Higson, the only one from the previous board even though the accounting period covered their time in charge. He, at least, still had feelings for the club and generously congratulated the new

ROOTS . . . Dad's old football team, Chickerell, with me as mascot, in their 1963 triumph in the Dorset League. Dad is front row, third from left.

AND WHERE IT ALL BEGAN . . . The old 'Rec', from where Weymouth FC moved to the Wessex Stadium in 1987. The Gasworks End was home.

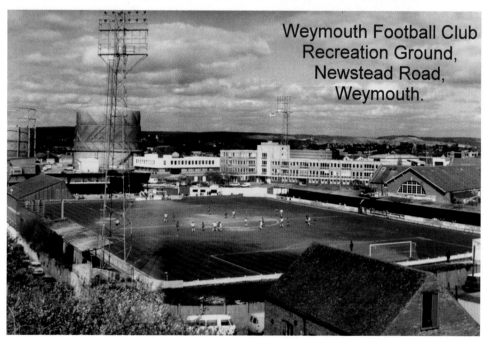

Weymouth Football Club
Recreation Ground,
Newstead Road,
Weymouth.

THE OLD GUARD . . . (from left) former chairmen Peter Shaw and Terry Bennett, and Mick Archer and Dave Higson of Park Engineering.

THE NEW BREED . . . (from left) Nigel Beckett, Andrew Brown, Tristan Murless, Jamie Lyones, Matthew McGowan, myself and Steve Claridge. Inset, Nigel Winship and Charlie Lesser.

FAMILY TIES . . . Me and my Dad, Bob. My daughter, Alex. Below: With my son Jack at the Wessex. The game was played in Dad's name.

VERY IMPORTANT PEOPLE . . . My sister Mel, the club's committed commercial manager. Bob Lucas, the club president and nicest man in the world. Below: with my partner, Vikki. She would have made a good football club director herself.

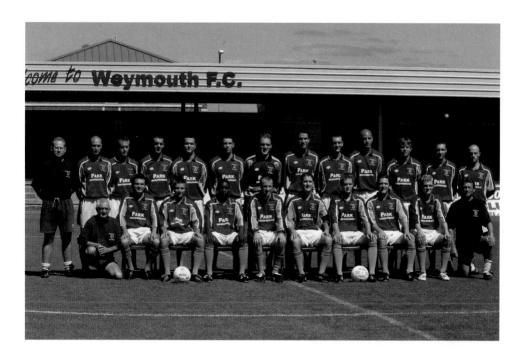

TEAM MATTERS . . . Weymouth Football Club, 2003/2004. The team that Steve Claridge took from 17th to 2nd in a season. Below: the press conference where Steve's signing to the club was announced.

POWER SHIFT . . . Challenging Martyn
Harrison (left, also below left), finance
director Chris Pugsley and accountant
John Tate at the AGM dubbed the
'Rumble at the Riviera'.

Below: Martyn Harrison with his new team
(from left) Kevin Hales, Garry Hill and
Gary Calder. Behind stand Tristan Murless
and Matthew McGowan.

SCENES WITH STEVE . . . In action (above), sent off for the first time in his career against Dorchester on New Year's Day (below left) and with Lee Phillips after both had scored hat-tricks in the 8-0 win over Dorchester on Boxing Day.

TERRAS AND SAINTS . . . Scenes from Weymouth's dramatic 3-2 win over St Albans City at the Wessex that all but confirmed them as Conference South champions. But Saints won promotion, too, via the play-offs.

board on the way they had started. He was less happy that we did not accord the old guard credit for keeping the club going when we announced their loss of £80,000, up from £50,000 the previous year, and I apologized.

He also raised the question of whether the current board intended to spend any money that might come from Asda in advance of building the new stadium. It had been the previous directors' intention, he said, to earmark £1 million to go into trust to provide a future income. It was a valid and interesting question. I said I wanted the same as the previous board. Only when the new stadium was built and we appraised where the club was, I added, would we decide whether it was financially feasible to go full time or kick on towards the Football League, if possible.

Otherwise the night was notable only for Duncan Stewart contesting a resolution required of us by the FA: that if we went bust and after debtors had been paid, if shareholders could not decide what to do with any money left over, it should go to the FA Benevolent Fund. Duncan said it was illegal. I could see his point, but couldn't ever see it happening and it was not worth worrying about. The necessary 75 per cent of the meeting agreed, not enjoying Duncan's own fondness for an argument for an argument's sake. One previous chairman had managed, Sarah told me, to get the AGM over in ten minutes. We took about two hours as I wanted all queries and questions to be addressed. After being frustrated with ignorance as a fan, I now wanted open government.

Having also promised to put on fundraising events, I had persuaded Tony Adams to agree to be the special guest at a sporting dinner. Now we were busy selling tickets and getting auction items. Having attended some of these events in London, I knew that people would pay good money for sporting memorabilia.

And so I drove up to Liverpool's training ground at

Melwood, where Gerard Houllier had prevailed upon Michael Owen to autograph an England shirt – 'To Weymouth FC, Best Wishes' – and the whole squad to sign a Liverpool shirt. Other items would be gleaned over the next few weeks when I could find time.

Now I took a few days away, left Steve and everyone else to get on with it. Sometimes, I concluded, it is best to let go rather than cling on, to work smarter rather than harder. Just as running players after a defeat can be counterproductive, so sitting in an office fretting can be self-defeating.

I was clearly missed. The miserable run on the field came to an end with an efficient win, 2–0 at Bath, Steve Tully and Lee Phillips scoring, and we climbed back to second in the table.

Then, the memory of the last-gasp 2–2 home draw with Merthyr was expunged by a 5–2 victory over them in the FA Trophy, Steve and Paul Buckle both scoring twice. Suddenly that competition, the equivalent of the FA Cup for non-League clubs, had become important to us. I was still a little concerned by the gate figure – 994 – but we were able to bank £750 in prize money, with the chance of more to come. It didn't compare with the FA Cup rewards but it was bonus material.

This was, too, a competition that we should seriously entertain thoughts about going a long way in, even if our record had been poor down the years. And, if we did, the bonus material turned into real rewards. For winning it, you would receive £20,000 in total. Neither was it too fanciful a notion since Southern and Northern Premier League clubs had a recent record of wins as Conference clubs increasingly treated it lightly, like some Premiership clubs with the FA Cup. Then there was all the gate money and some from television with the final being live on Sky. It could amount to a windfall of some £100,000.

Steve had been working hard to get new blood into the

squad and it had brought success. He recruited on a month's loan Tim Clancy, a young defender from Millwall. An old mate, Dennis Wise, had ended up with the player-manager's job at The New Den and Steve was quickly on the phone. It was great business, too. We had only to contribute £20 a week to Tim's wages along with paying his expenses down from London. Soon, a lively right winger from Yeovil in Andy Lindegaard would follow.

Back in the league, the following week we went to Merthyr again, this time winning 4–0, with Tim immediately strengthening us in defence and Lee Phillips scoring another pair. Suddenly we were back on top of the table. It was followed by a 1–0 home win over Eastbourne Borough, Steve grabbing the winner. The crowd, to my relief, was back up to 1159, though still short of what I hoped we might be getting.

But at least we were going in the right direction again and there was a good turnout for the Tony Adams dinner, a sellout of around 225 at the Hotel Prince Regent thanks to Mel's selling powers. We had had to postpone it for a week because Tony had since taken the job as manager of Wycombe Wanderers and an away game at Rochdale had intervened. Jamie, a qualified pilot, had offered to pick up Tony, fly him down and back in the helicopter he said he had, but I knew Tony would not be keen. Tristan also wanted him to say in his guest annexe and photograph him there to put it on the Internet to advertise it as a holiday let, but I knew, too, that Tony would just want a bed at the Regent ready for an early trip back to training in the morning.

Tony signed an Arsenal shirt. Vikki, when going about her work as athletics correspondent of *The Sun*, had also pitched in by obtaining a signed Sydney 2000 shirt from the Olympic sprinter Darren Campbell, once a Weymouth player – and who, with his pace, would have been a world-beater had the game not involved a ball – and a London Marathon shirt signed by Paula Radcliffe. In addition, Jamie had offered a trip around the bay in his helicopter.

The Michael Owen shirt went for £800 and I thought Jamie was being exceptionally generous in bidding £930 for the Liverpool one. It turned out, though, that he was only driving the bidding up and got lumbered with it. Tristan later managed to find a Liverpool-supporting mate who gave £700 for it.

Other mates helped out. Jimmy Mulville, co-owner of the Hat Trick Productions TV company, a major force in British comedy and drama, offered two backstage tickets for the recording of his series *Have I Got News for You* and Garry Richardson of BBC Radio offered two more, plus breakfast in the notorious Beeb canteen, for his Sunday morning show on Radio Five Live, *Sportsweek*. When all was totted up, we made an impressive £8000. Enough for a week's wages, including bonuses.

It had been a good, sociable and lucrative night, captured by *Football Diaries*. I managed, also, to have a word with Dave Higson. Of the four directors who had resigned, he was the one who regretted it the most, I suspected. He still had the club at heart, still came to the odd game and supported nights like this, still had much to contribute, I reckoned. I wondered if he wanted to come back on the board? Despite the disagreements we had had, we both knew that we had the club at heart. He would think about it, he said, and I would discuss it with the new board.

All were in great spirits two days later for the home match against Hinckley United. The Leicestershire side had been on a good winning run since we had won at their place and came to us in second place, able to overtake us by winning. We billed it as a top game and Jamie and Tristan organized fireworks for after it. From being the Chuckle Brothers, they became the Dangerous Twins.

To my relief, we attracted our biggest attendance of the season, 1573 – bettered by only Shrewsbury Town and Aldershot in non-League football that day – and a brace of goals by Lee Phillips gave us a tense, hard-fought 2–0 win. It was blood-and-guts stuff on a cold and damp afternoon, the sort made for football.

Our goalkeeper Jason Matthews sustained a badly gashed forehead and had to go to hospital to have it stitched. Lovely lad, Jason. An electrician in Bath, he was as daft as a brush and happy as Larry. I went down to the dressing room to check on him as soon as he was carried off and it was a gruesome sight. Jason was dazed but the physio told me that, being Jason, he would probably not have noticed much anyway. Goalkeepers really were crazy.

An hour later, there he was, swathed in bandages having a drink in the bar to celebrate a result that would make Steve manager of the month in November for the second time in four months and put us top of the table by five points. The cut glasses he was awarded would at least make the trophy cabinet look less forlorn.

Now we had thirty-six points from eighteen games – that two-a-game championship yardstick. In a highly competitive league of such 'big' clubs as Nuneaton, Worcester, Stafford and Crawley, it was quite a feat. It surely couldn't get much better than this. When the sponsors and the visiting directors had left, I sat in front of the TV staring at the league table on teletext. We now had double the amount of points we had at this time the previous year and the same as Tamworth, who had then gone on to win the league and promotion to the Conference.

It was around the time of Vikki's birthday and she had rented a cottage for a group of her friends deep in the west Dorset countryside near Bridport. Some came to the Hinckley game, where she was match ball sponsor, and were impressed, particularly the poor old Bath City fan,

Matthew, a lecturer at Manchester University, who never thought he would sit in the directors' box at Weymouth and have to endure a day of success for bitter, local rivals, taking it all with such admirable equanimity.

Vikki's good friend Janet, a journalist on the *Western Morning News* in Plymouth, was at her first match and loved it. 'Is it always as good as this?' she wondered. 'I'll look for the results now.' She was told she could sponsor a player, if she wanted. 'What, like African children?' she asked.

It was an idyllic weekend, the damp, the mist and the rolling countryside evoking the green Hardyesque landscape, the match and the company – football and friends – being all you could want from life. All I did, anyway.

That week, I wrote a piece for the *Echo*. It was a crucial week, with West Dorset District Council meeting to decide on their ten-year plan and I wanted to influence them, do what I could to ensure that the club's scheme, in conjunction with Asda, would be included in it.

'A scheme is proposed by the Asda/Walmart company,' I wrote. 'They want to build a superstore to serve the increasing retail needs of Weymouth on our Wessex Stadium site. In return they will build Weymouth FC a new stadium complex.

'It ought to be simple enough. The people benefit from an outlet that meets their modern shopping needs. The town benefits by the easing of the traffic bottleneck around the current Asda harbourside site. Weymouth FC and its supporters – along with all the youth team players and their families associated with the club – benefit from better facilities. Town and community are properly served, enhanced indeed.'

The problem was, I outlined, that by an accident of geography, our land was in West Dorset, even though we were emotionally and culturally in Weymouth and Portland, who approved the scheme.

'I know this is a far-reaching decision for West Dorset, to be made by people who do not necessarily have a close working knowledge of our town,' I added. 'But I would urge them over the next month, as they consider what should be included in their 10-year plan, to show foresight and look at the wider, integrated picture in harmony with local representatives. And with a feeling for opinion and the common good.

'Weymouth, football club and town, are on the up. It would be a shame to interrupt that journey now.'

I was fearing the worst, however. While everyone in Weymouth surely wanted a better Asda on the edge of town, and a new football stadium with community facilities, the concern was that the decision was being made in Dorchester where our town was viewed somewhat differently.

In addition, and most important to be fair to the council, they had technically to consider the merit of the scheme in terms of planning need and gain, whether Weymouth needed more retail space and whether the Wessex Stadium was the best place for it, since government guidelines were now geared to regenerating town centres, rather than building edge-of-town retail parks. There had, indeed, been an about-turn during the eighteen years of Tory government, with the American-style shopping parks having done damage to towns, both commercially and architecturally.

As a citizen, I could see the need to safeguard town centres. As the chairman of the football club, I wanted what was best for it, and this deal was certainly the best thing that could happen to us. We needed revenue-raising conference and hospitality facilities. Above all, if we were to become a League club, we needed a bigger stadium with more ways of making money than simply on match days and not dependent on results. I became an expert on the relevant government guideline, PPG6, liaising with transport and environment consultants hired by Asda.

Unfortunately, it didn't seem that the middlemen developers, Trent, had enough of a sense of urgency. I always felt that, with their metropolitan hauteur, their two representatives, Alistair Jespersen and Toby Atkinson, were treating us as country bumpkins, as perhaps they had with the old board, and were condescending in their dealings with us, dilatory in their work on behalf of Asda. At one point, I deliberately met them in the Mayfair offices of our director Charlie Lesser to show them that they were dealing with people of consequence here. Well, in Charlie's case at least.

We had become a more professional club, and were at last getting some luck. I recalled the story told by the golfer Gary Player. Once, having holed out from a bunker, he overheard someone in the crowd saying, 'That was lucky.' He turned round and looked at them. 'Yeah,' he said. 'And the harder I practise, the luckier I get.'

We had had yet another dispute with the company in charge of our pitch. I had arrived at the ground one day to find deep tyre indentations across the surface. They had, after much badgering, finally agreed to vertidrain the pitch – a technique of making deep incisions to improve drainage – as we had wanted but, I was told, the proper vehicle with smooth tyres was not available so they had used a tractor.

I threatened them with cancelling the contract again, at which point a new man suddenly arrived and was devoted full time to us. Mark Reynolds had once worked at Coventry City's Highfield Road and had moved to the area. Quickly he was nurturing a flat, green pitch suitable for our passing football. He was a real find.

For the following Saturday's game at home to Ashford Town in the FA Trophy, I wrote in my programme notes, referring to the Hinckley game: 'It was certainly one of the proudest days of my life. Many people have done a lot of hard work over the last six months to try and help the club fulfil its huge potential. Last Saturday it all came together.

The sight of so many people enjoying their day and the sound of such a buzz around the ground made all the hard work worthwhile.'

Pride comes before a fall, however, and I soon appreciated how the game could burst bubbles. Ashford were but a mid-table team in the First Division West of the Ryman League, two steps below us in the football pyramid. Steve decided he could afford to put himself on the bench.

I was covering a game at Aston Villa and the text messages alarmed me. With fifteen minutes left, we were 3–1 down. For Ashford, coming to Weymouth and playing to a crowd of 876 – not great by our standards but six times what they were used to – was their final. We were, by the sounds of it, complacent.

In my fury and concern that a revenue source was drying up, I picked up the phone to Vikki, who was on holiday down there, and told her to go down to the bench and tell Steve to get himself on. There was a silence. Not surprisingly, she didn't feel it was her place. Actually, it wasn't my place either. In hindsight, I sounded like an old-fashioned, meddling dictator. Then, relief in her voice and in my mind, she told me that he was coming on anyway.

Five minutes later came another text. I shuddered as I opened it. 2–3. Phew. Come on. Then another, and another shudder. 3–3. Claridge equalizer. Full Time. Thank God for that.

An hour later I phoned Steve, still angry. He asked me if the team could have a meal in a hotel on Tuesday afternoon before the replay, and some rooms booked for a nap. I told him he must be joking – reward them for that? We agreed a compromise: if they lost the game, the players would pay it all rather than their usual third. If they won, then the club could pay out of the prize money for getting into the next round. It wasn't budgeted for, it was a bonus, after all, wasn't it?

There remained this boyish charm to Steve, this winning way, though when I calmed down it also made sense. If the players were properly prepared and went on to win, then we would be getting the chance to make more money. And like a kid, you couldn't stay angry with Claridge for too long. It was one of the many things I liked about him, one of the things that made him a proper football man. In this mad, knockabout world, you could fall out but get over it very quickly.

And, I also realized, I could get to Ashford for the replay, it being less than an hour's drive from my home in St Albans. Great. Watching Weymouth on a Tuesday night.

It was not so great, though; a foul, wet and wintry evening. Vikki, Jack and I left early to avoid the M25 rush hour. We found the ground, somewhere at the end of runway four at Heathrow, and then a local pub to have a meal. But I was looking forward to it, my black mood of Saturday night gone.

They had made a real effort at Ashford and were warm, hospitable people, though the setting was bleak and spartan. A marquee had been erected as an overspill bar. The boardroom was tiny, but a picture on the wall touched me. There, in Ashford's unusual and charming orange and white striped shirts, was a team in Africa they were helping out.

I went to the dressing room to see Steve and see how everyone was doing. As I walked in the mood was sombre. I thought it needed livening up. 'Where have you brought me?' I said to Steve, and I later heard from two of the players that when they were warming up, they saw a couple rats behind one of the goals, where a sewage farm was fenced off. 'I've just been to a pub round the corner that had a quiz on,' I added. 'The place was so hard, the first question was: "What are you looking at?" '

Nobody, it seemed, dared laugh – well, I thought it was funny – though I noticed a smile playing on the lips of Steve

Tully, who fancied himself both as a player and a bit of a lad; with some justification on both parts, being a raiding right back and a favourite with the lady fans.

'Can I have a word outside now,' Steve said, more an instruction than a question. He still hadn't quite grasped the chairman–manager relationship.

'What the fuck are you doing? I've just told them how pissed off you are, how much we need this tonight and you come in cracking jokes.'

I simply said sorry and left.

I was nervous as I contemplated the kickoff from their small stand, Jack wandering off as he liked the freedom to roam of non-League football. I noticed that the halfway line had been marked out across the soggy surface with a wobble in it. I hated losing, hated being humiliated, and was as competitive as Steve, even if I did try to keep my reactions as understated as possible, tried to look as positive as possible.

I certainly had to when Ashford took an early lead. It got worse when we lost our central defender, Lee Russell, in what looked an innocuous challenge but produced what was to be a serious injury. The half-time tea tasted sour.

Gradually, though, we found our feet on the treacherous surface and drew the sting from a young, enthusiastic team rising above themselves. Lee Phillips equalized. Then came a penalty. Later, Steve would tell me that he was as nervous taking it as he had ever been – this from a man who had played in a Worthington Cup final and a play-off final at Wembley – but thankfully he converted it. Scott Partridge confirmed the win and we were into the third round. Another £1000 banked.

I had learned another lesson to put into my personal bank, too. Steve had been right. In this instance, it was me who hadn't quite grasped the nature of the chairman–manager relationship.

I was an informal chairman who liked to have a benevolent relationship with Steve and the players, thought that
they would perform best in an atmosphere of bonhomie
rather than fear. I preferred the light touch to the heavy
hand, thought it got more out of people as well as tallied
with my own personality. But Steve had used me as the
hard-man villain of the piece for motivation to the players,
and I had undermined his work.

I knew that from then on, I should never go into the
dressing room – his dressing room and their territory – without an invitation or without seeking his permission first.
There had to be a demarcation. Nothing wrong with them
thinking I was a good bloke, and like any human being I
wanted to be liked, but sometimes they had to know there
was a divide and that I could be tough. I had crossed it, not
them. It was not always about being liked. It was about
being respected. And successful.

CHAPTER ELEVEN

Because of Boxing Day

Being something of a compulsive – so people tell me; can't see it myself – life became a series of lists: of jobs to do at the ground, people to phone, see and write to, meetings to attend, players we wanted. Sometimes I did something not on the list and added it to the list just for the pleasure of immediately crossing it off.

It had become tiring. I would drive down from St Albans to Weymouth to the rented house on a Sunday night, always looking forward to the sight of the sea from Ridgeway Hill and the lights snaking down the main road to it. Jack, another fan of the film, always said that it looked like the final scene of *Field of Dreams* where the car's headlights wend their way to the baseball diamond.

I would then work at the club on Monday and Tuesday, drive home on Wednesday afternoon to do some work for my day job, then cover a game on a Saturday.

One week included hanging around Sopwell House in St Albans at the time when the England players were threatening not to travel to a World Cup game in Turkey, in solidarity with the banned Rio Ferdinand who had driven away from a drugs test. This pampered lot should lead the lives of the Weymouth players, I thought, working all day then training two nights a week, playing twice a week, for an average weekly footballing wage of around £350. They would go out to Turkey in their places for nothing, would probably even pay for the privilege. As for drugs, at our level the lads struggled to afford Nurofen.

We were still owed sponsorship money, mainly from Park Engineering, and Jamie and Tristan had still not bought any shares, taking our overdraft beyond the £50,000 limit, up to £80,000. The bank were ringing or writing to me weekly. I kept telling them that it was just cash flow, that the figures would eventually add up. I told them that, surely, they could see how the club was in better shape than six months ago. They had had too many bad experiences with the club in the past, though, to be overly sympathetic.

People remarked how thin and weary I was looking. I was certainly smoking heavily, up to thirty a day, driving sometimes more than 1000 miles a week and eating fitfully. Without my sister cooking for me on the nights I was in Weymouth, I probably wouldn't have bothered eating some days. Now and then, Vikki would come down and feed me fish fingers from Somerfield. Adrenalin often felt sustenance enough. But somehow I loved every minute of it. I had a drive and a passion and you couldn't ask much more from life. A lot of people never find it.

And sometimes I did get a free meal out of it. I was invited to a dinner at Weymouth College, who were looking to set up a football academy and wanted it to be under our name, and took up the offer so that I could meet Oliver Letwin, Conservative MP for West Dorset and Shadow Chancellor, to canvass support for our new stadium. He said he would do what he could, that he sympathized with our cause. I later emailed him to ask if he would put that in writing to West Dorset District Council.

All the irritations and sometimes criticism when we lost a game – of too many players living away, of us not training enough; sundry other irrational complaints that do not surface when a team is winning – were worth it whenever I took my seat to watch Weymouth play. Sometimes, poor Pete Saxby, ever a fusser, would get short shrift from me if he came to me during my ninety-minute oasis with a problem, about car parking or something footling. In addition, some of the football we were playing, with Paul Buckle and Lee Philpott outstanding in midfield, was delightful. As well as Steve's second manager of the month award, our goalkeeper Jason Matthews won the 'safe hands' accolade as recognition of the defence's improvement.

Steve gave an interview to the *Echo*. 'All the players have worked really hard and if anyone deserves the award it's the chairman Ian Ridley because he has worked his socks off to turn the club around.' It was touching. I also knew that Steve was a canny old bird to flatter his chairman.

The traditional curse of the award did not strike this time. We immediately went to Chelmsford, or rather Billericay, where they were playing before their new ground was ready to occupy, and won 3–1 to retain our lead at the top of the table, and remain unbeaten away from home halfway through the season. We had also recorded five consecutive league wins. How different it all was from when I had taken Jack to Ian Dury land in the Terry Bennett era and watched us lose.

Even the *Echo* were getting excited. They got our permission to produce large 'Living the Dream' posters of our players to give away with papers – and gave us some to sell at 50p a time in the club shop.

We were having a little run in the Dr Martens Cup, too – unfortunately. I had made the mistake when negotiating the players' bonuses of including the competition in them. It meant that we were paying top dollar when only getting crowds of 400, still the best in our league for such games but not enough to make a profit. It was daft of me. During one win, Steve, who had rested himself, could not resist turning round from the dugout, looking up at me in the stand and smiling and rubbing his hands with glee.

Two weeks before Christmas we entertained Weston-super-Mare. It was a match, given league positions, that we should have won but we could not break down a resolute defence and drew 0–0. It was a disappointment as Ricky George, who once scored a famous FA Cup goal for Hereford United against Newcastle United and was now writing about non-League football for *The Daily Telegraph*, had come to pen a feature about us. Still, he would give us a good write-up, even describe our football as lower-level Arsenal.

That night, we had the Christmas party for more than 200 staff and supporters at the Pavilion and even the chairman was seen to dance, though only briefly. Steve was another matter. For some reason, he liked to dance on his own, and didn't care about looking daft, his moves a cross between a barefoot man on hot coals and a gibbon. Actually, I envied him his ability not to care what people said about him.

Each game was revealing more. Lee Russell's injury sustained at Ashford was worse than feared and, just at a time when he was playing well, we suddenly looked short in central defence. Neither, as the goalless draw against Weston showed, did we have enough ingenuity to break down teams who defended in depth. We could do with a tricky wide player to provide the service for Claridge and Phillips. It would be nice to find some money to get one into the club.

But even though Steve and I suspected that without reinforcements we could not sustain our form, I was reluctant to find money we would have to borrow. I had been back to Tristan and Jamie asking for the share money they had promised but yet again they had stonewalled. Tristan said he was still owed money and would put in at least £5000 in January. We were now unbeaten in ten games, having won eight of them, and were going to Nuneaton Borough, our main title rivals at this stage, in good shape the following Saturday so I didn't press it. Except that we weren't going to Nuneaton. It lashed down in the Midlands and the game was postponed. It was a shame. Nuneaton, their early promise fading, were going through a bad patch.

It meant that we went into the Christmas programme not having played for two weeks. I wondered, and worried as usual, about how that might affect us as we approached the game against our nearest rivals, Dorchester Town, at home on Boxing Day. They were struggling, having just been promoted from the division below, but were still dangerous, especially in a festive derby.

I had done the usual on Christmas Day, went to St Albans Cathedral, cooked the turkey for the kids. Vikki had done me proud by giving me a new car number plate – T12 WFC. I was delighted. But Boxing Day was my real Christmas Day. I awoke as if six years old again at 6 a.m., dragged Vikki out of bed for the drive down to Weymouth. As we passed Dorchester's ground, the sun barely up, I felt just like a fan again. 'We'll have you today,' I said out loud. 'Don't be so childish,' Vikki said.

Today the *Football Diaries* crew were up early to be there, too, and, as usual, the house that I had rented had been taken over by a group of our players. There was Lee Philpott, who lived near Doncaster, and, being a mature family man, always looked after the place, was always polite. His wife always used to send him down with home-laid eggs and the others, probably jealous of his happy domestic situation, poked fun. Often he would offer to go and get the shopping from Joy's Convenience Store, down the hill at the end of the beach road.

Martin Barlow, up from Devon, was similarly adult. No sign of men behaving badly, or footballers on the rampage, here, though plenty of laddish banter and mickey-taking. I did find a 'men's' magazine around the place, which I told

Steve I did not like with Jack using the house, and Steve tried to blame it on Lee Philpott, but the real culprit was fairly obvious.

Then there were Lee Phillips, up from his home in Cornwall, and Luke Nightingale, who travelled from Portsmouth with Steve. Luke was the quietest bloke I had ever met, just sat there reading *The Sun* and *FHM*, speaking – tersely – only when spoken to. The most I ever heard him say was, during some *Pop Idol*-type game show on the TV that was never off: 'I've seen this. That bloke wins.' Naturally, he was pelted with water bottles and papers. He was often the butt of the ribbing as well, probably because he had an English O Level and footballers always take the mickey out of 'boffins', but just sat there and smiled good-naturedly.

It was something I had spoken about with Steve before. Some players love all that. Often at the highest level, you hear of players sad about retiring, saying that what they will miss most is the banter, the dressing-room atmosphere. But sometimes they have to be strong to survive it, to give as good as they get. Many fail to make it not because of a lack of talent, but because they shrink in such a macho environment.

Steve was naturally the lord of the manor. It was him who left empty water bottles and apple cores around – he just could not eat enough fruit – as well as leaving the washing-up for well-brought-up young men like Leon Green, a young striker from London who looked as if he wasn't going to make it with us.

Steve was always big on preparation, and expected it of the players, too. He always came down the night before a game – extending even to Christmas night – and those who lived more than two hours' drive away were expected to as well. He insisted on the right foods, and eating at the right times. Breakfast was cereal, toast and fruit, lunch –

or a late-afternoon meal before a night game – pasta and chicken. Baked beans were also big. Nothing was to be eaten less than three hours before kick-off.

I stole a moment away from the TV cameras to speak to Steve privately that Boxing Day morning. 'I haven't asked much from you,' I said as I sat with him at the kitchen table, me with my own pre-match meal of coffee and a cigarette, 'but win this one for me.'

Fortunately, to them as professionals it was just another game and I did not want to build it up for them too much, didn't want their emotions to get in the way. Being too wound up can be counterproductive. I remember writing in my day job, having been privileged enough to be in Munich's Olympic Stadium the night England beat Germany 5–1, that Sven-Goran Eriksson had succeeded immediately where Kevin Keegan had failed because he took the sting out of the occasion, reminded his players that this was not a war but a football match that needed cool, clear heads.

Even the players who did not live in the town, though, realized how huge this game was. The natives – Simon Browne, whose brother Alex would be in the Dorchester team, John Waldock, Mark Robinson and Ian Hutchinson – had been telling them. Now they would see for themselves.

The car park was virtually full by 1 p.m., the bars already crammed. With Gordon gone, Jamie and Tristan were stretched in overseeing them. I had come from the cemetery, where I had had a quiet word with my dad. It was a cold, stormy day, but already I was sweating.

This time I was mine genial host to the Dorchester directors, not a word out of place. I wanted us to kick off on the dot of 3 p.m., to show that we could handle a big crowd, but no matter how hard we worked, we just couldn't get the amazing number of 3734 through the turnstiles in time, since many still expected to turn up at five to three, as you do in non-League football. It is one of its beauties, unlike the traffic-jammed, turn-up-early-or-else Premiership. We managed to start at 3.15.

It was to be the most astonishing game, all captured by another TV crew, from ITV's *On The Ball* programme. Simon Browne opened the scoring within a few minutes, heading home a corner. On the television later, you would hear Steve shouting to the Dorchester fans: 'Already.' We would also hear Andy Townsend, once a Weymouth player now an ITV pundit, wonder with a laugh whether chairman and manager were on the same wavelength when we were separately interviewed, blaming the corny 'Live the Dream' catchphrase on the other.

After that, the goals went in at barely believable intervals. When we went 2–0 up, I feared the worst from our early season squandering of leads. At 3–0, I was simply relieved, believing that – surely – we could not lose from here. Still they went in and, to my own astonishment, I even began to feel sorry for our visitors, feeling their directors' embarrassment and hoping I would never be in such a position. Steve scored a hat-trick, Lee Phillips another three as Dorchester crumbled. Lee Philpott completed an 8–0 rout with a curling free kick.

'Alex, Alex, what's the score?' our fans sang and our former stalwart Alex Browne, now at the heart of the Dorchester defence, simply scratched his head as if trying to remember and smiled. It was the sort of reaction that endeared him, once anew, to our fans. 'Can we play you every week?' they chanted on, Dorchester's humiliation compounded by the sending off of their midfield hard man, Jamie Brown.

The Dorchester chairman, Eddie Belt, a polite and civilized man, offered his hand and I genuinely did feel sympathy. 'You've got some good players there,' he said generously, wistfulness in his voice.

I couldn't resist going into the home dressing room

unbidden. The door closed behind me, I bellowed with delight and kissed Steve on the forehead. The team laughed. I asked Steve if he had heard the chant about playing Dorchester every week. 'Heard it? I started it,' he said.

Up in the bar, a delirious crowd high on Christmas, the result and ale, cheered Steve and the players when they appeared. A few even hugged me. 'I don't care what happens from now on,' one supporter told me. 'You've given me the best day of my life.'

We had taken around £20,000 through the gate, another £4000 at the bar. That would get the overdraft back down. Now the bank had to see our potential and I resolved to write to them requesting our limit to be increased to £80,000 now that the club was dealing in bigger figures. We would cover the next three weeks' wages comfortably. The only blot on the landscape was a couple of disturbing things that I heard. Stressed, Jamie had gone for Tristan over a dispute about running the bars. Two fans also phoned me to say they had seen Jamie in a local club on his way home carrying a bag of the day's takings, he and Tristan having agreed to take them back to their personal safes since we did not wish to leave them in the ground overnight. I also took a bag to lock away until the banks opened again. Tristan said he didn't want to take the Jamie incident any further and Jamie himself denied the club episode so I let both matters go.

Besides, now was not the time for conflict, with everyone pulling in the right direction. The town was buzzing with the excitement and, due to the quirks of the Southern League fixture programme, we were sent back to Dorchester's Avenue Stadium just six days later, on New Year's Day. Some bright spark in our Supporters' Club came up with the idea of using a picture of the hat-trick heroes Steve and Lee holding the match ball after the Boxing Day game under the line 'Who Eight All The Magpies?' on a T-shirt and putting them on sale for £10 each, half the proceeds going to a charity for a local boy who needed expensive surgery. Our Supporters Club asked Dorchester if we could sell them inside their ground. 'Over my dead body,' came word from their secretary, David Martin, but a higher, less bitter, authority on their board prevailed.

We knew that the Martin attitude would be the prevalent one amongst the Dorchester players, though, and understandably so. Ours too, I hope, would have been smarting, would have wanted revenge after such a drubbing. It was to be an acrimonious day.

Mostly Dorchester's directors were a decent bunch but David Martin was a precious character. I had been told by various sources that he was known to be very resentful towards our club, always seeking to get one up on us. And he had written to the local paper back in the summer criticizing me for comments I had made about us deserving the Boxing Day game this year.

At the fans' forum I had lightheartedly commented that our fans should boycott the game if Dorchester were awarded it when it was our turn. This was because I knew that Dorchester budgeted for this day. Their average attendance was around 500 but today it would be over 4000, all because our 3000 fans would be travelling up, to go with the doubling of their own support that such a local event produced. The 8−0 made people even more curious. And so on the day, I gave a surly, taciturn Martin but a cursory shake of the hand.

He was typical of so many in these parts, I was coming to believe; say all manner of things behind your back, not brave enough to say anything to your face. As I took my seat and read the programme, neither was I best pleased by a piece accusing Steve Claridge of being a diver. They simply had not seen some of the treatment he had been receiving this season.

We started badly, fell a goal behind but worked ourselves

back into it. Steve scored, then Luke Nightingale put us ahead. Steve was now playing him wide on the right, since Luke had been missing a few chances and was not better as a striker than Steve and Lee Phillips, but talented enough nevertheless to deserve a place.

All of a sudden, though, Steve was poleaxed by a tackle from behind by Jamie Brown. A melee broke out. In the confusion, the referee raised a red card. It was for Steve. I could not believe it. Brown at least also saw red.

I stood up. All around me was a braying crowd cheering as Steve trooped off. I turned round to the man sitting two rows behind me who I recognized as the writer of the article in the Dorchester programme, Rob Hodder, also their supporters' liaison officer. He was known to our fans as Itchy, and another outspoken Dorchester fan as Scratchy, after characters in *The Simpsons*. 'What's the matter with you people?' I said. 'We bring you a proper footballer who will entertain you and this is how you treat him.' He said something back which I didn't catch. I tossed the offending programme in his direction. Dorchester equalized courtesy of a late, dodgy penalty.

I went down to the dressing-room area. 'You'd better get your manager out of the referee's room before he gets into trouble,' a steward said to me. I went in and Steve, animatedly but not abusively, was asking the ref and linesmen what they had seen.

I hadn't noticed it but it seemed that he had been sent off for a kick to Brown's head as he lay at the bottom of a ruck of angry players standing over him and the linesman had witnessed it. Steve insisted to me that he hadn't kicked out, but that it might have looked that way as he walked – or limped – back to the scene of the incident. Someone else might have kicked Brown and it might have been mistaken identity. I said we would back him if he wanted to appeal.

I went back to the Dorchester boardroom. Our lead at the top was still intact but had shrunk, with our rivals winning. Oh well. I shook Eddie Belt's hand, told him that his team had restored some pride. He thanked me. As I left, the Dorchester vice-chairman Colin Clark turned to someone and within my earshot announced: 'I don't care who wins the league as long as it's not Weymouth.' I thought better of it. Leave it.

Out in the car park, Jamie Brown was giving an interview to a local newspaperman. 'Telling the truth are you?' Steve asked as he walked by. 'You got a problem with me?' asked Brown in return. 'Yes I have,' replied Steve, who moved towards him. They had to be separated. I told Steve to go home.

The aftermath was more unpleasant. The kickoff had been delayed by half an hour as our 3000 fans in the crowd of 4116 were shoehorned into an area not big enough to accommodate them. There was overcrowding and younger fans were frightened. My sister and her children, as well as my Jack, were among it.

I had floods of complaints and took up their cases with the *Echo*, saying that I hoped Dorchester would learn the lessons for the future. It annoyed me that our fans were being portrayed as yobs when Dorchester should be grateful for all the money they brought in and should have treated them better.

Dorchester retaliated by claiming that Steve had made offensive gestures to their fans, and that they had had to confiscate dangerous weapons, including razor blades, from two of our fans. I made my own enquiries. One of the weapons was a tin of beans, the offender just having been shopping for his tea at the adjacent Tesco. The other was a Stanley knife which was handed in by the Weymouth fan, a carpet fitter who had come to the game straight from work. I also pointed out that one of our injured players had been pelted by home fans with plastic bottles as he was limping along the sideline back to the dugout.

Later, the local police would send me a copy of a letter they had received from David Martin complaining about our fans' behaviour. There was also a copy of a reply from the police. They would be taking no action. It said everything. I was again the villain with Dorchester but I was not going to be diplomatic and polite when David Martin was doing his damnedest to malign us. I cared more about our fans than I did about a club whose fortunes and sensibilities were none of my concern.

All this at a Southern League match, and in deepest rural Dorset. It may not have been Liverpool v. Everton, Celtic v. Rangers, United v. City, Arsenal v. Tottenham or even Portsmouth v. Southampton, but it meant a lot to us. And never let it be said that passion for the game does not run high in our little south-west county.

CHAPTER TWELVE

Creepy Crawley

It was gone five o'clock and still the result hadn't come through. I was about to ring the ground, Mel, anyone I could get hold of, when there came that gut-wrenching beep-beep just as I was about to drive away from a petrol station on the way home from having covered an early kickoff in the Premiership. 'Lost 1–0. Steve missed pen', said the text. I slumped forward over the steering wheel. Now it was getting serious.

It was a cold Saturday in early January and this was a big game. Crawley Town, after a mediocre start to the season, were emerging as serious rivals for the title. We had led them by as much as eight points, though they had had a game in hand, but their win at the Wessex today had thrown new light – darkness in our case – on the Championship issue. We now led them by just three points.

We had battered them, apparently. They went down to ten men with their goalkeeper sent off for a professional foul but we could not force the equaliser after they had taken a thirty-fifth-minute lead. Steve's penalty was saved by the Crawley left back, Ian Payne, who had taken over in goal. Just a point would have been enough, to deny them three and keep a six-point difference between them and us, but it was disappointment for an excellent crowd of 2016.

Steve was depressed when I rang. He needed help, a

shoulder to cry on, and the squad needed a boost. So did he. And so I drove to Portsmouth the next day to talk it all through with him. I could tell how low he was before I even got there. That morning, he told in his *People* column about how tired he was of some of the tackling in this league.

'There have been three or four tackles on me that have been nothing short of dangerous, made by people who are just trying to make a name for themselves,' he wrote. 'If that's what football at this level is all about – Sunday afternoon refereeing and Saturday night tackles – then I'm not interested.'

Threatening to quit playing did not sound like him. He loved it, reckoned he could go on at a high level well into his forties. Players differ. Some, like Tony Adams, prefer to end at the top, rather than go down through the divisions. But then Tony saw life beyond football. Steve did not yet and wondered what he would do without it. I could see him turning out for the Dog and Duck at fifty.

Missing three games because of the suspension forthcoming as a result of the sending-off at Dorchester was crippling him emotionally, on top of the tackles that had threatened to cripple him physically. The Jamie Brown episode on New Year's Day had taken a big toll.

We went through the squad, for a start who was and wasn't fit. Lee Philpott, our creative engine, was injured, hence the lack of ingenuity against Crawley. Our central defender Jamie Impey had damaged a shoulder. This on top of Lee Russell still being absent and likely to be for a long time. Steve had brought in Lee Molyneaux, a defender he had known at Portsmouth, but one half at Dorchester had shown him not to be what we were looking for.

And so we identified the areas where we needed new blood, mainly central defence and a wide player. I had hoped the group we had would be good enough, but it was becoming clear that we needed reinforcements.

I had much on my mind. The home games against Dorchester and Crawley had eased the financial position considerably but looking ahead at the fixture list, things could get tricky. Cup competitions were taking over – we had been drawn away at Lewes in the third round of the FA Trophy and at home to Bath City in the Southern League Cup – but they did not bring in much income. The more lucrative home league games could be postponed, because of either the cups or bad weather at this time of year.

In addition, we were coming up to the crucial West Dorset District Council decision on whether the Asda/Wessex Stadium scheme should be included in their ten-year plan and I had meetings to attend with the developers, reports to write. Football, though, had to be the priority right now, I concluded, if this season that was promising so much was not to peter out.

The budget was tight, I told Steve, but I would go to the board and see what we could do. In the meantime, if he could offload on loan a couple of players who weren't figuring much, then he would free up wages for new people. I asked him to supply me with a list of players he wanted or thought he could get.

Steve also said that he found it difficult without me at games on Saturdays. He was concerned, he said, by the lack of football knowledge some of the directors showed in their conversations with him and the negative comments they made. He wondered if I could be there on Saturdays as well as in midweek. He liked me as a sounding board, to throw ideas around with, and as a buffer between him and a few of the directors.

I asked him who was troubling him. Jamie Lyones, Tristan Murless and Matt McGowan, he said. The first two knew little about the game, he reckoned, but insisted on telling him something wasn't working or that something else wasn't very good. Matt was more dangerous, he added. He was more confident in his knowledge of the game but was behind the times.

I told him that these were good men with good intentions. Jamie and Tristan had done a lot behind the scenes, particularly in increasing our profits from the bars lately. Matt had been a player, manager and chairman of the club and knew the local scene. That was the trouble, Steve said. The game had moved on and Matt had not been around it for years.

It was a delicate subject and I had to be loyal to both Steve and my board, I had to pour oil on any troubled waters. It was also delicate trying to get any more time off work. *The Observer* was already giving me leeway here and there but asking for every Saturday off was a big request. I broached it tactfully and after sensitive negotiation, my sports editor Brian Oliver agreed, though with reservations. It would mean a pay cut of a third of my salary, however. This was getting expensive. And my contract was due for renewal in a few months. It would not go down well. Such had my commitment to the club become, though, that I was prepared to place my career in jeopardy.

Now I was struggling financially myself. I was living on a promise of selling off my dad's house and waiting for the proceeds to come through. I wasn't sure how Dad would have taken it, the fruits of the only real thing he had to show for his working life going on a football club. I was a mixture of guilt and gratitude. As for my own kids, there wouldn't be much of a legacy for them at this rate.

What was emerging in my talks with Steve around this time was a theory that we shared. He had imported winners into the club, like Paul Buckle and Lee Philpott, but too many of the existing players had never known a promotion campaign. They were more used to relegation. The stresses of leading the league pressed heavily on some shoulders.

When the pressure was on in games, some buckled mentally. And this was before the business end of the season.

I had spoken of this before with sports psychologists in the course of my work. There are indeed many players, strange as it may sound, who have a fear of winning. The tension and emotional demands of going through what it takes to be a winner are too much, not worth it. They prefer to be in the comfort zone, where you can make money without the pressure that comes to the very best.

We had also done our best to promote young local players but they were either tiring or not physically or mentally strong enough. It was a problem for kids in Weymouth. It being a footballing outpost, they grew up mostly playing against other kids in Dorset, believing themselves to be better than they were. Then, when they were exposed to tougher and better competition, they were found wanting.

Steve also felt that Scott Partridge was not working out. He had had chances up front but was still not going to displace the first-choice pairing – anyone sensible's choice, really – of Claridge and Phillips, a partnership that had already produced twenty-seven goals midway through the season. Steve apart, Scott was our most expensive player. He had also been to see Steve to say that he wanted to play more regularly, and would prefer to go elsewhere if he didn't.

Steve made some enquiries and Bath City were the only ones who bit. They could only afford £300 a week, however. It was unfortunate that Steve's call to me about Scott came when I was being filmed by *Football Diaries* with Nigel Winship going over some accounts and I felt uneasy, but it was the price for full access to the club and I just had to think of the fee it was bringing in.

I was reluctant to let Scott go, especially with Steve's three-game ban for the foul at Dorchester, but I saw it as my job to back the manager. His way, we would save £300 for another player, a defender hopefully – and we made enquiries about a stopper at Tiverton by the name of Nathan Rudge without any joy – but would have to come to an arrangement to pay the difference over the remainder of Scott's contract.

We agreed a reduced figure, paid every six months, the sort of deal that football clubs at any level do maybe once or twice a season. I had not wanted us to get into that sort of thing, believing that we could conduct our business differently, but I was seeing from the inside how the game made you pragmatic, forced you to compromise on certain principles. The board agreed, and also allowed Steve to do what he could to freshen the squad, within limitations.

It meant that Steve had to get in another striker, and he did well to agree a deal with Plymouth Argyle so that we could take their promising young goalscorer Stewart Yetton on work experience without it costing anything. We also took, initially on a month's loan, Robbie Pethick from Brighton for £300 a week. Robbie had been a folk hero in his first spell at the club a decade earlier, before being sold to Portsmouth for £10,000, and he could play either at right back or central defence. He was the sort of tough, forceful player we needed.

Steve wanted a full back, Graeme Power from Exeter, a left-winger and a driving midfield player, with injuries and weariness affecting the squad. He had identified a hard-tackling midfielder from Havant and Waterlooville, Shaun Wilkinson, but Havant, unlikely to do Weymouth any favours, wanted money.

I was reluctant to pay transfer fees, believing that we should be able to get players out of contract or through our scouting. But this was a tricky time of the season, and this was a tricky season in particular. Next year, the three feeder leagues to the Conference, the Southern, and Northern Premier and Isthmian Leagues, were to be consolidated into the two Conference North and South competitions.

We would comfortably finish in the top thirteen and qualify for Conference South and that had been the first goal of the season, something that might have been beyond the club had the old guard still been in charge. Now the championship, and thus promotion to the national Conference, was our aim, having come this far. If it wasn't, we had just as well cut our losses and finish thirteenth. But to do that would be to alienate a now expectant support and return to the low crowds and cynicism of the recent past.

The problem was that every other club was jockeying for a top thirteen position. In any other season, with just the champions promoted, those who realized it was beyond them after an expensive, optimistic start would be cutting their own losses and ready to let players go. Not this year. Against my better judgement, we might well have to pay to get in what we needed. And Havant knew it.

I wrote to our bank manager, Geoff Light, who was questioning our overdraft, which had now reached £72,000, £22,000 over our limit, and more payments due out imminently. We were also waiting for £20,000 we were owed, Park Engineering now saying that they could not pay the next sponsorship instalment agreed until February.

'Clearly our costs have risen as we have attempted to turn the club around,' I said. 'You will be aware that the previous board's strategy of cost-cutting led to a loss last year of £80,000. We have been trying something different and it has paid off. Crowds are averaging 1500 (up from 650) and we are top of the Dr Martens Premier League.

'We cannot afford to stop now. If we do cut back, crowds will dwindle and our income go down. We have to see this through to maximize the potential of the club.' All this as prelude to seeking an increase in the overdraft limit to £100,000.

Geoff was sympathetic, agreed that the cash flow forecast to the end of the season looked feasible and said he would see what he could do. In the end, a few weeks later, he came back from his regional office with an offer of an £85,000 overdraft limit. It was something and it would mean that we had more grace before incurring high interest charges. He also suggested that we could repay the inherited debts over a twenty-year period, rather than the current ten, which would mean a saving of £700 a month.

In the short term, though, we needed some money in. As I had written to Geoff Light, we could not afford to stop now. I also told the board, reminding Tristan and Jamie once again that, yes, I had wanted them for the work they were willing to do but that they had also agreed to put in money to buy shares, which they still had not done. *Now* was the time I emphasized. On the promise of Dad's house being sold, I had personally borrowed £10,000 to put into the club as a loan and I wanted some support.

Andrew Brown and Nigel Winship gave some by offering similar sums in loans. Jamie and Tristan twitched uneasily in their seats and I began to have my doubts about them. I was beginning to feel let down. Matt McGowan was also unwilling to invest, having put in plenty during his previous time on the board, and I had never expected him to. It was part of the condition of him returning. I couldn't help hoping he might change his mind, though.

Amid all this, I was seeing the dilemma for a board, for a chairman. You could budget and plan all you liked, draw up a business plan, but at times like these, with players injured or suspended, action was needed. Not to act might be to squander this rare chance not just of winning the league but of the increased revenue, through gates, television money and prizes, that being in the Conference would bring. The ship would be spoiled for a ha'porth of tar.

I phoned Tony Adams to ask him if he had any players we could take on loan from Wycombe. He said come and look, that they had a reserve game that week at home to a West

Indian touring team. On a freezing night, Steve and I went along to watch. I liked the look of a big central defender called Luke Oliver, who was only on £300 a week. Steve was not so keen and nothing came of it.

Personally, I thought Steve made a mistake. Oliver could have headed and kicked it away for us, plugged a hole, intimidated the opposition, I thought, but I still believed that it was not a chairman's role to foist players on to a manager who did not want them. Oliver went on to sign for Woking, play in the Conference and make the England non-League team, before returning to the Football League with, of all people, Yeovil.

Instead Steve looked far and wide, and even made an attempt to sign Nuneaton Borough's ageing but towering centre half Terry Angus, as they had financial problems of their own with their chances of a quick return to the Conference disappearing. Angus decided against the move. Instead, Steve concluded for the moment that with Jamie Impey coming back to full fitness and Robbie Pethick having been signed, we could manage. Initially results proved him right.

My first Saturday away from my job and with the team took me to the charming Sussex town of Lewes for an FA Trophy tie. Jack came with me and the hospitality and atmosphere at the progressive little club, in their quaint stadium called the Dripping Pan, on the site of an old monastery and where the pitch was below the level of tall grass banks around it, was far more enjoyable, more like real football in England, than any Premiership experience.

In as bizarre a game as I have ever seen, we won 8–5 with Steve and Lee Phillips each scoring twice and Luke Nightingale, from his position wide on the right, a hat trick. I was pleased for Luke, who had had the fans on his back at the Wessex after some of the chances he had missed.

We were always at least two goals ahead but still I was

worried anew. Our comical defending had kept them in it and there was indeed an urgency for another defender. The fact that we were now in the fourth round of the FA Trophy, the last sixteen, with £1100 in prize money to come, and a home draw to follow against Altrincham, glossed over the anxiety.

It was further dissipated the following week when Robbie Pethick scored on his home debut with a brave header to unlock a tight game and we beat Hednesford Town 2–0 in front of another good crowd of 1474. We were surely back on track, as reinforced by another 2–0 win over Bath in the Dr Martens Cup, with Scott Partridge scarcely getting a kick in what looked like a team courting relegation.

Though the anniversary had passed me by, it had been exactly a year since I had sat in the car park that night waiting for the board, as it proved, to turn me down.

I was preoccupied with trying to balance the need to strengthen the squad with the need to keep costs in check. I had to emphasize this to Steve, as he was growing frustrated at our slowness in sanctioning new players. I pointed out the realities of our finances. The forthcoming Altrincham FA Trophy tie meant that we had to postpone an attractive home game against Worcester City and would forgo income. While we might get a crowd for Altrincham, the receipts would be shared.

Charlie Lesser was growing into the club as we had progressed during the season and coming to more games and board meetings. He offered to lend the club £50,000, repayable when the £70,000 due from Asda came through at the end of the season. I said that, given the pending West Dorset planning meeting, they could yet pull out and I did not want us to be that much in hock, nor Charlie that much out of pocket. Steve, remarkably, stepped in and offered to loan it instead as he was in the process of remortgaging a property he owned. Again, I was reluctant. If, for some reason, the Asda money did not materialize, I told him, we would struggle to pay it back.

Instead, I preferred the board to chip in to tide us over, with Steve's money a last resort. Matt McGowan was also reluctant to accept it as he said, validly, that Steve could then dictate where it was spent. We had enquired about two players from Havant and Waterlooville, the midfield player Shaun Wilkinson and, with Scott Partridge gone, a back-up striker in Chukki Eribenne. We were quoted £35,000. It was outrageous, but then we were Weymouth and they were Havant and ne'er the twain would meet. We could not have Steve insisting his money would go towards the two.

Finally, at a board meeting, Tristan agreed to put in £5000 now and £5000 in March. Jamie also suggested that we revamp our small Terras Tavern bar downstairs, which yielded little profit, and turn it into a café by day to serve the industrial estate and a bistro, called Claridge's, by night. It was a good idea, we all agreed.

The problem was that we did not have the £5000 Jamie told us it would take to refurbish the place and if we did, I thought we should spend it on football. Jamie objected, saying that sometimes we needed to invest in things other than football. And so I offered him a deal: if he bought £10,000 worth of shares, we would earmark £5000 for the café and £5000 for football. He just looked down at the agenda that Sarah prepared for board meetings.

And so we continued to beg and borrow players on loan. Coaches, too. Micky Jenkins had been sacked as co-manager of Havant and Steve took him on a non-contract basis as his assistant, to work with our coach Gary Borthwick. Steve was paying him just £50 out of his own pocket.

With John Lamb another of the injured, we also managed to find a left-winger by the name of Lewis Cook. Lewis was only on £250 a week at Wycombe and Tony Adams was willing to let us have him for a month. And so one Friday I made a mad dash to Wycombe, to sign the papers, then to Portsmouth where he could link up with the team for training in the afternoon – Steve liked to get in an extra session on the way to overnight stays for away games – ahead of a game against Dover Athletic the next day.

It paid off. Lewis did well enough in a splendid 3–2 win, after being 2–0 down, against a side then doing well, and Pethick and Yetton were on target again. It was an especially important win, being the final game of Steve's suspension following his sending off at Dorchester – and we had won all three. At five points clear at the top of the table, we were surely over our blip. I could rib Steve that we no longer needed him and get away with it. Three wins in a week had lifted everyone's spirits.

It is amazing in football what a win or three does, no matter what the undercurrents at a club are. Or what effect a loss or three has. When you win, the finances do not seem so serious, all those little annoyances round the club and fans' complaints – and we now had them about hypodermic needles near an exit just outside the ground, with addicts using the edge-of-town anonymity to shoot up – seem to go away. The players you have must be good enough.

Lose three and the fan hits the shit. That being me, the chairman bearing the brunt. Suddenly then, money is the issue, the problems pressing. Being realistic, still trying to treat triumph and disaster as equal imposters, I felt that we were somewhere in between. I suspected these players were not quite good enough, though I really wanted to believe they were. I hoped that Steve could keep on draining the last drop of talent and belief from them.

I also knew that as soon as you got the overdraft under control something came along to wrest that control from you, some hidden cost. I was hearing from the physio, Roger Hoare, that Lee Russell would be fortunate to play again this season, or possibly ever again, so badly were his knee ligaments damaged as a result of that clash at Ashford. It would mean we would have to think about reaching a settlement for the year left on his contract.

And as soon as you make headway on the field, something comes to take the wind from your sails off it. West Dorset District Council's environment committee had voted by nine to six not to include the Asda/Wessex Stadium project in their ten-year plan. The council said the developers, Trent, had simply not provided them with enough information, mainly in proving the case that the Wessex was the best site in the town, and the nearest to the town centre for a super-store, to enable them to give the go-ahead.

Trent, it seemed, had not done their job thoroughly enough and I was angry that this could slip through our hands. I put pressure on Asda to put pressure on Trent ahead of the vote of the full committee in a few weeks' time, which would be our final chance until a public inquiry into the ten-year plan in a year's time. Asda's go-between, Simon Hoare, a well-spoken, canny and erudite man, took responsibility and began to assemble a dossier that could go to every councillor ahead of the vote.

And so began a new to-do list. I had been keen to establish an academy at the club, to create a throughway to the first team from the youth teams for young players, and so met a man from an organization called PASE, who ran a competition for Conference academy teams, along with Stuart Bell, the head of sport at local Budmouth College and a well-respected coach of young players both locally and nationally. We duly agreed a tie-up with them, but it would upset Weymouth College.

I also met with the local Haven Holidays manager, Dave Bennett. They were interested in becoming our shirt sponsors for next season, thanks to Mel's wooing of them. It looked as if it could be promising, as we worked out how best we could promote their business in return. We suggested a blimp over the ground on match days as just one idea.

The next day, I drove up to the BBC as they wanted to know how the documentary was progressing. They were shown some 'rushes' by the production company and seemed happy enough that they were getting the inside story, the ups and downs – and there were plenty – inside the club.

While in London I met with Charlie Lesser. I wanted him involved in negotiations with Asda as, being a tough businessman on their metropolitan wavelength, he could show Trent that we were a little tired of being treated with a lack of urgency. I also wanted Charlie as involved in the club as possible, not just for the money he might be willing to invest but also because he was the sort of civilized, decent person we needed around the club if we were to take it forward. He was keener on becoming involved, was enjoying our season, and would look at investing more, he said. I was greatly encouraged.

It was FA Trophy week, at home to Altrincham. The FA rang and asked if they could bring the trophy itself down to Weymouth to be pictured with Steve for publicity shots. We had to agree, indeed welcomed the opportunity for as much publicity as possible to swell the gate, but it felt like tempting fate. I reckoned we had a good chance of going all the way in this.

The day of the game arrived and the heavens had opened, spilling thousands of gallons of water down on the whole country. I woke to hear on the radio that games all over the country were threatened with postponement. I was filled with dread. If we did not play today, it would mean that we would be going a whole month without a home game, apart from minor cup games, without any significant income.

At 8 a.m., as I drove down from St Albans through the lashing storm, I rang the fixtures secretary Pete Saxby, who had already alerted Altrincham that the pitch was under water. The Northern Premier League team from the outskirts of Manchester were due to set off and needed a decision. I told Pete not to call the game off, to tell them to travel. Paying for their coach was a risk worth taking.

Weymouth is a tidal town and the water could subside. When the tide went out the water table would drop, and some of the water would drain away from our pitch. This was more evident at our old harbourside ground but even here a mile from the beach and harbour it applied. We checked with the coastguard. High tide was around noon, after which it would get better. The only problem was that it was bucketing down and showed no signs of stopping.

I stayed in touch with Pete at regular intervals. We had put out an appeal on the website for fans to come and help with pitchforking the playing surface and when I arrived through the spray, at about 11 a.m., there was the magnificent, soggy sight of some forty or so. There were even four from Altrincham who had been staying overnight in the town.

Somehow, we did it. We forked and forked, brushed water from the surface to the sidelines, Jamie nipping over to B & Q to buy the tools, and at 1 p.m. the referee passed the pitch playable. We gave all the volunteers a voucher for a free drink in the bar. We would be one of the few games in the country going ahead this weekend.

Ninety minutes later, we wished we weren't. We pressed for much of the game but were hit by two breakaways and lost 2–0. Steve cursed the forty people who had got the match on. As a chairman, my view was different. It had been a gift as well as a curse. The revenue from a crowd of 1700 was needed, though actually it was not as huge as it should be.

Many clubs in the competition were happy to draw us – their directors, if not their players – because our crowds generated a good revenue that they would share. With the home club paying the visitors' travelling expenses, and the VAT on the receipts, we ended up with less than the visiting side. It struck me as an iniquity. Still, we had some money to pay into the bank on Monday to keep the other manager I dealt with quiet if not happy. I was, though, upset that we had lost £1500 in potential prize money, and a chance at £2500 from the next round.

And as a fan, I was annoyed that we were out of a competition I felt that we were capable of winning. That would be proven later in the season when the final at Villa Park was won by Hednesford, whom we had just beaten and taken four points off in the season. I guess I was annoyed that our profile would not go higher, too.

Still, we had the league and the championship challenge to look forward to. We had new players, too. There were three months and seventeen games left to go and we were five points clear. At the start of the season, as the saying in the game went, we would have taken that. Now it was all about the end of the season.

CHAPTER THIRTEEN

But February made me shiver

Charlie Lesser rang me. He had been thinking about the club a lot and wanted to present a business plan to us. I knew that it would be hard to sustain another season like this, with directors underwriting the trading loss. It was tough enough getting money out of some of them the first time round, let alone a second.

Charlie had been a Newcastle United fan for his forty-four years, his father even having served on the board at St James's Park. He saw many clubs, he said, living beyond their means and still believed they could be run as businesses, with income outstripping expenditure. His ambition was to show it to be possible. He now had a feeling for Weymouth and would like to try it there.

And so he arrived at a board meeting accompanied by his business partner, James, since their coffee trading company in London was the potential investor in the club. It was certainly a radical, high-powered plan.

Charlie was offering to invest upwards of £100,000 for shares and change the format of the club. He wanted me to remain as chairman, he told the board, as he believed it was my enthusiasm driving the club forward. But he would also want to install a chief executive with day-to-day responsibility, particularly for financial matters.

He proposed dividing the club into 'profit centres':

stadium, bars, lottery, shop and so on. The club should budget for players' wages only out of gate receipts and prize money. There should, he said, be lower basic wages with players receiving more in bonuses for achievement.

In future, should the club make a profit, a dividend could be paid to shareholders – he being a major one and expecting a return on his investment – and other monies go back into the club.

I was unsure, the board was unsure. We would be ripping up 100 years of unpaid tradition in running the club. The difference between them and me was that I knew Charlie. He was wise and benevolent and, though a businessman, would never have sought to asset-strip the very thing he was attracted to. We asked him to come up with more detail and return in a fortnight.

We certainly had to do something, both short and long term. Because of tax and VAT being due, the overdraft had crept up to £110,000 and there was not a home game on the horizon until the end of the month. In addition, the former chairman Terry Bennett had picked a fine time to ask for £9100 he had loaned the club a few years ago. By now I had sold Dad's house and bought another £10,000 worth of shares, taking my total to £25,000 worth. It would help a little.

If only we had the £50,000 that I thought Jamie and Tristan would invest, to pay off a few bills, maybe to get a couple of new players in. Tristan, despite having agreed to stump up the previous month, had still put nothing in. Jamie had his mind on other things, chiefly how to get his pet project of the café through. Charlie – who also said he would guarantee another £25,000 on our overdraft – had offered to loan some money but wanted interest. Steve's remortgaging and lending us some would prove too costly.

But another couple of potential investors, impressed with

what the club was doing, had emerged. One of our coaches, Gary Borthwick, was recommending a man called Martyn Harrison, the hotelier who had bought the Russell from Matt McGowan. Martyn was noting how well the club was doing, Gary said, and he would want only 5000 shares in return for loaning us £50,000. Unsold shares we had plenty of. There were hundreds of thousands of those.

Tristan and Jamie also approached me. They had someone, they said, interested in joining the board. He was a local accountant, their accountant, by the name of Chris Pugsley, and they reckoned he had pots of money. He owned racehorses and was willing to invest in the club. It seemed like a good lead.

I met him privately, along with Tristan, and he seemed a decent enough bloke. Balding, greying, in his fifties, he spoke with a West Country accent which can make people from the rest of the country underestimate the speaker. He seemed sharp enough to me.

He was, indeed, willing to buy shares and put money in. We danced around the subject of how much but it was best not to press for too much, too soon and risk putting him off. I felt, as with Charlie, that once the club got under his skin, he would want to ensure it all worked. Pugsley had his reservations, mainly about Jamie. He no longer did his books but was worried about some of his business dealings, including winding up his scaffolding company, which came as news to me. But he was another who liked what we were doing at the club. He had been asked to go on Dorchester Town's board, he said, but did not feel they were ambitious enough.

Beggars couldn't be choosers. In the six weeks between mid-January and the end of February, we would have no home league games, only the shared revenue from the Altrincham match. The Southern League Cup tie against Bath and a couple of hastily arranged games against local teams Portland and Wimborne in the minor Two Counties Trophy brought in peanuts.

At least we were not paying out win bonuses, for the Altrincham defeat was to trigger a bad run, unexpected as we now had some new blood. Robbie Pethick had signed for fifteen months. I had also been pressing the Supporters' Club for a mid-season donation from their profits from car boot sales, the tea bars and the club shop they administered and they came up with £5000 that enabled us to buy the tough-tackling Shaun Wilkinson from Havant and Waterlooville. Havant thought they had 'done' us, as usual, but it was a long way from the £35,000 they had quoted for him and Chukki Eribenne.

Shaun made his debut at Cambridge City as a substitute but could not alter a 1–0 defeat. We dominated the game but just could not force the ball into the net and were caught by a breakaway goal.

The next week we went to Eastbourne Borough in a howling gale, took an early lead through Lee Philpott but subsided to a 2–1 defeat. Fortunately, Crawley were beaten on the same day and I still felt we could, would, win this title but our lead at the top, with them having some games in hand, was fast disappearing.

In between, we played at Eastleigh in a Southern League Cup quarterfinal. The Hampshire side, a division below us, were becoming a force, with investors behind them now, and Matthew Le Tissier, the Southampton legend, who had even played a few games for them, was at the game.

Also there was Gordon Strachan, about – unknown to all except himself and his chairman Rupert Lowe – to quit as Southampton manager. 'You haven't come to pinch my centre forward, I hope,' I said to him. Funnily enough, he said, he had thought of trying to take Steve last summer when he was out of contract at Millwall just to bring a bit of nous and play a bit part in this season's Premiership campaign. I was taken aback, realizing again how lucky we had been to recruit Steve.

When I later told Steve about the exchange, he cursed me for talking him back to Weymouth, before agreeing that, as a Portsmouth fan, he would have found it difficult to turn out at St Mary's Stadium. He had done so for Millwall the previous season, joyously scoring their goal in a 1–1 FA Cup tie.

More important was the conversation I had with Chris Pugsley before kickoff. We had agreed for him to join the board and I asked him how many shares he would purchase. He said he would put in £2500 now and more later. I was taken aback, hoping for ten times that much. I hated this business of being a beggar and not a chooser.

I also asked Tristan Murless, yet again, if he was now able to buy the shares he had promised. He was waiting, he said, for a large sum of money he was still owed by Martyn Harrison – that name was cropping up a lot lately – for electrical work at his hotels.

Again I was disappointed, anxious even, but I was beginning to recognize what Mel had told me about certain Weymouth businessmen. They liked to portray to all they had money, but when it came to backing up that impression, they were less forthcoming. They talked a good game. But they didn't walk the walk.

Then there was Jamie Lyones. Jamie was still not coming up with any money, either, but he was going ahead with his latest plan. I was talking to Sarah in the office on the phone one day when she mentioned that Jamie was in the process of taking apart the Terras Tavern. The board had agreed that his idea for a café/bistro was a good one. It was used mainly as a base for the youth teams and for Mel to host her birthday parties for kids, which brought in a good profit on match days. It was only really employed as a bar for big games when the Wessex Lounge couldn't cope. Profits from it were small even then.

Jamie, it seemed, had interpreted the board's enthusiasm for the idea as a green light to start work. I rang Jamie, asked him to stop work. I asked Tristan and Matt McGowan to talk to him until I could get down to Weymouth and talk to him in person myself. When I did, I asked him about the business plan the board had asked for, and the cost of bringing in all the kitchen equipment. It varied from £3000 to £8000 depending on different versions. I told him the club did not have the money, that we needed proper costings. He said he was doing deals for all the equipment.

I had had this experience before. I hadn't liked the tables and chairs that Tristan and Jamie had acquired for the main lounge, as I thought they made the place look like some cheap wine bar rather than a football club, but I backed the two of them because I admired their enthusiasm. They had assured me they were cheap and we would have months to pay. Only when we got the invoices sooner than they had told me we would, from some bloke who was getting rid of them from a hotel anyway, did I wonder and worry. They had done this without reference to a board meeting but at the time I believed they should be allowed some rope. I trusted them.

I did not want the club to get burdened with more bills for an enterprise that might be a white elephant despite Jamie's insistence that a café would bring the club £2000 a week. I asked him again where all the figures were, how he worked that out. 'I don't have time for bollocks like that,' he said. 'I'm a businessman. A doer.'

Jamie had said that he would pick up the tab for it all, then receive it back in the form of shares, as Tristan had done in submitting bills of around £10,000 for his electrical work. But that work was necessary, this was a luxury. And we couldn't let someone dictate what their money coming into the club was going on. I hadn't wanted to pay off the debts last summer with my share money, would have preferred to invest in the team, I told Jamie, but it had to be done. If Jamie was willing to hand over £5000, then that should come into the club and the board would decide how it was spent.

It sparked fierce internal strife within the club. It seemed petty, an example of wills and personalities clashing, but it came to preoccupy us. Jamie felt my stopping of the project humiliated him. I felt he was becoming a loose cannon, off on his own agenda, trying to get a new business that he could run on the back of the club, his own having failed. Given the board's attitude, Jamie had to put the Terras Tavern back to its original state. The episode was closed. For now.

We had more important business than squabbling. Following West Dorset executive committee's decision to recommend to the full council that the Asda scheme should not go into their ten-year plan, we had one last chance. Asda rallied their experts in transport and environment consultancies and their go-between, Simon Hoare, decided that all the information drip fed to them over the last couple of years should be consolidated into a compendium and sent to every councillor ahead of the meeting.

I wrote a chapter on the football club, outlining the way the club had taken off again this season, and its needs for the future. We hoped to be promoted, it said, into the Conference and thence into the Football League, all within the next four years, and needed a new 8000-capacity stadium, to include 2000 seats. In addition, we would be providing community facilities alongside, with a speedway track and third element. I had thought of an indoor sports centre but artificial five-a-side pitches, open to the public, might well be better. I also wanted a players' hostel, to house the academy and first-team players staying overnight.

Despite the glossy and impressive document, it was still with trepidation that we attended the full council. We knew there were power struggles within, that the Tory group would oppose the Labour, that West Dorset needed to be seen as the prime movers of the scheme, to assert their authority over Weymouth and Portland, whom they felt should not be backing this as the majority of our land was within their jurisdiction.

We sat through the arguments, knew quickly which way the tide was turning. One councillor said she was not familiar with the location for this development. For pity's sake. The compendium made no difference, they said. The developers Trent had been slow in providing them with enough detail and this was simply too late for them to change the executive committee's decision, they added. The scheme would not be going forward to the ten-year plan.

I sat with Simon Hoare in the old adjacent courtroom, where the Tolpuddle Martyrs were unjustly tried and sentenced to deportation in 1834, and seat also of the notorious hanging Judge Jeffreys. We agreed that all was not lost, that it was now a question of throwing everything into the public inquiry into the ten-year plan, which would not start for another year. Even if the scheme had been accepted, any work or plans could not anyway have started until after the inquiry, which would last ten months. I told Simon that I had lost all confidence in Trent, that the club wished only to deal with Asda direct now. He agreed, and he would be the point of contact.

What with the financial struggles, it was a blow. As was hearing from our club secretary, Bob Mowlem, that he was finding the stress too much and wished to stand down at the end of the season. He loved the club, he said, loved the job but thought it was going to be more of a retirement hobby. We had become so professional, with all the extra work that entailed, that he could cope no longer, he said. He even brought his wife in with him to tell me one morning and I could see from his, and her, face that it was getting to him. I knew how he felt. I thanked him for his hard work, loyalty and his support and meant it. He was a lovely chap. I told him to go and spend some more time with the new Labrador puppy he had acquired.

I had by now remembered where I had met Bob before. As a teenager, I once went – whisper it – for training at Dorchester Town. Bob had been the coach. A couple of kids were talking behind his back. He turned on them. 'I heard that,' he said. 'I'm not blind you know.'

I also heard from Nigel Winship that he was finding it difficult to fulfil his role as finance director with a new business to run and a young baby to help look after. Chris Pugsley agreed to think about replacing him. Tristan Murless also told me that two of the club's former heroes, Anniello Iannone and Kevin Dove, were interested in joining the board. I asked him to talk to them, see what they could offer, though we were now only one short of the maximum number of directors permitted. I was still hoping that Dave Higson might return, though he was wary of all the hassle again.

The day of the board meeting to hear Charlie Lesser's revised plan for the club arrived. His company, Carlton Commodities, would be prepared to buy the remaining 659,000 unsold shares in the club for 20p each, bringing in £131,800, he said. In return, they would run the stadium, and maximize income from it. We would also prepare for Conference football by adopting their salary cap of 65 per cent of football income, with players on low basics and then sharing in a bonus pot at the end of the season if we exceeded expectations.

There was a silence while the board thought through the implications. We would be selling 50 per cent of the club for £130,000. I asked Charlie what would happen to the proceeds from pop concerts, which I thought we could put on and make money from. He said that Carlton would take the proceeds. I thought this could be renegotiated and he agreed.

I could see the board was unhappy with it all. Chris Pugsley said that the deal was heavily weighted in favour of Carlton and I could only agree. Charlie countered by saying that if the club made a loss, it would be Carlton that bore that responsibility, so therefore if they were taking the risk, they should take profits as well.

The mood was clearly not for such a deal. We were not that desperate. There was nothing that an injection of cash would not fix to cover the cash-flow problems, I felt. Charlie sensed the mood, too, and withdrew the offer. But I wanted to keep him on board. I still had this belief that the more he grew to enjoy the club, the less hard-nosed he would be in his business demands. He agreed to look at the possibility of making an offer for a licence to run the stadium, leaving the football side alone.

When we did talk football, finally, at the board meeting, the news was not great. Tim Clancy would be coming back from Millwall for a second month's loan but Lee Russell's career, sadly, was over and it would fall to me to negotiate a compromise payoff for the last year of his contract.

I said I would like to increase the wage bill for the last two months of the season, before the transfer deadline, to give Steve a real shot at the title, since cracks in the team were now only too evident. I mentioned £1000 a week. Chris Pugsley, notably, was in favour. None, though, was willing to invest personally. The matter drifted. I loaned the club another £5000 to pay off some bills. My father's legacy was dwindling.

These were hard times. We had slipped to second on the back of the defeats at Cambridge and Eastbourne and, with Crawley having won their games in hand by the time we played the Birmingham side Moor Green, who were on the slide themselves, we had slipped to second in the table.

Actually, these were worrying times, accentuated by all the off-field tribulations. Another home game, against Dover Athletic, had to be postponed because of bad weather. It was Valentine's Day and Mel had ordered roses for a promotion to hand out one to every woman who came to the game. Luckily the florist cancelled the order without cost.

To the relief of all, we trounced Moor Green 3–0, with Lee Phillips scoring twice and Steve once. Then, three days later, we beat Dover Athletic by the same score, this time Steve scoring twice and Paul Buckle once. Thank goodness, not just for six points that took us back to the top of the table, but also for the much-needed revenue from crowds of 1402 and 1352.

A huge weight was lifted from my shoulders. I was newly charged for meetings, with Asda, with potential club secretaries, with kit suppliers to work on next season's shirts – I wanted retro, feeling that if we were going back into the Conference after so many years away, we should mark the occasion – and with local companies to try to talk them into next season's shirt sponsorship.

Now we would go to Crawley on Saturday for a potentially epic contest. If not quite a championship decider, with plenty of the season still left, it was certainly one that would go a long way towards deciding matters. And the onus was on them to knock us off our perch.

Things were looking up. There was also a possible white knight on the horizon.

CHAPTER FOURTEEN

Beware the sides of March

It was an astonishing sight. Coach after coach, debouching fan after fan, drove into Crawley Town's car park at their tidy, municipal Broadmead Stadium on the edge of the town near Gatwick Airport. It was a far cry from my first game as chairman when we were beaten 5–0 and just twenty or so diehard stragglers had made the trip to watch a Weymouth side which had just avoided relegation. And half a dozen of those had stayed in the bar for the second half.

Now there were 850 packed into a segregated area, with another 100 or so in the stand, to watch a Weymouth side contending for the title. At one point, we worried about overcrowding. It all added up to a remarkable attendance of 4522, what would be the league's best crowd of the season.

It was all because this was *the* crunch match of the season. 'Race for the Championship' said the front cover of the programme over a cutout of the Southern League shield, a most magnificent, and huge, trophy, one that I had once seen years ago disrespectfully laid on its side behind a pool table in the then champions' Welling United club house. Our lead had gradually been whittled away by Crawley. Now we were just two points ahead of them with both sides having thirteen games to play.

I had travelled down early with Jack and met up with

Charlie Lesser at the team hotel. I wanted Charlie to have brunch with the players, to get him more involved and further his growing affinity for the club. Steve liked him immediately. 'He's proper, he is,' he told me.

It was, as expected, a tense, tight game, goalless at half-time. Then Crawley broke the deadlock, scored again soon after. It is a sickening feeling sitting there as a director and the team is 2–0 down, behaving with sangfroid when it eats at you so, hundreds of thoughts swirling through your mind. What would this cost us, on and off the pitch?

It is even more difficult to keep cool when you pull a goal back, as Steve Tully did; worse still when your player-manager misses a header from close range with minutes left. It would have given us a vital point, just as Steve's penalty miss against Crawley at the Wessex back in January would have done. Just after the final whistle, the *Football Diaries* crew wanted to interview me. They caught me on camera blowing my nose as I was talking to Mel, who had brought her husband Simon and three kids, Rob, Rosie and Lee, up for the game. It would later look on television as if I was wiping away a tear.

All week I had been liaising by phone with Crawley's charming and sporting chairman Jo Gomm about safety and refreshment arrangements for our fans in their segregated area. 'I don't think we'll beat you 5–0 this year,' she had said. But 5–0 or 2–1, it still meant three points to them as well as surrendering six to them this season, actually a twelve-point swing given that old cliché about a six-pointer. Had we won today, we would have been five points clear. Now they led us by a point, with twelve games left. All was not lost by any means – they had eight of their last twelve games away from home, we had six and six – but the momentum was definitely with them.

Mind you, some of their supporters did have a scare the next day. With the skies darkening, Crawley had turned on their floodlights at half-time and Steve Dadd posted on our website that we were appealing the result under FA Rule 37(b), which states that playing conditions must be the same in both halves. It prompted bemused debate, even renewed hope, among a few of our fans until people cottoned on to the wind-up, perhaps having even searched the FA handbook for a rule that didn't exist. He could be amusing, could Steve.

Two days later, the other Steve and I saw just how the pendulum had swung towards Crawley when we travelled with Micky Jenkins to Billericay to see them play Chelmsford City, bottom of the table. Crawley led 2–0 after twenty minutes. 'Claridge, Claridge what's the score?' sang a group of their fans when they noticed him in the stand. 'Come on, I've seen enough,' he said and, freezing, I wasn't too disappointed to leave. Crawley went on to win 4–0. They led us now by four points.

We had an immediate chance to cut it, playing Moor Green at their ground in a Birmingham suburb the next night. Three months ago it would have been three certain points. Now we were nervous, insecure about ourselves. It is true what they say about confidence in football at any level. When you play with it, you feel as if nothing is going to beat you. Without it, a pub team worry you. As Arsene Wenger once observed, confidence can take a long time to build but can disappear in a day.

Moor Green is a curious little ground. They have – or had, since an arson attack would later destroy it – an old wooden stand housing all the seats behind a goal. It was the result of having changed the pitch round at some point. Charlie Lesser had driven me up from London and for the first half we sat there, freezing.

For the second, we could take it no longer. We needed a release, and made our way round to the side of the pitch and shouted our lungs out for the team. We scored, they equalized almost immediately. We shouted harder, all the tension coming out. I behaved like a fan again.

'Get on with it,' someone shouted as their goalkeeper dawdled over a free kick. 'All the time in the world,' he replied, probably happy with a point. That's another thing about non-League football. Quite often you can hear pretty much everything that is said on the pitch.

Then – delirium – we pinched a goal through Paul Buckle, set up by our substitute Mark Robinson. 'Curly' had been a bit-part player this season, and the touch of others Steve had brought in did eclipse his, but he was wholehearted and devoted to the club. Tonight we had reason to be grateful for that commitment.

We led 2–1 with minutes left and the Moor Green goalkeeper rushed to take a free kick. I could not resist it. 'All the time in the world, goalkeeper,' I said. What a smart-arse. I would have disliked me at that moment, but football makes you do and say such things in the heat of the moment. It was why sitting in the directors' box was such hard work. Out here, within reason, you could vent the frustrations of your life. It was cheaper than a psychiatrist. It is the therapy of the working man.

By the same token, you do wonder how players sometimes keep their cool as well as they do, particularly in the non-League game where the purveyors of unpleasant remarks are so close to them, so easily heard. Eric Cantona was vilified for his two-footed lunge on a fan who had called him a 'French motherfucker' at Crystal Palace and was punished with a long suspension. The only surprise to me is that it doesn't happen more often. Through my experiences at Weymouth, I was actually coming to admire more the restraint of those within the game.

And so we clung on for a vital win to cut the gap back to a point. Crawley was just a blip then, otherwise we had won three of four games. It was still all to play for. Actually, not quite. We hadn't played well, weren't playing well. We were just hanging in there. We were beaten 2–1 at home by Welling United in our next match. A familiar pattern had developed. The opposition camped in their own half at the Wessex, daring us to break them down. If we couldn't, they would hit us on the break.

Afterwards I sat with Steve in the dressing room. 'We're not quite good enough are we?' I said, acknowledging that it was beginning to look all over for us. Shattered, after an hour's inquest with the players, he could only nod in agreement.

It did hurt, though, when Steve Dadd went on the website to say that certain fans had reckoned that the performance had been as bad as anything the previous season. I couldn't accept that. Even at our worst we were certainly better than the best that Geoff Butler had sent out last year. At least we were still trying to do the right things, to pass the ball as befitting the club's tradition for playing the game the right way.

It was not the best time to be holding a fans' forum, but I had committed to having one at least every three months and would not duck it. In fact, I went prepared for a good old debate if the fans were turning. 'Where has it all gone wrong?' was inevitably the first question.

I didn't think it had gone wrong; just not as right as we would have liked, I said. People would have settled for this position at the start of the season but in a way, we had done too much too soon, raised expectations with the form of the first half of the season. I pointed out that we were still on course for our highest league position since finishing runners-up in the Alliance in 1981, and our best in the Southern League for almost forty years.

Besides, I added, people had to remember that this was the first year of the five-year plan to get into the Football League. We had made significant progress. Next year, two promotion places would be up for grabs, rather than this year's one, and we would be well placed to claim one of them. This was a rebuilding year that had gone better than expected.

But we hadn't given up on the title, I added. We were still looking to strengthen ready for a final push. We now had to rely on Crawley losing some games, but a lot can happen, I said. Hadn't Newcastle United once squandered a twelve-point lead, Manchester United once blown a five-point advantage in the last week of a season? We just had to win games and be ready to take advantage of any slip-up.

In addition, after January and February's problems with the development, we were now progressing on the new stadium and I had had some exceptional news from Asda, I said, without divulging the details of a letter that I had just received.

With Trent now out of the picture, I had been dealing with Simon Hoare and Andrew Westlake, the estates surveyor for Asda, who was quiet, efficient and businesslike. Meeting them again with Charlie Lesser, the four of us were on the same wavelength and progress was swift, the atmosphere one of mutual respect.

Charlie and I told them that since they did not have a history of building football stadiums, that we would prefer to get in our own specialist architects. We wanted a price for our land, so that we could cost the whole project. And it had to be higher than the deal negotiated by the previous board where they bought us adjacent land, built the stadium and gave us £1.5 million on top. We reckoned that deal added up to around £7.5 million. Charlie had consulted with property developers and knew the value of our twelve-acre site. It was at least £1 million an acre, possibly £1.5 million if they wanted it badly enough.

They went away to think about it, assuring us that despite

West Dorset District Council not including the scheme in their ten-year plan, Asda were committed to the project and would be pulling out all the stops for the public inquiry. I was confident that their resources would ensure that it went through.

A letter came back. They were offering £11.5 million for our site. They would, when I spoke to Andrew to thank them for the offer, also consider raising the £70,000 annual interim payment to £100,000. Now we were getting somewhere. And if they could respond that quickly, there was surely more to come. I had already consulted with a firm of stadium architects recommended to me to by Simon Inglis, author of the definitive *The Football Grounds of Britain* and a good contact. For an 8000-capacity stadium and a training ground with another stand so that it could host speedway, along with an artificial pitch for community use and a hostel for players, they reckoned it could be done for around £7.5 million.

Asda had told me that it could take between £1 million and £1.5 million to secure the adjacent land – cheaper farm land – which meant that in total, as well as all the new revenue-generating facilities, we would have around up to £3 million to put aside for the future of the club. It was a good deal. 'You've cracked it,' said Charlie when I rang. The board, naturally, was delighted but I still felt that Asda might go higher.

It made our cash-flow problems look trivial by comparison, but without the result of the public inquiry, without planning permission, it would still not impress the bank unduly. Still, we had home games now, with Worcester City to follow three days after the Welling United match. I still couldn't get money out of Tristan and Jamie but by now I had fixed up a meeting with this Martyn Harrison. As well as the Russell, he had bought one of the biggest hotels in Weymouth, the Prince Regent, along with the old art deco

Riviera holiday complex at Bowleaze Cove, once a Pontin's. He appeared to be a man of means.

One morning, I met with him at the Prince Regent. The man who carried out Harrison's building works, Ramin Hidari, was also there, along with Gary Borthwick. I trusted Gary and he spoke highly of Martyn. In a corner, as we sat drinking coffee in the clean, main bar, lolled Harrison's teenage daughter, Faye, looking bored.

Everyone, except her and Gary, both of whom said nothing, smoked a lot and Harrison and Hidari were clearly sizing me up. I was gauging them, too. Hidari was clearly the 'gofer', doing the bidding, relishing a little bit of power by association. Harrison, in slacks and open-necked checked shirt, dressed sloppily for one so supposedly wealthy. Indeed, with his mop of unkempt curly hair, he did not give out the impression of money. He did give out an impression of power, however. As hotel staff came and went, brought us coffee, they seemed on edge.

After uncomfortable pleasantries and a bit of dancing around the subject – I was always uncomfortable asking people directly for cash – Harrison supposed we had better get down to talking about money. He said he would buy £10,000 worth of shares and loan another £15,000 and I duly offered him a place on the board. Hidari, who would not be joining the board, offered to lend another £10,000. This would certainly ease the overdraft, now running at around six figures, and help get players in ahead of the transfer deadline.

Hidari signed a cheque and there was a pause. 'Oh,' said Martyn, 'you want a cheque from me?' It would help, I replied. At length, he got Hidari to sign a cheque, saying that he would pay him back.

'Don't worry about it, it's just his sense of humour,' Gary would say to me later. 'He likes to think he is in control.'

I was a little puzzled at this game-playing but delighted nonetheless that we had some new money and a man with more of it than me on the board.

I was even more delighted the following Tuesday night when we beat Worcester City at home 3–1. Luke Nightingale scored twice from his position wide on the right in what was a game we simply had to win if we were to retain any hopes of the title. We had attracted a healthy crowd of 1702 for the Welling game and I had feared it would drop considerably for the next home game. Instead, the figure was one up at 1703, though it might have nudged 2000 had we won the Welling game.

The Worcester goal was scored by a tricky little left-winger called Adam Wilde, who impressed us all, Martyn included. 'See how much he costs,' he said, so, after consulting Steve, who had also liked him, the next day I did. Worcester wanted £20,000. We all agreed it was too much.

But it was encouraging that we could be in the market and Martyn gave Steve the green light to sign players. The problem was, no clubs of any standing were willing to let go any player of stature without a ridiculous fee at this stage of the season.

Again, Steve drove all over the place to games and meetings, made calls everywhere to try to recruit, but that centre half eluded us. With Jason Matthews looking wobbly in goal lately, we did get in Jimmy Glass, who once famously scored a last-gasp goal to save Carlisle's League status, having dashed upfield for a corner. He was now playing Dorset League football but, still only in his late twenties, was keen to get back into the semi-professional game at least. He certainly impressed on his debut against Worcester.

That win had made it four from our last six games and had taken us back in with a sniff of the title. If we could get another from a trip to Grantham, the longest on our roster, then we might just be prompting some nerves in the Crawley camp.

It was, though, the gloomiest of days. A howling gale at another stadium that had an athletics track around it made for a ridiculous game. When the ball went out of play, it often took a ball boy, as if chasing a beach ball along the shoreline, up to a minute to retrieve it. You didn't get replacement balls being chucked on instantly at this level. Not unless the home side was losing, anyway.

Grantham were a poor side, now bottom of the league having slipped from a promising position early in the season. We, in these conditions, were just as bad. After they had taken an early lead, it took a late Claridge goal to rescue a point. And Crawley had won again.

What made it worse was that Paul Buckle was sent off in the first half in one of those incidents that can make you despair about the game. He was fouled from behind, then stamped on as he clutched his ankle. Prone, he responded with a kick upwards to the perpetrator. Naturally the ref saw the retaliation but not the stamp and Paul was sent off, the real offender seeing only yellow.

From then on, I had to endure people in and out of the directors' box yelling abuse at our team, Claridge in particular. 'Three grand a week? Waste of money,' someone shouted. Three thousand quid? I would have shouted rubbish, too, if that's what Steve was really getting. I noticed a couple of kids at the front of the directors' box yelling at him that he was an overpaid joke.

The perception seemed to be that we were the fancy dans of the league, spending fortunes. If only. I knew that Crawley were paying more than us, along with a few others, and what we had achieved had been amazing on the amounts we were actually paying. A lot of it, I had become convinced, was because of jealousy. Clubs averaging a few hundred through the gate envied our attendances and the size and potential of our club.

That view was clearly prevalent among opposition players, as well. As I made my way to the dressing room, I began chatting with a Grantham director and lamented Paul Buckle's dismissal, wondering why it is that the instigator of an incident rarely receives the same punishment. He shrugged his shoulders diplomatically. A Grantham player walking by must have overheard.

'What you moaning about, you fucking big-time charlies?' he said. I was taken aback and asked him what he meant. He pressed his chest to me and we started arguing the toss, interrupted only by two of our players, Ian Hutchinson and John Waldock, intervening. I was grateful they did. The bloke was a brick outhouse.

Up in the bar, I had a quiet drink with Steve amid fans now sheepish after the roasting they had given him all afternoon. It struck me as cowardly. The two young lads berating him all afternoon now approached him for an autograph. I pointed out to them that Steve had been gracious to them, perhaps in return they would not shout abuse at him next time. They were only kids, so I couldn't be too upset with them. It was the parents they returned to in the corner of the bar with their autographs who upset me. 'You take it all too seriously,' Steve said. He had become used to all the double standards in the game down the years.

Crawley were now getting away, five points clear, and three days later we reached a turning point when we had to go to Nuneaton Borough for the match rearranged from just before Christmas when it was rained off. At that time Nuneaton had been struggling. Now they were in a rich seam of form.

It was the sort of game home fans and neutrals love, a nightmare for us as the away team. Sloppiness in defence saw us go 3–1 down before we recovered to 3–3, only to concede a late winner. I knew now how Kevin Keegan felt that time when Newcastle, the Premiership title slipping away from him and them, lost 4–3 at Liverpool. The then Newcastle manager was shown on television slumping over an advertising hoarding in disbelief and frustration as Liverpool grabbed a late winner. What made it more galling was that Crawley had been unexpectedly beaten at Merthyr Tydfil on the same night.

Football Diaries wanted to interview me after the game and I sat in the dark, alone, in the dugout by the side of a soggy, muddy and deserted pitch. This is a maddening game, I told them. I hate it. And I love every minute. Knowing the stick he had got, I didn't dare echo Kevin Keegan's 'I'd luv it, just luv it, if we beat them to the title' tirade directed at Sir Alex Ferguson.

Afterwards, I drove our loanee Tim Clancy to Coventry station so that he could get a train back to London. It was a difficult twenty minutes or so. I knew Steve was fuming with him, the whole of the defence indeed, and that this would be Tim's last game on loan from Millwall. We would not be signing him. Probably, he was glad to get away, too, but it would not be easy for him to find a club as good as Weymouth if Millwall, as looked likely, were going to release him at the end of the season. He eventually ended up at the South London side Fisher Athletic of the Ryman League.

Now we were playing catch-up – now we had to go for broke. Next Saturday, at home to Chippenham Town, a side we had defeated comfortably early in the season, we just could not break down their defence, ending up throwing men forward only to be caught on the break and losing 1–0 to another late goal. With Jimmy Glass also wobbling at Nuneaton, Jason Matthews returned in goal but could do nothing about being so exposed. The crowd slipped to 1465. Had we won at Nuneaton, been just a couple of points behind Crawley, it would probably have touched 2000. Crawley themselves, on an inexorable march, had won again and were eight points clear.

One point from three games was not title form and the transfer deadline had arrived without us able to recruit the players we needed. Now it was probably a question of winning our last six games and hoping that Crawley suffered a serious bout of nerves. I wasn't giving it up and I wasn't about to let Steve and the team do so either.

It wasn't just because as a fan I wanted that title and promotion. I wanted as much prize money as possible, with £6000 going to the winners and £3500 to the runners-up. I also wanted gates to stay as high as possible. We needed the money, even if we did now have some wealthy men on the board. At least this year we would be getting in some £60,000 from speedway, with Brian White and the Weymouth Wildcats having had the go-ahead to stage thirty meetings this year.

Deep down, though, I began to realize we would not be in Conference National the following season – although at least we had qualified for the new Conference South setup, something that would have been uncertain had the club not undergone a revolution – and that it was time to start planning for next season.

Off the field, there was much to attend to again, no time to lick wounds. Nor for the chairman could there be the luxury of wallowing in gloom. There was a sponsors' night, to thank all those who had returned to the club this season and to try to recruit more for the next season.

There was a new secretary to appoint, and, having interviewed three, I decided on Liz Bell. 'Good shout,' said Matt McGowan when I mooted the idea with him. Liz had once covered the club for the *Dorset Echo* and, though from Coventry, had become a fan after leaving the paper. She was efficient and enthusiastic, bright and personable and though nervous about taking on the job, extremely capable. I thought she could also help with the programme as she could write well and actually spell.

Even if things were fading on the field, I hoped we would be more settled off it, with the board now all in place. But Jamie Lyones and I were still at loggerheads and the issue would not go away. Thankfully Jamie took the heat out of the situation by taking his family to France. I only discovered he was gone when I came across a letter in the office from the stocktakers looking at our bars. I had left the running of them to Jamie and Tristan and was shocked to find out that proper records were missing, despite them having installed, at considerable cost, modern new tills. 'The gravity of this situation cannot be over-emphasized,' said the letter. In Jamie's absence, Tristan and Chris Pugsley told me not to worry that there was any irregularity, that it was just admin.

I was more buoyant about the possible concert that we would be staging this summer. I had tried myself in the autumn to get an act, even went direct to Eric Clapton's agent but was told no-go. And so I decided we needed professional help. At first I rang a contact at the Professional Footballers' Association, Christian Smith, formerly commercial manager at Leicester City, having been told that he had influence with Rod Stewart. He came back to me saying that Rod would cost £1 million but Christian did know two people who might be able to help.

Lester Holcombe and Mark Abery, he said, ran two successful specialist events companies called Toast Events and Cup Promotions and were the organizers of an event called Soccer Six, a successful celebrity tournament at Chelsea featuring such stars of the pop world as Robbie Williams. I recalled seeing pictures of the event and the celebrities in magazines.

Lester and Mark had been my guests at the Worcester

City match and, yes, they thought they could do something for us. I presented the results of my discussions with them to the board. I wanted the hot new band McFly, I said. They said they would try. They reckoned it would cost us about £100,000 to put on but the profits were likely to be at least that amount.

This perked everyone up. Our new board member Martyn Harrison, decidedly unimpressed in board meetings by the time-consuming acrimony of the Jamie Lyones saga, now looked rather more interested.

CHAPTER FIFTEEN

The cruellest month

It was time to try something different. The previous summer at a charity golf day, I had met a prominent former jockey named Michael Caulfield who had become a sports psychologist and was then working for a company called Trained Brain. Having persuaded the *Football Diaries* makers to pay for it, I gave the company a call and one Thursday night, along with players and coaches, I found myself in the Wessex Lounge in a deep and meaningful session with one of their trainers, Jamie Edwards.

I warmed to it, and many of the players did too. The session was all about mental toughness, how to turn negatives into positives, how to make the most of oneself. One little tip about reacting to adversity seemed perceptive. The psychologist suggested that after conceding a goal, the players should look up at the opposition's crossbar, rather than down at the ground. Literally, get your heads up. Some fifteen months later, Jamie would be working with Andrew Flintoff, turning him into Freddie the warrior who would help win back the Ashes for England.

This whole theme had been a continuing topic of discussion between Steve Claridge and myself for a while now as we continued to take stock of the club and work out what it needed. Players had come to the club, not least Steve himself, with experience of being winners. But we also had a core remaining from previous regimes where struggle had become a way of life. It was easier, subconsciously, to lose than to win, not to have to undergo the physical and mental commitment needed in the pursuit of achievement.

There was also the question of the expectation of the club, particularly from fans. Yes, we had a remarkable support for this level of football and a stadium, though leaky, much better than most at our level. It added up to a package that should take us into the Conference, at the very least, but there almost seemed to be a mental block preventing it.

It had produced a frustration among fans that meant they would turn very quickly when results did. Disillusioned at yet another false dawn, the sense of negativity around the place only increased, despite all best efforts to cheer and brighten the place up. Robbie Pethick was quick to sense it in his second spell with the club. He had been at Brighton, where fans were simply grateful to survive in the Championship. He had not there felt the same degree of expectation he experienced at Weymouth, he said.

Steve and I had come to the conclusion that we probably needed seven new players in the summer, more physical defenders certainly and at least one new wide player with tricks who would unpick the seams of well-stitched defences who came to the Wessex for a point. They should also be mentally strong, used to the rigours of promotion campaigns rather than relegation battles or mid-table mediocrity.

To instil a winning culture into the club would take more than a couple of hours with a sports psychologist, though, more than this one season indeed, but we did seem a more buoyant bunch than latterly when I met up with the team at a West Bromwich hotel for a match at Stafford Rangers the next Saturday.

We took the lead, only to concede. Just lately, that had been the signal to collapse and give away another goal soon after. I saw something interesting, though. There had been times when players had been at each other's throats, blaming each other. I said to Steve that I thought it sent the wrong message to fans and to opposition, showed that we were disunited and easily wound up. Steve said he wanted players who cared. I said I didn't want to see it happening. This time, though, there was no getting at each other. Just looking ahead towards the opposition's crossbar.

Our perennially optimistic and ever-present president Bob Lucas had made the journey but as the only director at the game – interesting how a bad run of results can also lead to a fair-weather board – I grew bored with sitting in the directors' box. And so I went to join my sister Mel and her family on the terraces. Again, I couldn't help myself.

When the Stafford goalkeeper attempted to drop-kick the ball upfield, it merely rebounded from the back of Lee Phillips and looped into the net to put us 2–1 up. It would later make a video collection of footballing bloopers that I saw advertised on television. The goalkeeper immediately raced to the linesman to protest, me directly behind the assistant, whom the referee quickly joined. 'Don't blame the lino for your mistake, keeper. Stay strong ref,' I shouted, trying to influence the officials.

I don't know if it worked but they kept their nerve and we held on for a morale-boosting 2–1 win. Perhaps Crawley might yet fold. Perhaps, if we won all our games, we could yet win the title. It was the anniversary of Dad's death and I, and Mel, were in need of some cheer and optimism.

The next Saturday was Steve's thirty-eighth birthday and we were away to Havant and Waterlooville. I had resolved not to enter their boardroom after all the bad blood earlier in the season and instead took Jack and stood on the terraces. On the way, I picked up a present for Steve. Knowing his fondness for fruit, I bought a pineapple at a fruit and veg stall. It raised a smile when I presented it to him in front of the team in the dressing room before the game.

The game could only be watched with hands over eyes. Our session with the sports psychologist had applied sticking plaster to the wounds but here they gaped again and we haemorrhaged goals, losing 4–1, a late goal by Lee Phillips providing minimal consolation. Soon fans would be asking why we hadn't bought their striker Gavin Holligan, who scored twice, from Wycombe Wanderers when we had the chance. Tony Adams, though, had told me that he was moody and injury prone and would not last a full season with any club. So it would prove with him at Havant.

At least I did not have to face Havant's gloating directors in their bar. In fact, I left a couple of minutes early to beat the traffic. The mobile soon rang. It was the suspended Paul Buckle, wanting to know how we had got on. 'Same old, same old,' he said when I told him. Indeed it was. Things were going to have to change.

The game was up and we all knew it. Stafford had been straw-clutching. It was now a question of finishing the season creditably and respectably, securing that runners-up position and its prize money.

Looking at the fixture list when we were top of the table, we pondered our run-in to the end of the season and thought we would have as comfortable a passage as it was possible to get for our last four games. We thought that if we could just hang in there and keep the pressure on Crawley, we could then beat such lowly placed teams as Tiverton Town, Chelmsford City, Welling United and Grantham Town, all but Welling at home, and perhaps pinch it.

But now we were struggling against anybody. The wind had gone from our sails and the opposition were all fighting to avoid relegation or secure a place in the top thirteen to qualify for Conference South.

Tiverton, Chelmsford and Welling yielded three feeble draws, the latter fortuitously coming about due to two goals in added time, by John Lamb and Robbie Pethick. 'We didn't so much get out of jail as escape from Alcatraz,' I told the *Dorset Echo*'s Matt Pitman and it duly formed his intro for Monday morning.

The crowd had been 1465 for the Tiverton game on the Easter Monday but, understandably given our flagging fortunes and the opposition, fallen to 1101 for Chelmsford. It would be another 1100 figure for our last home game, against Grantham, for which we reduced admission to a fiver as a thank you for such good support during the season. The gate was a disappointment as I had wanted to finish with an average of 1500 for the year and we fell short by just ten. But with Grantham certain to finish bottom and us limping to the finishing post, it was still remarkable given where we had come from a year earlier, on and off the field.

I interviewed Steve, with a hand-held mike, on the pitch after a 1–0 win that confirmed us as runners-up – twelve points behind Crawley – him asking the fans to view the season as a success even if we had just fallen short of winning the title. He urged them to keep in mind the bigger picture of a club now back on the way up, more profession-ally run. We should, he said, be proud of ourselves after years of underachievement.

We were not going to get away with it that easily, though. You sensed that the fans were sceptical. Had we come with a late run to finish second, they would have been encouraged. But we had squandered an eight-point lead and this felt a very different type of second place, the mood less forgiving. 'You've failed really, haven't you?' opined a Grantham director ungraciously. It was a bit rich given that his side had just finished bottom of the table, but one of those moments, having learned from our visit up to his place, when I decided to bite my lip.

I knew a lot of people would be thinking the same as that director, though, both within the town and non-League football in general. I did not want it to happen again. My determination to win promotion for the club was even stronger. The next season there would be play-offs, and that meant a greater chance. Runners-up the next season would not be a similar letdown.

The Player of the Year dance at the Pavilion that night, with Steve Tully cleaning up the awards, was a night of mixed emotions for players, staff and fans. It had been a good season but so nearly great. I did discover one benefit of being chairman. Every restaurant was full but the owner of a curry house recognized me and found a table for Vikki and me.

The players could afford to let their hair down. They were now off for eight weeks, the next season twelve weeks away, but for everyone else at the club, once again, the summer would be our busiest time.

Jamie Lyones had now returned from a long break in France, having left Tristan to run the bars, though Martyn Harrison had now decided to take those over and was using his staff from the Prince Regent. I was all for it. He said it would cost the club only £6000 a year, compared to more than double that previously.

I had been annoyed that Jamie had not told us of his absence, nor said for how long he'd be away, and that I had heard it only via Tristan. Jamie appeared to expect to return as if nothing had happened but I was not so sure, and told him so at a board meeting. It transpired that he had been tape-recording board meetings and I got to hear of it via Tristan. We were also upset with him going to the *Echo* to complain about the board, me in particular. It may have been coincidence, but certain stories were appearing about the club, like the details of Steve's contract.

The *Echo* had clearly seen a copy of the contract and concluded that Steve was about to earn £100,000 for the season. He wouldn't, but I conceded that he could have done had we been promoted. Steve himself was not happy that it all came out, and I could not blame him, though being a journalist, I could not get too upset with the local paper.

What concerned me more was Steve Dadd posting on our website that he had been informed that we might lose £400,000 on the season. It was untrue and damaging and I asked him to come to the club. His main job now was to take photos in in the sponsors' lounge and I told him I thought he should take a break from the club, and he conceded that it would be a good thing. I hoped that maybe there would be a role for him in the future, when the dust settled, as he was a bright bloke.

Jamie and I clashed again in a board meeting, in which I said that due to recent leaks, I was uncomfortable talking about anything to do with financial, commercial or playing matters. Martyn Harrison did, though, raise the subject of our assistant manager Micky Jenkins. The fans were unhappy with him, he said, and thought he should go.

I was taken aback. Sometimes you do listen to fans, of course, other times you back your own judgement. Micky was not to blame for the sequence of bad results, I felt. It was just a coincidence. In fact, we still won a few games soon after he came to the club. Besides, I said, it was the manager who decided who should be his assistant and not the board, though I would communicate any misgivings to Steve.

Charlie Lesser sought to smooth things over with me and Jamie, seeing that we were both stubborn. He was probably right; but then something happened from which there was no going back.

One day I was sitting in the boardroom after a day working on club admin, drinking coffee and smoking profusely, as usual, in Matt McGowan's company. He had been told by Jamie, he said, that if I didn't change my attitude towards him, I would find myself 'face down in the backwater'. Jamie's bark was always worse than his bite but Matt suggested I inform the police. Two detectives arrived at the club the next day, just to get the threat down in the records in case something did happen.

A board meeting then decided that this kind of threat against the chairman was unacceptable and that Jamie should resign, something that I wanted. He refused, however, telling the *Echo* that the boardroom was no longer a democratic place and he did not want to let the fans down by resigning. It was a bit rich, given that he had ignored a democratic board decision when he began tearing apart the Terras Tavern and had let everyone down by disappearing for so long.

And so an extraordinary general meeting was called so that shareholders could vote on his removal. It would be an annoying cost, both in money and time, but it had to be done we decided. As the EGM date approached, Jamie offered a deal. If we did not say anything about the whole episode, if we granted him £6000 worth of shares to cover the work he had done at the club – ground maintenance; his scaffolding company erecting the WFC sign on the side of the grandstand the previous autumn – he would resign.

I thought it outrageous, considered it blackmail. I was certainly not charging the club for three days' work a week, plus matchdays. In fact, this was costing me plenty. I wanted to go ahead with the EGM, to ensure that the full story was heard, but the board, chiefly Matt, persuaded me to agree to the deal to get him quietly out of our hair. Finally, I did. A horrible, unhappy episode was over. I thought.

Finances were still the overwhelming concern. I particularly wanted to find a new shirt sponsor as we had received a letter from Dave Higson and Mick Archer at Park Engineering saying that this would be the last year they would be putting their money in. Indeed, they would want the money back they had loaned the club, around £33,000. That meant, with Terry Bennett's £9000, we would have to find £42,000 soon. We had already paid back Peter Shaw's £5000. It was a blow. We had had Asda's annual end-of-season £70,000 payment, the overdraft now at a manageable £50,000 with £60,000 to come in from speedway over the summer, but the repayment of loans – and I was now owed £15,000, Steve Claridge a similar sum, though we would not press for the money back – was not in the budget.

Nigel Winship's figures for the season, we could see as we now took stock, had been spot on. There had been months, because of postponed games, when income did not reach the projected figure, and months when we brought in more than we expected, but overall we had hit the targets.

The trading loss for the season, we reckoned, would be about the expected £150,000. It was supposed to be underwritten by the directors buying shares, allowing us, in cash-flow terms, to break even. I had bought £25,000 worth of shares and the total of the others was about another £75,000. Lyones, Murless and Pugsley's failure to invest despite all the promises meant that we were some £50,000 down on the year.

Now it was a question of looking forward and we scheduled a board meeting for three days after the end of the season. We would not have quite the same costs next year, with ground repair work mostly done, but we did have the old directors' loans to pay off. We were, as I saw it, faced with three alternatives:

1. We could do the same again next year, the board again underwriting the loss by buying shares.
2. We could cut the wage bill.
3. We could work harder commercially to make up the shortfall.

Personally, I could not put in another £25,000 and there seemed little appetite elsewhere on the board for doing so either. Besides, we had to get this club standing on its own two feet sooner or later. Though I was confident the Asda deal would ultimately go through, it was by no means certain and it was not sensible to keep racking up debt hoping that the new deal would pay it off in years to come. Always assuming that the bank would allow us to rack up debt, that was. The Asda money represented the club's future and I at least did not want to mortgage that future.

But neither did I have the stomach for cutting the wage bill. In fact, we wanted to increase it to attract the seven players Steve reckoned we needed. We had come too far, everyone agreed, and we were not far off being a promotion squad. The play-offs in the new Conference South season even offered hope of new income. Who knows, we might even get some luck in cup competitions and bring in more revenue. But again, we could not budget for that.

Commercially, Mel had done brilliantly. Sponsorship of club and matches had yielded some £120,000, up from the £16,000 shown in the club's books the previous year. There was still some extra mileage in attracting more, I reckoned, though not much more. This was not a hugely wealthy town and those who had invested had done so out of goodwill towards Mel, Steve, even myself. My cousins, for example, had put in £7500 from their company, ASM, and we thought they might go to £10,000 as they had enjoyed the season, but there were not too many benefactors like them about.

I had been working hard on a shirt sponsor, talking to some serious regional businesses, such as Condor Ferries. A local Haven Holidays park was still making some encouraging noises. Above all, I had been playing a softly-softly game for six months with New Look.

New Look were one of the major success stories in British

retailing, their low-cost women's clothing having exploded on to the nation's high streets over the last decade. They had been founded by a man who lived in Weymouth, Tom Singh, and he had made the town their head office.

I had always imagined they would have wanted an alliance with the club but the previous board had told me they were an impossible nut to crack. It had, I came to realize, a lot to do with their profile being female while football's was largely male.

But I managed finally to get a meeting with their managing director, Phil Wrigley, and he seemed impressed by my vision for the club and what we might offer his company in return. I foresaw them as sponsors of every team going right down to Under 8s. For a sizeable fee, I even saw our new ground being called the New Look Stadium.

It was encouraging, but not enough on which to base a budget for next season. There was, though, another potential income source. I had been liaising closely with Lester Holcombe and Mark Abery and they had been working on getting together a line-up for the concert. If not McFly, they said, they would try for Busted, then riding high in the charts. Mark also had ideas for a celebrity football tournament, along the Soccer Six lines he and Lester had successfully promoted, as part of a weekend festival.

It might, if all went well, bring in about £100,000 for the club, they said, and the board was impressed by the plan. Martyn Harrison was proving a good acquisition to the board as he volunteered to host the artists at his hotels. But still, we could not factor that figure into next season. It was all yet to be confirmed.

Actually, Charlie Lesser piped up, there was another alternative. His plan to restructure the club and take a profit had not been welcomed by the board but clearly he still wanted to be involved, to do what he could. He would, he said, simply buy £100,000 worth of new shares to enable us to increase the wage bill. He needed to go back to his company to talk it over with his business partner but having grown to enjoy his involvement with the club, he wanted to take more of an active role.

The meeting was amazed and touched, none more so than me. I always felt that if Charlie got involved, it would get beneath his fingernails the way it had me. Charlie added a few caveats – that he would need to look at the figures in more detail, and have more of a hands-on role in the business affairs of the club – but he had seen what had been achieved this season and wanted to help us go even further. It was based on my committing to the club for the next few years as, he insisted, I had been the catalyst for it all. I said I would.

Leave him, he added, to go away and prepare a business plan and we would meet again in three weeks, at the end of May, to crunch all the numbers for the following season and enable Steve to start assembling his augmented, improved squad.

I could have cried I was so grateful, not for Charlie's testimony and vote of confidence in me, but because the club would be secured. The money worries that had kept me awake at nights for most of the winter appeared at an end. The strategy of speculating to accumulate had worked. The club had become an attractive proposition again, with investors appearing. Someone was going to save this football club.

CHAPTER SIXTEEN

Day of the jackal

Weymouth Football Club had known some significant moments since its founding in 1890. Unfortunately, not enough of them. The events of a May day 114 years later, though, it is fair to say, will probably go down as the most pivotal in the club's history.

By and large for fans, the highlights, or lowlights, are all to do with playing: great Cup days against giants, igno-minious defeats by minnows; joyous promotions, or the disgraces of relegations. Even Manchester United supporters would probably place fifty memorable moments above the takeover of the club by Malcolm Glazer, though the picture may change as the implications of his takeover, just as that of Roman Abramovich at Chelsea, unfold in the coming years. For us, what would unfold would be momentous.

Three weeks had passed since the end of the season. The days were lengthening, the weather was balmy and the traders in our seaside town were awakening from their hiber-nation ready for a summer of selling. We had not stopped at the Wessex Stadium. The players may have been on holiday, the fans beginning to grow edgy without their fix of football, but the work at the club had actually increased.

I gave up a Sunday to go to watch the Soccer Six celebrity event organized by our two concert promoters, Lester Holcombe and Mark Abery, at Reading Football Club's

Madejski Stadium. I wanted to see how they operated, perhaps even meet some of the bands to talk them into performing at our ground. The concert, along with a similar football tournament, was beginning to take shape.

Organizationally, it seemed to go well enough, though I was a little concerned that the crowd seemed to be only around 6000. I was hoping that we would attract 10,000, which would mean a profit to the club in six figures. With Busted now getting too big – and too costly at around £100,000 – I was still pressing Lester and Mark to try to get McFly.

In addition, the *Football Diaries* series, chronicling our season along with behind-the-scenes glimpses from higher up the game's food chain, had begun on BBC2. The reaction was so far encouraging, and when I appeared on the Simon Mayo programme on Radio Five Live, the feedback was positive from a panel reviewing the first programme.

Our struggles, and enthusiasm in overcoming adversity the previous summer, were playing well as counterpoint to the wealth of Reading's owner John Madjeski and the glitz and glamour of the Premiership. Watching a sequence with Kieron Dyer, the Newcastle and England midfield player, I couldn't help musing that his diamond-encrusted watch alone would have solved quite a few of our financial problems.

The reviews in the paper were also enjoyable, notably from Martin Kelner in *The Guardian*. 'Ridley took over his home-town club a year ago and installed Claridge as player-manager, presumably because he decided he had reached that stage in his life where he needs more grey hair,' he wrote.

'While Claridge chuckles, we see Ridley wearing what I can only describe as an expression of resigned indulgence. At this point he is absolutely Bob to Claridge's Terry.'

As well as *The Likely Lads*, we were described by

Dominik Diamond in the *Sunday Star* as natural successors to Jack and Vera Duckworth in *Coronation Street*. Jim White in *The Daily Telegraph*, who also described me as looking like Eeyore, noted this exchange:

Director: You're like an old married couple.
Claridge: If we are, there'd be divorce papers coming
    through the door any minute.
Me: Yeah, I'd be able to file for unreasonable
    behaviour.

A subsequent episode went down less well in club and town, however, when Tristan Murless was shown driving around pointing out the fleshpots and where – he thought – the players liked to drink. I had tried to get the programme-makers to show sunny shots of bay and beach and they had done, but they could not resist this part of the town's underbelly and Tristan was happy to oblige.

'Tristan proved conclusively the recently discovered law of television which proposes that when confronted by a camera, 80 per cent of the British population turn into David Brent,' wrote Jim White. He should have seen some of the more mocking shots I asked the makers to edit out. One sequence, showing Tristan and Jamie Lyones buying a toy helicopter for the auction at the Sporting Dinner then promptly crashing it on a test run in the car park, did not make it because Jamie had refused to sign a release form giving his consent to appear in the programme after leaving the board.

It was all a bit of fun and I did not mind too much Tristan being so laddish, unlike others who thought he made us look a laughing stock. We had done well out of the programme, in publicity and financially, and you had to take the rough with the smooth. What would disappoint me was an episode covering the Dorchester matches over the Christmas period. In it, Steve confessed to having kicked Jamie Brown, having denied it to me. As the chairman, who had defended him in public, I felt let down.

It was bizarre being recognized in strange places. One day at Bond Street tube station in London on my way to Charlie Lesser's office, two blokes approached me and asked for a photo with them on a mobile phone.

Charlie had asked to see me on a much more serious, and significant, matter. Further to his offer to buy £100,000 worth of new shares, he had been working on a financial plan for the future of the club. Now he was willing to invest £300,000 to buy the remaining shares and would outline the conditions at the next board meeting. In the interim, we should put signing new players on hold. I was touched anew. It was getting even better.

I phoned the members of the board individually, to say that Charlie was going to come up with a package far bigger than originally proposed. It would mean, I hoped, that Steve would be able to go out and find the players he reckoned we needed to move from second to first, increasing the wage bill from a basic £6500 a week to £8000 – the sum he reckoned he needed. These were exciting times, I said, but I would leave Charlie to explain properly himself.

The board gathered at 2 p.m. that May day: me, Matt McGowan, Martyn Harrison, Chris Pugsley, Tristan Murless, Andrew Brown, Nigel Winship and Nigel Beckett. Charlie had driven down from London to present his plan.

I gave my introductory speech outlining the financial position of the club. We were in a far better position than twelve months ago, before the pumping in of money from directors. We owed around £125,000 to the bank, which had come down from around £150,000 since we had kept up monthly payments during the season, plus about £75,000 to various former directors, who were now pressing for payment.

On top, our overdraft was running at around £100,000.

The bank, however, had notified us that we should be getting it down to £60,000 out of the football season, which meant that we needed an injection of cash.

That made total debts of £300,000, roughly about the same as we had inherited. It was not a bad position for what was, in effect, the first year of a new business, when we had to pay to improve the stadium and invest to get the buzz back in the town and the spirit back in the club. And we had succeeded in doing that. The problem was that although in real terms we would break even, because of the buying of shares by directors, we would have a significant trading loss for the season and we could not do that again.

The Asda deal was pending, the concert was taking shape, but still we needed short-term financing – the concert costs would probably be around £100,000 – and longer-term certainty. I turned the meeting over to Charlie.

He had clearly done his homework and presented us with a glossy document to peruse. It included projections for the club, set within the wider context of other football clubs' finances.

Charlie said he had looked at football with astonishment over the last few years. Clubs had been spending beyond their means, always chasing the best players, frightened not to compete, without the income to match it. They relied on directors' money or the indulgence of banks. It was not a recipe for financial success.

The only two clubs which he admired – financially speaking – were Manchester United (then before Glazer) and Newcastle United, the team he supported. They kept wages to a manageable percentage of their income, so that they could then offer shareholders a dividend.

It was hard to disagree with him. Stories abounded in the game of unbelievable sums of money being paid to players, and the annual report into the game's finances issued by the consultants Deloitte showed that some clubs' wage bills were actually more than 100 per cent of their income.

Charlie had a vision, that he would like to try to run a club along stricter financial lines, income and expenditure bearing some relation to each other. Yes, he admired our vision of Conference, then League, football in five years in a new stadium – but only if the club could sustain it. It may well be, given our history, that we were no more than a Southern League club but the market would decide that.

I began to feel a little uneasy but I trusted Charlie. I knew him well, knew him to be an honourable man with integrity and good intentions. I only hoped the board would see that, too.

Yes, he went on, he would buy the remaining £300,000 worth of shares – there were just under 600,000 still unissued of the 1.2 million available at 50p – but he had certain ideas in mind.

He would approve an increase in the playing budget initially, as he wanted to honour the commitment he gave at the board meeting three weeks earlier when he made the £100,000 offer, and would be seeking to use the stadium more for events to bring in extra income. He would bring in a man from his London office to oversee the financial running of the club though he did not want to make any changes to board or management.

His company would also buy up other shares from existing shareholders who wished to sell so that he could hold a controlling 66 per cent stake, which would enable him to change the articles and memoranda of the club and make it a conventional limited company, his company, taking a profit and paying dividends to shareholders.

It was becoming clear that this was not an entirely altruistic offer, and was including many elements that I had not spoken about in real detail with him. I had expected him to want to revamp the players' wages, particularly the too-high bonuses I had negotiated, and I knew he had a good plan to defer all extra payments to the end of a season, and only if promotion was achieved, Steve willing to sell the idea to the players. But then Charlie was a businessman – a benign one but a businessman nonetheless – and I should not have been surprised. He liked a deal.

The moment of truth arrived when he outlined what he wanted in return for his investment.

First, he believed, that the club should be able to turn a profit, assuming we kept costs down, the main one being players' wages. It should then be able to pay a dividend, with one third of the profit going to the club, one third to community causes locally to provide goodwill for the club, and one third to shareholders. That meant him and his company, who would own two-thirds of the shares, receiving a sizeable payment. It was hypothetical, he added, as it might be a while before we turned a profit, but it was feasible.

Second, as controller of the club, he expected to have the main say in how the Asda money was apportioned. He would, he said, build the club an 'appropriate' stadium, depending on where we were at the time and whether we did indeed show signs of being a League club, or whether we were just a Southern League – or next season Conference South – club. He would then, for the risk he was taking and the money he was pumping in, expect to receive a sizeable, unspecified, sum of money out of the Asda deal.

The board was rendered silent, me included. It would mean handing over the control of the club to one person for the first time in our history. There were some pressing questions, such as how much he would take out of the club, but he said that circumstances at the time would dictate how much the club could afford. 'If I am taking the risk of investing and making losses, then I would expect to be rewarded for profit,' he said, and the board accepted that argument.

Martyn Harrison chimed in, with Chris Pugsley not far behind. Would Charlie mind leaving the room so that we could discuss his proposal? He had no objection and departed to enjoy the sunshine of a glorious spring day outside.

I had been hoping it was going to be glorious for other reasons. Instead, I felt a little empty. I had not realized that Charlie would be so hard-nosed. In my naivety, I thought we were getting a benefactor rather than a businessman.

It had always been my personal belief that clubs should not be in the business of making money. As a chairman, of course, I had a duty of financial care to the club, to ensure that debts did not get out of hand and the club enter either administration, which these days brings a ten-point penalty, or bankruptcy, which brings even worse punishment. But I did not believe that clubs should exist for making big sums of money for owners or shareholders. I had not come into the game to make money, just to enjoy my club performing better. I personally would have handed any dividend on my own shares back to the club. It was where I differed from Charlie on Newcastle United, where Freddy Shepherd was taking huge sums for running the club and debt was mounting beneath the glossy surface.

The aim, in my view, was to break even each season. It would be a sign that you were doing the job properly, putting as much money as you could into the team, providing the fans with the best team they could see without getting the club into trouble. Any profit or windfall, such as from a cup run, should go into improving the team or facilities the next season.

As the man who knew Charlie best among us, knew his trustworthiness, I found myself defending him and his plan in his absence. I felt that if we just got him, and his money, more involved, Charlie would relent in his financial demands. He had, after all, been bitten by the football bug. He would, I felt sure, come to love it so much that he would not wish to take money out, but instead use any personal profit to invest in the club.

I believed we should negotiate with him, try to reduce his demands, and I felt he would be open to that. Besides, in the absence of other plans or pledges of capital investment, it was the best deal we were likely to get, I thought. Then Martyn Harrison, between deep puffs on his cigarette, spoke up.

'Well, I can do better than that,' he said.

There was a pause while we took it in.

'What do you mean?' I asked.

'I'll buy up the remaining shares,' he said.

Again I was stunned, this time more pleasantly. All of a sudden, we had two people wanting to invest money in a club that a year ago could not find anyone to touch it with a bargepole. Apart from a mug like me.

'No strings attached?'

'No strings attached,' he echoed.

There was what seemed to be genuine amazement all round. Here was a man going to pump £300,000 into the club without wanting anything in return? He would also pay off the loans of the previous directors and offer main sponsorship of the club for £30,000, he said. In addition, he would approve an increase in the playing budget. Chris Pugsley and Matt McGowan both asked him if he would be willing to sign a legal document saying that he would not benefit in any way from the future development of our land. Yes, he would sign one.

It was scarcely believable but Martyn Harrison assured us he was to be believed.

I thanked him for the astonishing offer and asked the board for their comments. There were none. A show of hands agreed the deal – well, the offer – pending the signatures on the legal document, to be drawn up by the club's solicitors, with Chris Pugsley detailed to liaise. I was asked to remain as chairman – and it was strange, that the possibility that I could be deposed had not troubled me, nor even occurred to me. Martyn would become chief executive.

I went out into the sun to sit with Charlie and tell him about what had just happened. 'I can't match that,' he said quite simply. 'It's a fantastic offer.'

Charlie returned to the boardroom, listened to some other business that now seemed minor – including an offer we had had from a lottery wanting to take over our troubled one and guaranteeing a better return – then asked if he could address the board without Martyn being present. Chris Pugsley was against it, but I thought it only fair that Charlie should get his moment.

It would be better, Charlie said, if he resigned, as he felt there was little more he could contribute to the club. He wished us well and took his leave.

As I heard his car pull away outside in the car park – knowing the feeling of rejection that went with that myself – I was terribly sad. Charlie had been a financial blessing, but more than that the sort of man of probity and quality that we needed on the board of the club. I was sorry he would be going but, I have to confess, delighted that we had, I believed, secured the immediate future of the club and new funding for a promotion push. The thought of cutting back the wage bill and slipping back into the pack in the league did not fill me with enthusiasm for a new season. Unconditional money seemed preferable.

And so we celebrated our good fortune quietly, invited Martyn back into the room and talked about a little left-winger from Worcester City by the name of Adam Wilde that we were interested in buying. Now we could. This was more like it.

CHAPTER SEVENTEEN

Harrison afford?

Martyn invited me to breakfast at his flagship hotel, the Prince Regent, the morning after the day before. I was happy to go, to enjoy these moments of optimism. The club was secured, the sun was shining. We could recruit the players we needed and plan for a concert that would make a lot of money.

It was a pleasant enough meal, and nice to get a fry-up free of charge after mostly making do with tea, cereal and a cigarette before going into the club for the day. Afterwards, we strolled along the esplanade, stopping for a coffee at the old Tea Cabin by the King's Statue. I had always loved the site. When I was a boy I had sold newspapers just here for a summer job starting at 7 a.m. and I had relished their steaming mugs of tea and the silent anticipation of a sunny day with few other people around.

Now the coffee came in polystyrene cups but this was not a day to complain. Nor, if there was something wrong with the world, was this the morning to be contemplating it.

Martyn reassured me that he wanted me to remain chairman, that I was a vital figure for the club and he saw no reason for me not to continue the good work. I was grateful to him. I thought that with his promise of money and my determination to see this club succeed, we would make a good partnership. Then he said something that took me aback.

'What do you think will become of the rest of them?'

I wondered what, and who, he meant.

'The board. I mean, it's a dictatorship now, isn't it? The club only really needs you and me.'

I smiled at him. I would, he was forever telling me, get used to his sense of humour and so I let it go. The words kept going round in my head, though, as he made it plain he didn't think much of the board and, one by one, went through them, disparagingly listing what he saw as shortcomings.

To be honest, there were those I wouldn't have minded resigning, or him getting rid of, but I was straightaway concerned about what shape the club might take now. If it was the price of moving the club on, achieving the success we all craved, I was willing to lose Chris Pugsley, who seemed to enjoy the perks of his position – free admission, acting important in the lounges – without putting in the effort or all the money he pledged. Also, Tristan may have done a lot of work, but had charged us for a fair bit of it and not put in a penny.

I was concerned, though, that good men like Nigel Winship and Andrew Brown would be affected. Nigel had already conceded the job of financial director to Pugsley because of his professional and family commitments. Andrew had not been a 'doer' around the ground, living in Bournemouth, but he had provided real financial help when it was needed and was a solid and loyal board member of sound judgement. They would now have to do more, take on more responsibility, Martyn suggested.

But now was not the time for that, nor to worry. I drafted a press release for the *Echo* about the man who had saved the club – a bit of a dramatization but a good story – and posed with him, shaking hands, for a picture in front of the Prince Regent.

I also filmed the final scene for the BBC2 documentary on

the beach, giving Martyn the credit for his investment. It had been a tough season, uplifting but ultimately disappointing, but now we could relax and enjoy the moment, I said. For some reason, the cameraman wanted shots of me buying and eating an ice cream on the beach – the cat that got the cream? We had to do two takes, needing two cones, as he had forgotten to switch the camera on first time round. It cost me £1 times two. The cost of being a chairman.

'There is a happy ending,' I said to camera. 'Bring me sunshine.' And I felt like doing that little Morecambe and Wise jig down the beach.

I went off in good heart to the Nationwide Conference annual general meeting in Eastbourne on a sunny weekend. There at the Winter Gardens in between more ice creams and afternoon tea we completed the signing with Worcester City of Adam Wilde for £12,500. The only minor event to mar the day was the election of the Dorchester Town secretary David Martin, an ambitious man in the world of football administration, to the Conference board.

In the evening, Vikki and I went to the dinner dance and came across the Crawley chairman, Jo Gomm. 'Congratulations,' I said. 'You deserved it.' 'We've waited long enough,' she replied. I wasn't going to get into competitive waiting.

We got some stick for not attending the Southern League dinner in Torquay. However, it was nothing to do, as was believed, with us being ungracious losers not wanting to see Crawley being presented with the shield. Unable to make it myself, I asked the Weymouth-based directors to go. They did not.

I returned to the club for a fans' forum night to introduce Martyn to the supporters. He wowed a couple of hundred of them, telling how he had bought the club on the spur of the moment. Fans loved the smell of money. I was pleased when he admitted that he knew little about football and was happy to let Claridge and Ridley deal with that side of the club. I was less happy when he began to talk of Charlie Lesser as a man who wanted to make money out of the club. I was not the only one concerned. 'He shouldn't have said that,' said Matt McGowan.

This summer, my work was taking me to Portugal for Euro 2004 and I felt as if I could go now knowing that the club would not miss me for a few weeks. It was a re-markable experience, suddenly being recognized by England fans as I travelled around the country as that bloke off *Football Diaries*. They wanted to know what Steve Claridge was really like – as if the show hid any of the warts – with many offering their recollections of his stay at their own particular club, from Aldershot to Millwall and points in between.

The most embarrassing moment came after England's 2–1 defeat by France at Benefica's Stadio da Luz. I was travelling by underground back to my newspaper-rented central Lisbon flat when a Leeds fan suddenly announced: 'Eh, it's that chairman of Weymouth.' Suddenly the whole carriage became involved as I answered their questions. Sometimes England fans abroad are badly maligned – occasionally justifiably – but these were men and women who took defeat with stoicism and loved the game. In fact, that was the whole experience of Portugal, with England fans travelling in huge numbers and behaving well.

Some wanted to know who that 'dork' of a director was. They were referring to Tristan, that Weymouth tour guide who had insisted to young ladies that if they wanted to pull a player, best not to leave it until the Surfside Diner at 2 a.m., where only reserve team players would be finishing the evening with a kebab and chips. It was news to me.

Tristan had also focused on the delights of the Jacuzzi in his garden, which 'had seen plenty of action, I can tell you'.

'Isn't that a bit unhygienic?' the director asked.

'Oh, it's got a very good filtration system,' he replied in his broad Dorset accent.

I was willing to defend Tristan, locally and to fans on Lisbon tube trains, because I always thought his heart was in the right place. It was his sense of humour, I said; he was saying it all with tongue in cheek. I wasn't sure he was capable of being quite that clever, though.

With Wayne Rooney's injury in the quarterfinal against Portgual went England's hopes and I was soon back at the club. Suddenly, the misgivings I had been dismissing could be ignored no longer.

There had been a board meeting when Martyn said that he thought we had taken a decision to sack Micky Jenkins the assistant manager. Martyn had, apparently, not been best pleased when Micky asked some sponsors at one game to move seats in the directors' box so he could sit down. I had known nothing about it. I repeated to Martyn that it would be the manager's decision to dismiss his assistant and Martyn did not look happy.

Now I was surprised to find that the boardroom was being completely redecorated, with a new carpet and a sideboard installed. The materials were clearly remnants from one of Martyn's hotels, the sideboard even having a plaque on it saying 'minibar'. I kept waiting for a trouser press to appear.

What upset me most – quite apart from no board meeting having sanctioned this work – was the disappearance of the magnificent boardroom table that seated twelve. It was a lovely old piece of oak, donated to the club by HMS *Ark Royal* in 1955, the year of my birth. We had needed to modernize but there were certain elements of the club's tradition and culture that should not be thrown out, I believed.

I went to Ramin Hidari, Martyn's clerk of works on his hotels, to ask where the table was. He said it was safe somewhere. I then asked Martyn to get Ramin to return it. He said he would, if it meant so much to me, but nothing happened. Eventually I located it myself behind a skip. It was in pieces. I asked Ramin to restore it but he never did. Then it conveniently disappeared one day from the corridor outside the boardroom where Tim Davis and Kevin Frampton had helped me carry it.

We had also had another lounge decorated only a year earlier as part of a deal with the brewery who supplied our beer. Now Martyn was, unnecessarily in my view, redecorating that too, though the painting work he had ordered around the ground was an improvement. At a board meeting, I asked him how much it was all costing. He said not to worry, that he enjoyed this kind of renovation work and he was good at it. Three times I had to ask him to reassure us that the club would not be footing the bill.

I calmed down. He was saving us money in other areas, by allocating staff from his hotels to bar and cleaning work, rather than us footing the complete bill for full-time people. Or so I thought. Another letter from the stocktakers warned of a 'grave situation' with a six-month deficit on the bars of more than £13,000. How could this be? Chris Pugsley and Tristan told me again not to worry, but I did.

I had been expecting a cheque for £300,000 to have been lodged in our bank by now. That seemed to be the deal. Martyn again seemed horrified to be questioned when I asked why it had not. I told him it was my duty as chairman to oversee the financial position of the club. In effect, he told me, it was no longer any of my business.

He was almost insulted, saying that he was negotiating to pay off the loans to previous directors, and underwriting the overdraft. I was concerned that he would do like Tristan and Jamie, and take shares in return for the redecoration of the lounges. The work had probably cost upwards of £50,000. My feeling was that, with the stadium likely to be bulldozed in a couple of years, it was wasted money and we would be better investing it in paying off our debts or investing in the team.

Martyn also announced that, for tax purposes, he needed to own 80 per cent of the club so that he could claim back losses and he began buying up the shares of previous directors, doing deals with them in return for them getting back their loans. Men like Peter Shaw, Terry Bennett and Mick Archer were easily persuaded though Dave Higson, clearly still a follower of the club, retained his shares.

I went to Matt McGowan, who had always been my confidant, and voiced my worries to him. Let it settle down, he said. Martyn was a man with a new toy and would calm down and let us as a board have more say. I was unsure, and thinking about resigning. I still had a big role to play in the club, Matt insisted, and should not even think about resigning. I went along with it, for three reasons.

First, Steve Claridge needed an ally on the board as he sought to augment the squad. This was shaping up to be a tough challenge, as we were hearing word from Hornchurch, who would be joining us in Conference South from the Ryman League, that they had hired the former Dagenham and Redbridge manager Garry Hill for £125,000 a year. He was to have a wage budget of, astonishingly for our level, £20,000 a week, some players on £1500 a week, one even on £2000, along with flats and cars. We had wanted Kirk Jackson, a striker from Yeovil, but he had gone to Essex. Our wage bill would be around £10,000 a week now and we could not match that.

Along with Adam Wilde, though, we had signed Lee Charles from Aldershot, who could play wide right for us, and were hoping to get Dean Hooper, a tough defender, from the same club. Nathan Bunce, a rugged centre back who had played for Farnborough against Arsenal in that FA Cup tie at Highbury, was also in Steve's sights. Steve valued my opinions, and I would offer them and help him, but I knew that when it came to the budget and what we might pay them, he was now dealing with Martyn. Steve knew who was now the keeper of the purse, where the real power lay.

Second, we were close to agreeing the Asda deal and I did not want it being jeopardized. We had realized that simply to take a lump sum would leave us open to all sorts of hassle that we were not qualified to deal with. Best to let Asda acquire the land we needed for a new stadium, pay for all the planning costs, though their estimate now of £4 million to acquire the new land was surely too high. There was clearly still much negotiation to be done before we reached a final figure.

In the meantime, I met with another stadium developer, a system-build company who had done two of the Euro 2004 venues, and they reckoned that we could get the 8000-capacity stadium, the training ground with grandstand and speedway track, as well as a hostel and revenue-generating all-weather pitch, for around £6 million.

Third, the concert plans were taking shape. We had settled on a date in August at the end of Carnival Week when we knew that 200,000 people would be in the town. It would mean that we would have to ask the league for an away game that weekend. The promoters were now talking about Will Young as the headline act for the Sunday, with a celebrity football tournament for the Saturday and parties involving the stars at a local nightclub, Banus, on both nights. Lester and Mark dubbed it Pop 4 Weymouth. The original idea to hold a concert had been mine and I was staying on because I did not want anyone else having to carry the can if it ran into problems.

But before that, I needed a holiday, my first for two years, and so did Vikki and my children, Alex and Jack. I had promised them a really good one after they had missed out the previous summer due to my work at the club and we

went on a luxurious and relaxing Mediterranean cruise.
It was a bizarre experience having a conversation about
Weymouth, somewhere between Rome and Barcelona, with
someone else who had seen *Football Diaries*.

Having resisted the temptation all week, the day before we
docked at Barcelona I decided to log on to the Internet in one
of the ship's lounges, just to check what was happening at
the club. I could not believe what I read. A fan, Mike Francis,
who seemed to have attached himself to Martyn, was
announcing on the forum that he 'had been given permission'
to tell people that Micky Jenkins had left the club.

I was furious. A fan knew this before I did? And I hadn't
even been consulted, let alone this decision taken at a board
meeting. Martyn had waited until I had gone on holiday to
do the deed despite telling me that I was in charge of football
matters. I immediately rang Steve, who was annoyed but had
been in football long enough not to overreact. I told him I
would speak to Martyn as soon as I got back, see if we could
get this reconsidered, perhaps the four of us meeting up to
iron out any problems. Though angry, I decided not to act
until I had calmed down, to try to smooth it over rather than
go in guns blazing.

Steve and I met Martyn but without Micky. We agreed a
compromise, with Micky continuing to do scouting duties
but not attached to the first team and not on the bench.
Martyn, I discovered, felt that Micky was rude and no more
than Steve's driver from Portsmouth. Again I repeated that
we should trust the manager's choice of assistant. He needed
someone he felt comfortable with. Martyn compromising
was a good sign, I thought. Indeed, he told me again how
valuable I was to the club, how much respect he had for me
and what had been achieved here.

Again, I was placated and I continued to nurture hopes
that it would all work out, that Martyn would realize that
other people in the club did have a contribution to make. He

would get used to it, Matt McGowan repeated. It was just that he was used to running his own company his way and needed to adapt to a new way of working.

It helped that Martyn was going on holiday for a fortnight and that we were already playing pre-season friendlies. And looking good. We had a good crowd of more than 1800 to play our local rivals Bournemouth, losing by a very unflattering 3–0. Steve's recruiting was going well and he had now also acquired two defenders with good Football League pedigree in Matty Bound and Dave Waterman from Oxford United. We had also signed Chukki Eribenne from Havant and Waterlooville. The £10,000 price, though well below what we had been quoted the previous season, was inflated, with them knowing we now had some money and their dislike of Weymouth undiminished. Martyn seemed not to mind paying it.

With Vikki's help, we had also attracted Sheffield United to the Wessex, them being the club she supported and their manager Neil Warnock a good contact. We lost 5–3 but it was a wonderful night, with Vikki's mum, Jean, her auntie, Rita, and uncle, Brian, making the long trip down from South Yorkshire as Vikki and I jointly sponsored the game in memory of our late fathers.

I also got Derek Dooley, legendary figure for Sheffield United, and Wednesday, to present the team with their Southern League runners-up medals. We only received nineteen, so I paid myself for a Weymouth company to make another twelve so that I could give them to deserving people around the club, including the board.

Tony Adams also brought his Wycombe Wanderers team down and we drew 0–0. Then, when we beat a strong Exeter City side, who would go on during the imminent season to draw 0–0 with Manchester United at Old Trafford in an FA Cup tie, we sensed we were going to be fine.

I wish the same could have been said of the concert. By

now, Martyn had taken over the running of the whole event. In fact, he was billing himself Event Controller.

My concept had always been that we would provide the venue, pay for the costs and leave the rest to the professionals when it came to booking the bands, putting up the stage and hiring marquees, temporary toilets and all the other paraphernalia that comes with staging an open air event. Our hands-on involvement would be in supplying all the stewards from our club and publicizing the whole shooting match.

Martyn had other ideas. He reckoned he could do it better and cheaper, thought he had the contacts that would make it work. I was coming to see that he loved being in charge, loved a project, loved giving orders and expecting them to be obeyed.

A couple of months earlier, Lester and Mark had supplied a list of acts they reckoned they could get for the £100,000 we were prepared to pay. They included popular acts such as Lemar, Jamelia, D-Side, Mark Owen, Paul Young and Tony Hadley and Spandau Ballet. I looked at them and was sure, with modification here and there, they would work. After all, 15,000 people had turned up on Weymouth beach for Holly Vallance and the Cheeky Girls, for goodness sake, for *Children in Need* night. It was free, mind.

When I emailed the list to Martyn, I was astonished to receive his response. His 17-year-old daughter Faye, he said, had decided that they were 'rubbish', that 'young folks' would not be interested and I had to do better. 'And now my head is on the block – it is not good enough,' he added. My initial reaction, having my work so far scorned, was that we should therefore leave it all to Faye. I decided not to interfere with Martyn's plans any more. I would do what I could, by using my skills to publicize the event, but the rest was best left to him. With the promoters Lester and Mark also in the mix there was a danger of too many cooks.

I was constantly receiving phone calls from the two of them, bemoaning Martyn's interference with what they were putting together. He had insisted they get Girls Aloud, the winners of the ITV series *Pop Idol*, they said. He was making all sorts of demands on them. I told them it was best to let him have his way. Anything else led to conflict, then him getting his way anyway. Besides, I said, to be fair to him he was the one advancing the money for the bands up front and he who pays the piper . . .

At first I had been miffed to be sidelined again when I felt I had much to contribute but I acknowledged that others knew better in this instance. I was a football man, not a pop impresario. Lester, sensing the tension between me and Martyn, tried to bring us together, suggesting that Martyn should be the Roman Abramovich of the whole operation, staying out of the public eye but with everyone knowing that he was the real power broker. It was, however, like asking a piranha not to bite.

Martyn could not, for example, resist going on to the fans' website. Unbeknown to me, Lester had been barred from organizing such events due to a previous insolvency hearing. Martyn's attention had been drawn to it by a fan, an intelligent one at that, Nick Brailsford, who had heard about it. Nick mentioned it on the website, sparking Martyn into a furious reply, which went, spelling mistakes and all:

> I am a very relexed sort of person – many people will tell you this is fact.
> However, you are getting right up my nose.
> I have paid the full costs of this concert out of my own pocket and I decide who I do business with. Did I ask you to either pay or give an opinion?
> It is none of your business – AND I have told you that before.

PLEASE keep your nose out of this before it gets burnt.
You are making me very angry . . .
Go away – you are causing me personal greef – STOP
IT.
It's folks like you who cause a war and walk away to
   leave people to die.
Get off my back.

Not for the first time, I was taken aback by Martyn. This
was a side that I was coming to know about but which
he usually kept private in his attempts to charm the fans.
His fabled sense of humour – and his barbs, I was also
recognizing now, always contained truth amid the sarcasm –
was failing him under pressure. 'Money, you know,' as
Cervantes noted in *Don Quixote*, 'will hide many faults.'

And so I contented myself with writing press releases,
appearing on the local radio station Wessex FM, who were
doing their best for us, to promote the show. Vikki also
managed to get a few paragraphs for us on to the Bizarre
page in *The Sun*, quite some publicity, and I pointed it out
to Martyn. 'It helps if you're sleeping with someone on the
paper,' he said. I resented such a tacky remark but bit my
lip. Martyn's sense of humour, I guessed.

I also attended meetings that Martyn chaired with his
staff at the Prince Regent to co-ordinate the whole event.
From toilets through car parking to scaffolding, Martyn
delegated someone for everything. He could do it cheaper
and better than the promoters. The problem was that little
of it was getting done properly.

The whole thing was giving me the shudders when I
contemplated it. The show was now being run by amateurs
rather than the professionals I had envisaged. All manner of
problems arose, from the council insisting that an advertising banner outside the Prince Regent be taken down as
it was a listed seafront building, to the spaces hired to sell

tickets on the esplanade on Carnival Day being just bare patches of concrete instead of containing the stalls we were expecting.

We were also told by the council we could not distribute leaflets on the promenade and in the end, though against my better judgement, we antagonized them by going to the *Echo* with a 'Red Tape is Killing Us' story. Some of the relationships being damaged by this event would take some time to heal. Marytn's staff at the Prince Regent were blaming those at the football club for bad organization and ticket sales. I would not have that and angrily let them know one morning.

All the while I was getting calls from Lester and Mark telling me that Martyn would not let them do their jobs, that he and his henchman Ramin Hidari had taken everything over, doing more expensive deals for such things as portable toilets.

Then I would get calls from Martyn, bemoaning the incompetence of Lester and Mark. Despite the fact he had been to Florida, he also did not like it that I had been reporting on Euro 2004, then was away with my children for a week, while he was doing all the work. I had been trying to run a football club as well, I pointed out. I was more interested in attending the funeral of a Supporters' Club stalwart, Pete Johnson, than worrying about portable loos. Martyn was doing enough of that for everyone.

One night, after a hard day at the club, I took Alex and Jack up to the hills at Bowleaze to fly a kite for a bit of fun and relaxation. Martyn was driving by in his Jaguar and shouted out of the window, 'It's all right for some.'

Anything I did or said counted for little anyway. Best keep trying to work on, and with, sponsors. A final meeting with New Look bore no fruit and I finally understood why they had been stalling. They were about to announce a series of redundancies and were moving their distribution centre to the Midlands. Now was a bad time. A worse one for all the local workers who would be out of a job.

But even though I was still meeting with stadium designers, still working with Steve to strengthen the squad, I could not escape the concert. I was unhappy with myself that I was trying desperately to promote it in the press and on radio and local television, while not really believing in the way it was being organized. But I did what I felt was right for the club rather than myself. I even fell out with the *Echo*, goaded by Martyn into berating them over a lack of coverage. It saddened me. I had always recognized their contribution to the club, had a good relationship with them. Martyn threatened to withdraw the advertising for his hotels, about £20,000 a year apparently.

Ticket sales were not going well. My daughter, Alex, came down to help out, fronting a ticket booth on the seafront. She sold few and after a couple of days moved over to help with promoting the event. It seemed we were looking at a crowd of around 3000 when we needed about double that to break even. Martyn, more used to London, had set prices too high at £10 for the celebrity football, £23.50 for the concert and £30 for a combined ticket.

It was all messy, all intense, all unpleasant. I would be glad when the bloody thing was over and we could just get back to playing football. I was reminded of Keith Burkinshaw's parting shot when he left as manager of an increasingly commercial Tottenham Hotspur: there used to be a football club in there.

At least we had the season to look forward to. Because of the travelling, Dean Hooper had decided against signing but Steve had recruited another full back in Paul Gibbs. With seven new signings, expectation was high. It might take some time to gel and developments at Hornchurch were frightening. However, even if they were to win the title this season, we knew we could still win promotion via the new play-offs with a squad that was stronger, mentally and physically, and deeper than the one which had finished second. Bring it on.

PART THREE

The end of the affair

Did I disappoint you,
Or leave a bad taste in your mouth?
You act like you never had love,
And you want me to go without.
Well, it's too late, tonight,
To drag the past out into the light,
We're one, but we're not the same.
We get to carry each other, carry each other.

U2, 'One'

CHAPTER EIGHTEEN

Flop 4 Weymouth

Actually, I had mixed feelings about the new season. I was growing increasingly concerned by Martyn's way of working and wondered how much longer I could continue under his influence, but I believed Steve had assembled an exciting team and I wanted to be around to see it play.

And so I was as optimistic as the town seemed to be on the 2004/05 season's opening day, which brought tricky opponents in Cambridge City, whose manager Gary Roberts I admired for working on a shoestring and moulding keen young players into an enthusiastic and capable unit. If ever Steve had left for bigger things, I might well have sought to bring Gary to the Wessex – going through all the right channels, of course.

Still, we should expect to beat them. According to the bookmakers, the title race this season was going to be between us and Hornchurch and in all honesty that is how I expected it to develop, too. When the fixtures were published in July, after checking the Dorchester games – as expected, them at home on Boxing Day this year – I looked first for Hornchurch, saw that we were away on August Bank Holiday Monday and at home on Easter Monday. You couldn't stop yourself thinking that the last one might be a title decider, though Grays Athletic, also investing heavily and now full time like Hornchurch, would also surely be challenging.

Cambridge City had other ideas, of course, and inflicted a surprising, if not shocking, 2–1 defeat upon us. It started well enough, with Matty Bound putting us into an early lead from a deflected free kick, but although we played reasonably well, we got hit by the old one-two. It was a terrible disappointment for the good crowd of 1568 after the summer's build-up. However, none of us was to know then quite how good Cambridge City would prove as they would go on to finish the season as runners-up, nor that our August fixture list would prove to be so difficult. From being outsiders the previous year BC (Before Claridge), we were now well known and there to be shot at by teams raising their game.

Newport County four days later certainly fell into that category. They took the lead against the run of play, though having a strong wind with them. We then battered them, missing a host of chances barely credibly. A late goal on the break then confirmed a 2–0 win for them. No one on our side could believe it, but at least we had played much better than the previous Saturday, created more chances.

Steve, out with a rib injury, was distraught. Afterwards I sat in the dugout at pitchside with him for half an hour analysing it all. 'What have you got to do to win a football match?' he wondered, exasperated. My attitude was not to panic, that this squad was too strong not to come good, and that it was a long season. The usual platitudes, but I felt and believed them.

I thought others would, too. But the short-termism and knee-jerk reactions that sometimes plague the thinking of football fans, seemed to be transmitting themselves to directors who were failing, in my opinion, to keep the big picture in view. Not just at Weymouth but up in Newcastle, where the knives were out for Sir Bobby Robson and he would soon be sacked. Panic, at every level, follows thwarted expectation.

At a board meeting, I sensed coolness in Matt, Tristan, Chris Pugsley and, above all, Martyn Harrison to what we were seeking to achieve. They began to talk about Steve having too many media commitments, about the team not training enough, the sort of any-excuse nonsense that comes up on the website after a defeat. Martyn was becoming especially interested in this forum, going on with little comments of his own, me advising him against disturbing what Alan Partridge would have called a nest of viper's eggs but being ignored. He also took too much notice of the noisiest, and sometimes most ignorant and emotive, fans at games.

'Hang on,' I said to the board, 'I'm getting the feeling here that you don't all believe in Steve.'

'Well, we're stuck with him, aren't we?' said Harrison. 'He's got a long contract.'

'It's a question of making the best of him,' said Pugsley.

Their attitude stung me. I could not believe this ingratitude and ignorance. It was hard to imagine anyone other than Steve who could have done so well the previous season. This was a man who was now attracting players who could have got more money elsewhere, with bigger clubs, because they wanted to play for him. If we all kept our nerve, this would work out, I said. The five-year plan should not be messed with for the sake of a couple of defeats.

I could tell, though, by the looks that Tristan, Matt, Pugsley and Martyn were exchanging that they were sceptical. I began to wonder what conversations they might be having behind my back. I began to feel isolated.

Thankfully for the moment, though, Martyn was too bound up in the celebrity football tournament and Pop 4 Weymouth concert – which, I later learned, Mel and Tim Davis had dubbed Flop 4 Weymouth – coming up at the weekend to concern himself too much with the football right now. It would not be long, though. His influence was now all-pervasive, as he had always clearly expected it to be, given the shares he had bought and despite his utterances otherwise. I still naively believed him when he said that he would be leaving the football to Steve and me.

Not that I could see any sign of his money coming into the club, with the overdraft still running at £100,000, as it had done all summer. When I asked, I was told that everything was being taken care of. When I asked Pugsley for the budget for the season at board meetings, none was forthcoming. The financing of the lounges, the concert payments were all a mystery to me, not part of my remit any longer, it seemed. They were Martyn's private world, with Pugsley seemingly the keeper of the keys to the kingdom.

Nor was there yet any sign of the finalized legal document between Martyn and the club that had been bandied about between the two sets of solicitors. I did get to see one draft, with a variety of clauses protecting the club from Martyn taking it into liquidation and preventing him benefiting from the sale of assets, but otherwise Pugsley kept saying that it was on its way. It had better be. We needed that £300,000 for the shares.

Even Pugsley seemed to be worried on occasions, though. On the Sunday night after the Cambridge City defeat, I received a call from him, saying that he was worried about not having a say any more and about the money. Could we do anything about it? I then rang the others and they appeared to feel the same way.

Thus I convened a meeting at Matt McGowan's house the next day, with Andrew Brown and Tristan also attending. Pugsley did not turn up. All had misgivings about Martyn's style of one-man-band management. 'I thought it was going to settle down but it hasn't, has it?' said Matt.

None, though, was willing to contemplate the alternative: that even now we turn down his money and instead club together ourselves. I said I could probably find another £25,000 if others would match it. None would. They also felt we were now in too deep with Martyn, though still the deal had not officially been done. I left deflated. I did not like the way the club was heading. And I suspected that Pugsley, now closely allied with Martyn, had set me up on his behalf to find out my thinking, with Tristan, also growing more in league with Martyn to whom he was beholden for the electrical work around his hotels, as the eyes and ears.

Now Andrew Brown and Nigel Winship departed. Martyn had been trying to get them to do more, to arrange golf days or sponsorship evenings. They did not believe in him, though, did not like his manner, and quit, doing deals with him for their shares. Charlie Lesser also sold his to Martyn. The board was shrinking, the good men were going. What, and who, was left was not inspiring me.

My own position was becoming all but impossible to sustain. I confided in Matt yet again that I thought I should resign. I did not agree with Martyn's autocratic style, his way of dealing curtly with people, his hiring and firing mentality. Above all, the secrecy about the money that was supposed to be coming into the club, and what was going out.

Matt insisted I should stay but I sensed he probably didn't believe it. He sounded as if he was getting fed up, too. In the end, I again decided against going for the moment. To leave now, with the concert coming up this weekend and Steve needing a positive face as his chairman after two defeats, would be to let everyone down.

When we went to Bognor Regis Town the next Saturday, an idiot in the crowd shouted, 'You're under pressure, Claridge,' as an injured Steve took his seat in the dugout. 'No he's not,' I turned and said with a smile. But then, what say would I have in it in the future?

Through Chukki Eribenne and Lee Phillips, we stormed into a two-goal lead inside half an hour. This was more like it. This was what we were capable of. I knew sooner rather than later someone was going to get a thumping.

I had reckoned without Luke Nightingale. Steve had let Luke go in the summer because he wanted to play as a striker rather than a winger. Now he seemed to be in his element at a club where there was little pressure on him in front of crowds of a few hundred and which played nice, passing football. You sensed they were lightweight and would struggle in midwinter but for now they were causing us problems.

Before half-time, Luke had reduced the arrears, then just after it equalized. Again we battered away, Paul Gibbs hitting the bar, but could not force the winner. One point from three games was unarguably a bad start but I needed to remain upbeat. 'Well done Luke,' I said afterwards as he was conducting a newspaper interview. 'You bastard.' We both smiled. The Italians call that phenomenon where a former player always scores against you 'the immutable law of the ex'.

My mood was not improved by phone calls coming from the Wessex as I drove back to Weymouth. A host of stars that Lester and Mark had billed, including Paul Gascoigne and Ian Rush, had not turned up for the celebrity football, which had attracted fewer than 2000 spectators, many of whom complained at the D-list soap 'stars' and pop figures on view.

Indeed, when I turned up at the stadium at 9 a.m. the next morning to do my bit for the concert, the first phone call I took came from an *Echo* reporter wanting a comment from me about the debacle. I asked him to come to the ground, to buy time while I found out what had gone on.

Again I found myself defending the indefensible. It was an inaugural event, teething troubles, the majority had a good time, I offered. I realized later that I, who had not even been there, was being put in the firing line. Martyn, whose show this had become, was otherwise occupied.

Now I was just a man who did the dirty work, quite literally that morning. The groundsman, Mark Reynolds, had failed to show and wasn't answering his mobile, clearly miffed that his pitch was in danger of being damaged by this concert. And so, with help from Jack and Alex, I took to cleaning the mess from the stand and terraces left by the previous day's event. There was perfect symbolism to it. I had never minded getting my hands dirty, doing whatever was needed, but this showed how I was becoming viewed.

I dreaded, hated the whole day, but fixed a smile on my face. I was staggered by the goodwill of our supporters in helping out with stewarding. One of our older supporters even stood at an entrance for eight hours without a break or complaint until I heard about it and stood in for him so that he could get a meal.

Though not my scene, the acts were good enough, the event entertaining. Girls Aloud entered by helicopter straight from a similar gig at Plymouth Hoe. The rain held off until the last act, Peter Andre, with Jordan in tow, but that was about the only thing that did go our way. I was grateful when it was finally all over. Not that it was over for me until I had been to the Prince Regent to get Weymouth shirts signed by the artists so that we could auction them.

The day, to my disappointment and even surprise, had not captured the public imagination. Around 4000 turned up and the next few days were again about dealing with the aftermath. Again at Martyn's behest, I argued with the editor of the *Echo* over the prominence given to stories of complaint, one from a local hospital radio DJ who had been ejected for trying to record part of the concert. I had known nothing about it. It did seem heavy-handed, but then he was pirating. Martyn said once again that he would have nothing more to do with the paper and would not advertise in it. I doubted that would last. He also said that he would never put on a concert at the Wessex again.

There were also people coming into the club claiming that they had not had value for money at the celebrity football and had not met the celebrities they expected at the Banus nightclub where we hosted parties. I always seemed to be the one there when they arrived to complain.

It was outside Banus that I had a curious exchange with Martyn, as we stepped out for some air.

'It's a good job I'm rich,' he said. 'But then again, what is rich? I can afford to give my kids £50 when they ask for money when most people would give them a fiver.'

Yet again, it was enigmatic. Martyn often talked about money. And I was always suspicious of people who talked about their wealth, and growing more suspicious of him by the day. It seemed to me that he was also trying to illustrate the power, over me and the club, that he now had.

Martyn was also unhappy with Banus. He thought they were ripping the club off by letting people in through a side door and pocketing the money. I would not believe it. I knew the owners and knew them as good people. He wanted me to take it up with them but I was not going to be used, yet again, by him for some dirty work. Let him do his own from now on.

We lost somewhere between £60,000 and £90,000 on the whole event. It was hard to get figures out of Martyn. It seemed he gave the higher figure when it suited to show how much it had cost him, the lower for damage-limitation purposes. He kept the true numbers to himself, again deeming it to be none of the club's business. I was not too concerned about that if he was genuinely underwriting it, but again I was worried by the absence of concrete answers and what it might mean for the club.

Football provided respite and rescue anew from the

problems and discomfort of daily life around the club. Soon, in midweek, we had our badly needed first win of the season, a more comfortable one than the scoreline of 3–1 at home to Maidenhead United indicated. Martin Barlow's looped shot that somehow went in was, I hoped, the turning of our luck.

But we faced a really tough August Bank Holiday weekend. A 1–1 draw at home to Grays on the Saturday struck me as a decent result against one of the pre-season favourites, especially when we dominated the game and only conceded a late equalizer, but Martyn was not happy. I could see him, Tristan, Matt and Pugsley muttering in a corner of the boardroom when I entered. They suddenly stopped in the way people do when they have been talking about you behind your back.

I couldn't take much more of this and spent the rest of the weekend pondering my resignation. The harmonious and progressive atmosphere I had helped create at the club was fast disappearing. A mood of distrust and disharmony was growing and I felt out on a limb, powerless to do anything about it. I also felt powerless to protect Steve. I was a lone voice giving him encouragement.

Two days later I made my way to Hornchurch with Jack. After taking only one point from their opening two games, they had swept all before them since and were clearly going to win the league, such was the power of their full-time squad, so deep their resources. To me, their financial outlay of more than £1 million a year in wages, which would be the envy of many a Football League Club, seemed like madness, a sledgehammer to crack a nut.

Although their Bridge Avenue stadium was a ground nowhere near to our standard, there was an air of prosperity to it. Their full-time chief executive, Gary Calder, was charm itself as the public face of the club, though the real power lay with a mysterious figure by the name of Karl

Williams, owner of a double-glazing company called Cold-seal Windows.

I met Pete Saxby outside the ground. I remembered that we had a home game against Redbridge in six weeks' time on the same day that England were playing Wales in a World Cup qualifying match live on television. I asked him to see if Redbridge would be willing to rearrange for the Friday night or at least bring the Saturday kickoff forward a couple of hours.

'Martyn has already told me to do it,' he said.

I once read a story about a man who left a suicide note saying that he was being driven to it because the potatoes had boiled over. I sensed something of how he might have felt. It was the final little thing that tipped him over the edge after a series of big things. I wasn't even to be allowed to be the club administrator any more. Despite Martyn's assurances and protestations, he was running everything now.

I sought out Martyn in the Hornchurch board area of their club bar. 'I'd like to resign,' I said. 'But on three conditions. First, I want to see your money for the shares going into the club. Second, I want to ensure that the Asda deal goes through, and third, I want back the £15,000 I have loaned the club.' He simply nodded.

I took Jack to the stand and told him what was happening. Best to level and be honest with him. He burst into tears. The club had become a big part of his life, too. He now supported the club even more than Tottenham Hotspur, loved going down to Weymouth and to away matches. 'I hate that Martyn Harrison,' he said, between sobs. He had been seeing how unhappy I had become working around Martyn.

We watched sombrely from the seats as we went two goals down early on. Hornchurch were indeed a powerful side. Then we got a penalty, Steve converting. Right on half-time, Lee Phillips missed a one-on-one with their goal-keeper, the ball drifting inches wide. When our own keeper Jason Matthews was sent off – mistaken identity; it was Robbie Pethick who had brought down the striker – things couldn't get much worse.

Surprisingly, we dominated the second half, even with ten men, and should have eked out a point. Garry Hill seemed taken aback by a side running his all stars close after a series of easy recent victories and did not quite know how to react. But we couldn't get a goal. A 2–1 defeat it was, a mere five points from six games.

I was angry, not so much at the defeat or the points tally. We had shown, in the performance against the runaway leaders – even this early – that we would be a play-off team if we held our nerve. During the second half, as I took Jack to stand on the terraces, unable to be around Martyn, Matt, Tristan and Pugsley any longer, it dawned on me that I had played into Martyn's hands. That to get rid of me would have been a public relations disaster for him but my resignation was what he wanted. I was not going without those three assurances, though, and they could take weeks.

I no longer felt the need to humour Martyn or be polite to him. 'Now you can sack Claridge,' I said sarcastically as I met him in the bar. He shrugged. Pugsley said I was behaving like a kid who had just had his toys taken from him. It was a pathetic image. As if the club was a toy, as if I owned it. I was always only a steward, privileged to serve. Now the club was in unsafe hands, I believed.

I rang Steve to tell him what was happening. He told me to reconsider and, indeed, he and the others I had brought to the club were the only reason I would. But, I added, I would not be leaving for a while yet. There were things to sort out. My voice at the club was diminished, I said, but I had left him with a long contract so they couldn't sack him.

Over the next few days, Martyn and I exchanged emails,

which grew more unpleasant as the week went on. He had authorized Sarah Redford to send me a cheque for £15,000 – that surprised me: coming out of club funds and not Martyn's supposedly deep pockets? – and since I had given a statement to the *Echo* that the Asda deal had been agreed, I should go immediately. I was right. He did want me out and had kept me on only for PR purposes. Now my use was at an end.

I responded by saying that it wasn't that simple. I still hadn't seen his cheque for £300,000. The *Echo* story was simply a rehash of a recent programme column when I said that the Asda deal had been agreed in principle. It was not yet signed, though, and I thought we could still improve on the £11.5 million package on offer. Neither was the deal that gave him control of the club signed and my signature would be needed. We still had a board, in name at least, I said.

Back he came, outlining what he claimed he had put in. There was £90,000 to pay bills (which ones – the refurbishment of the lounges?) and £141,000 for the concert costs, he insisted. With £50,000 from concert tickets to be banked, he made that £181,000 due in for shares. He had paid off the previous directors, he added, and taken over the bank loan. I couldn't argue. I was no longer privy to Martyn and Pugsley's accounting. The club's banking was in the process of being transferred from Weymouth to west London. But my suspicions were correct. Martyn was not putting money directly in the club for a board of directors to decide how to apportion. He was underwriting payments that I had no knowledge of and taking shares for them.

Then came the knock-out punch. 'Pugsley/Merliss/ McGowen have today agreed the contract for the sale and payment for the shares,' said his email. He couldn't even spell his own directors' names.

It was over. The directors had signed a document that I

hadn't even seen and handed the club over to him. I was worried about Steve, about my sister Mel in the commercial office, about the Asda deal, about Martyn getting his hands on the club. But even if I wanted to stay, the rug had been pulled from beneath me.

'So, Ian,' Martyn concluded, 'it looks like we have no further need to wait and I would appreciate a formal letter from you to confirm your departure from the board.' I replied that I would come down for the game at home to Bishop's Stortford on the Saturday and, if the document signing the club over to him was satisfactory, it would be my last match.

Naturally, it was leaked. The day before the game, I got a call from Matt Pitman at the *Echo* asking if it was true I was resigning. I said I would issue a statement after the game the next day. Later in the afternoon Mel rang me. The back-page headline, she said, read: DISILLUSIONED TERRAS CHAIRMAN WILL QUIT THIS WEEKEND.

As I sat at home that night trying to take in the implications of it all, a text message came through on my mobile. It was from Jamie Lyones, and it said: 'Good things come 2 those who wait! Mine was 2nites echo, he he he.'

I texted back urging him not to be bitter, as I was not. It simply led to more gloating and abuse, ending with 'See u soon.' I wondered what he meant. 'U never know, small town,' he replied. Best to end it there and then before it got worse.

Unnerved, I was reluctant to answer the next phone call but fortunately it came from Bob Mowlem, our former secretary. 'I can't believe it after all you've done for the club,' he said. 'Can't you do something about this bloke?' I told him that it had gone too far.

The first Saturday of September dawned bright and Vikki, Alex and Jack piled into the car with me as we left for the seaside at 8 a.m. Jack was especially sad, and angry, but I told him that we went to Weymouth with our heads held high. Today was a day to be enjoyed and savoured.

I had arranged to meet the board at noon for my first glimpse of the document signing the club over to Martyn Harrison. The legal papers flying between parties were becoming too complicated and it needed something simpler.

Harrison, McGowan and Murless were there, but not Pugsley; a good job as I would have given him a piece of my mind. He had been especially cowardly and duplicitous, I believed, asking me to meet him to see if we could sort out an alternative to Harrison but then not showing.

I perused the document. It was simple all right, ludicrously so, and was already signed by Harrison, McGowan, Pugsley and Murless. It said that Martyn would not profit from the sale of the ground to Asda, but there were just too many loopholes. First, I said, I have seen no evidence of the £300,000 for shares. Martyn protested again, saying that he had pumped huge sums into the club this summer. I wondered why, then, the club's overdraft was still around £100,000.

Crucially, too, the page and a half of A4 – on Hollybush Hotels notepaper – said that Martyn would not PROFIT from the ground. But it said nothing about him not taking money out of the Asda deal as payment of what he could claim he was owed or had pumped into the club. He could say, for example, that the concert had cost him £90,000 and the lounges £60,000, and take £150,000 off the top of the deal.

I refused to sign, could not in all conscience be associated with a deal that drove a coach and horses through the club's culture and even its articles and memoranda, which Martyn, as 80 per cent owner, would now be able to change at will. I shook hands with them and went back to Mel's, where I had left Vikki, Jack and Alex. I worked on a statement for the *Non-League Paper*. My relationship with the *Echo* was no longer what it had been and they had swung, in that way that local papers do – must, I suppose – behind the man now in power. The King is dead, long live the King. I tried in my statement to sound as reasonable and dignified as possible, hoping everyone would read between the lines.

'I am sad to be going after such an exciting year,' it said, 'but the traditional role of chairman of a democratic board of directors was effectively rendered redundant with Martyn taking full control of the club and all its decision-making. I felt my contribution and value to the club was diminishing in its importance.'

I changed into the claret suit I had bought in Harvey Nichols' winter sale, matching it with a white shirt and light blue tie. I had worn the outfit only once before, deciding it was unlucky because we had lost to Altrincham in the FA Trophy that day. But I was determined to go out showing my true colours. The club's colours.

I did my duty, greeted the Bishop's Stortford directors, wished the players well, and went round and thanked every-one, in the club shop, the office and selling programmes, for all the help they had given me. Lee Philpott wondered how I was going to manage without the club. 'I've never seen anyone in football that loves their club like you,' he said. Then I wanted a moment of solitude and shut the door behind me in Steve's office.

It soon flew open and in came Martyn, face white but sweating. 'Could you have a word with Mrs Ian?' he said. It was what he called Vikki. I asked him why. 'She has just accused me of being sexist and unpleasant.' He related how Vikki had confronted him about his remark to me about gaining publicity in *The Sun* because I was sleeping with someone on the paper. He said he did not remember saying it. I assured him he had. I told him that Vikki was her own person and I would not be having a word with her. He should have one himself. He had no stomach for it, however.

Briefly, he was as vulnerable as I had seen him. He said he regretted taking on the club, was sorry that I was leaving and never wanted that. For a moment I actually felt sorry for him and believed him. It was a deceptive moment. I told him, commanded him, to take care of this club. As W. B. Yeats wrote, 'Tread softly because you tread on my dreams.'

As I went up to find Vikki, fans approached me, urging me not to go, trying to get me to deny that I was leaving. It was a 'say it ain't so Joe' moment. But it was so. I asked Vikki about the exchange with Martyn. 'He's a typical bully,' she said. 'Runs away when confronted.' She had not liked Martyn from the outset but then even if I had trusted her intuition, I was powerless given other board members' wishes.

Steve went out and turned it on, scoring a hat trick in the 3–2 win. Fans were wondering why Chukki Eribenne had been relegated to the subs' bench after scoring three times in three games, and Martyn, again reacting to fan criticism, even came to me with their concerns. The answer was that Steve, fit again, formed a formidable partnership with Lee Phillips. After the second goal, Steve held up two fingers at the directors' box. After the third, he held both thumbs aloft in the same direction. 'Did you see my V-sign to Harrison and the thumbs up to you?' he would say later. I had wondered if it was the other way round.

The only dark moment was when the Bishop's Stortford chairman swore very loudly for several minutes and I went over to ask him to tone down the language as there were children about. I was not about to let the standards of dignity and behaviour that I believed we should be setting drop, even if this was my last day. He clearly had no hard feelings. After the game, he said that he had heard I was leaving and gave me his card. 'I hear you live in Hertfordshire,' he said. 'Come and join our board.'

What sickened me was Martyn in the boardroom basking

in the glow of the victory, congratulating Steve. The night before, he had phoned Steve to say that his job was safe for now but he had better deliver. 'I don't know how you can shake hands with him,' Vikki said to Steve.

When Martyn had left, Steve came to me with the match-ball, signed it and handed it to me. 'Thanks for everything,' it said. 'We all owe you a lot.' On a very emotional day, I was touched even more.

He was soon back in character, though. As we all piled into my car, Jack still sad and angry, a voice came from a window. 'Fuck off Ridley. Good riddance.' I looked across, stunned. There, head poking out of the dressing room, was the beaming face of Stephen Edward Claridge.

CHAPTER NINETEEN

Three sacks full

They had been kind on the day of my departure and now the fans were generous on the website. Many posted to say they were saddened at me leaving, thanked me for my contribution to the club and understood, in the wake of my statement to the *Non-League Paper* that told of my feeling 'redundant', why I could not stay. I thought that would be the end of it and, free of all my daily anxieties about running the club, I would get my life back.

I felt satisfied that I had left a legacy, even though my tenure as chairman had been brief at sixteen months. Financially, the club was better off than it had been for a while – even if needing new finance to kick on yet again – and the Asda deal had been progressed. We had established an academy and the club, with an average attendance of 1490 for league games, was a far more vibrant concern, finishing runners-up and entering a new season with a strong squad and high hopes.

But in some ways, that had been the problem. The club was revitalized to the point where it had become attractive to people never previously interested in it, and I still worried about the motives and intentions of people who might know the price of everything but may not comprehend its value. And expectation is the biggest burden to any football club. If the fans expect you simply to avoid relegation, they are delighted when you do. If they expect you to win a championship, they turn when you don't.

I had wanted to do five years, to see genuinely if we could take this club to the Football League in a new stadium, as I believed possible. Still, at least I went having set the club on the right path, I believed, and brought in new investment.

Also, in the fleeting, fickle world of football, I knew there would come a day when I was no longer flavour of the month. As Matt McGowan always used to say: if you can say you got out with a draw, then you've done well. I felt I'd almost got out with a win.

I planned from now on just to go to games, watch the team and cheer them on to promotion from the terraces. I would not be one of those former chairmen who expected a free seat in the stands as reward for service. And I would keep my own counsel about the internal politics and economics of the club, letting Martyn Harrison get on with it. Steve was still there and I was really rooting for him and the team. I felt sure that after the Bishop's Stortford result we would go from strength to strength.

So relief was my first emotion and I began to sleep properly again, figures on a balance sheet no longer the last thing I visualized as I drifted off. Then, for a few days, I felt terribly sad and empty that something I had given so much to for the last year and more was gone.

A joke went through my head. Somebody once wondered why the man whose job it was in the circus to clean up the elephant dung kept on doing it. 'Doesn't it ever get to you? Don't you think of doing something else?' 'What,' came the reply, 'and give up show business?'

I could now see, in hindsight, that Jamie Lyones and Tristan Murless had been rather too keen to get Chris Pugsley on to the board. I could understand their concern if they thought that the finances were getting out of control, but they had, I reckoned, panicked because they were finally getting close to having to put their hands in their pockets and were unwilling to do so.

Now I began to piece events together. The way I saw it, Pugsley and even Matt McGowan had been having meetings with Martyn Harrison without telling me, long before he was introduced to the board. Neither did I believe any more that his offer to buy the club was a spontaneous gesture the day of that fateful board meeting. I believed that they, knowing I was seeking to bring in Charlie Lesser, were working on a deal all along.

A posting by an embittered Jamie on the website, soon after his own departure, now made sense. There's someone willing to take over the club, he had said. Jamie's motives had probably been to regain his own position on the board with Martyn in charge. He was in dreamland. Martyn had long ago told me he had no time for Jamie. Martyn was clever, though. He had used Jamie to good effect.

It was all a horrible revelation. I had always sought to create an environment of trust and openness, in which I believed people – from manager through coaches to players, staff to volunteers – would flourish. Now, I could see the deviousness behind the scenes. Deviousness I had written about for years and often seen through but which I had not seen coming when I was inside the game. Welcome to football.

Martyn had issued a statement to the *Echo* forty-eight hours after mine in the *Non-League Paper*. 'Myth and legend do not pay the wages,' he said. 'Unfortunately "Living the Dream" is not always the reality – the reality is that the financial responsibility comes much higher in the pecking order than knowledge especially when our club was in such a precarious financial position.' It was a distortion, a clear attack on me, but I was not going to get drawn into a slanging match.

He also said that he had no desire to become chairman.

A week later he was chairman. It was announced a month later when someone on the website wondered if the club had a new one yet.

The Saturday after Bishop's Stortford, still wanting to support Steve and the team, I went with Vikki and Jack to a game away against Margate. Although it wasn't pretty, we eked out a 1–0 win courtesy of an own goal. Two wins in a row and now up to eleventh in the table after being twentieth after the first week of the season.

I phoned Steve on the way home and congratulated him. One of those scrappy games and bleak places where you get the result, get on the coach and get home, I said. He thanked me and asked if I could ring Martyn to tell him that. He had simply said to Steve at the end: 'Well, that wasn't very good was it?' It had taken the wind out of the team's sails, Steve said.

I also went to watch a home game against Basingstoke, one of the surprise early season leaders in this period where optimism was still high for most. We took the lead, dominated the game, only to concede a late equalizer with a familiar defensive flap. It was part of another patchy run of results but a victory over Redbridge Forest had taken the team up to tenth, just half a dozen points outside the play-off zone.

Everyone in the league always expected Weymouth, with this squad, to get stronger, and a recent tally of twelve points from seven games was play-off form. Soon, the company backing the league leaders Hornchurch would go bust and they would lose their highly paid manager and players – mainly to Grays Athletic, who would go on to be class-apart champions – and the task would have grown easier.

Then came a night that was to alter everything.

Steve had achieved a really good result in the second qualifying round of the FA Cup, a 1–0 win at Dorchester in one of the toughest draws we could have been given.

A picture from the day that appeared in the *Echo* amused me. In it, Martyn Harrison was leaning over a railing to congratulate Steve, who looked unaware and was walking on, ignoring him. Steve was never the type to play a hypocrite for the cameras. He knew Martyn was privately unsupportive and was sceptical of the public image.

After that came a home draw against Thame United. It should have been a foregone conclusion against a team in the First Division of the Southern League but the vagaries of cup competition are time-honoured and Thame battled bravely for a 1–1 draw.

The next Tuesday was dank and dark as Jack and I travelled to the replay in the sleepy Oxfordshire market town, where we stopped for fish and chips. As we arrived at the spartan ground, Martyn approached me to offer a handshake. The supporters' coach had just arrived and he was in full view.

The pitch was a mudheap. It would not be a night for quality, but courage instead. Steve, carrying a slight injury, had named himself as a substitute. A defensive mix-up gave Thame the lead and it took us another hour to equalize. Now we would surely go on to win. Instead, it was they who grabbed the winner. We were out of the FA Cup, yet again, at an early stage.

The reaction of our travelling fans shocked me. 'Resign Claridge,' screamed Merv Sharpe, one of our stalwarts. 'Don't you start,' I said, knowing that we now had a knee-jerk board of directors, led by a new chairman with a jittery trigger-finger. 'Sorry, I got carried away,' he said. Jack wondered how fans could be so fickle.

Driving home, my mobile rang. It was Steve. 'Sorry,' I said. 'It happens. Better make those play-offs now.'

'He's sacked me,' he replied.

I was stunned. I had to pull over in the car.

Actually, Martyn had not quite done it himself, it turned

out. He had sent Tristan Murless to fetch Steve, within minutes of the match finishing, then told him that it wasn't working out and that they should meet the next day to discuss a pay-off.

When I got home, still furious, I phoned Tristan's mobile, told him he was spineless and just doing Martyn's bidding without using his own judgement. He denied it, saying he, too, thought Steve should be sacked. It confirmed to me his lack of knowledge of football. I asked to be put on to Matt McGowan, who I knew would be travelling with him. 'He'll never make a manager,' said Matt. I could not believe it of someone I thought knew the game better. Just an unlucky thirteen league games after taking a team from seventeenth to second in the space of a season, Steve was never going to make a manager?

The next day, at 5.55 p.m., Steve phoned me to say he was just going into a meeting with the three of them at the Hilton National hotel just outside Southampton.

Now Steve was a canny professional who had been in the game a long time, Martyn, Matt and Tristan mere amateurs by comparison. The reason he had wanted a five-year contract was now seen. He knew that if someone like Martyn Harrison deposed me, he needed some security.

In these situations, negotiations can be long and difficult, as mine with Geoff Butler had been. The sacked manager is trying to get the most he can, the chairman the least he can get away with. A compromise is normally agreed, payments made in stages if the sums are large. Sir Bobby Robson, for example, was still waiting for his a year after being dismissed by Newcastle United.

In Steve's case, he had almost four years left on his contract. At an average of what he had earned the previous year, around £85,000, that would be £340,000. But no one would have expected to get anything like that. Steve certainly didn't. After all, he would then be free to find another club, where he would be earning again, and he would not be short of offers.

A mere fifteen minutes later, Steve phoned again. He was laughing. I asked him what had happened.

They had offered him a drink, he said, but he had told them that he wasn't here to be sociable, just to get his money and go. There had been a silence, broken by Martyn blurting out: 'We're not going over £200,000.' Steve was laughing because he was going to ask for £100,000, along with £38,000 he was owed in expenses and loans he had made to the club.

'If it had been you,' he added, 'I wouldn't have asked for even a hundred grand. But it's Harrison.' I told him that had it been me in this situation, he would still have been in a job, that there was a long-term plan rather than one bad Cup result at issue. Steve now understood better why I had resigned, that any decision Harrison made was not open for negotiation and that I could not have prevented this. Had I not resigned seven weeks ago, I would have now had to anyway. It was just a question of time.

Steve had also asked them where the money was coming from, since the club had been struggling financially for so long and he had not had the money to spend he had been promised by Martyn. 'Matt McGowan told me it's coming out of the club's money in the future,' Steve told me.

That could only mean the Asda deal. It was outrageous. I could stay silent no longer. It disturbed me deeply that Martyn might be underwriting the sums of money but that the Asda money would be going to fund his running of the club. In effect, we were mortgaging our future, when Harrison was giving out the impression to all and sundry that he was a sugar-daddy benefactor pumping in huge sums. After all, the *Echo* had told us that he had already put £700,000 into the club when I left, so it must have been true.

I posted on the fans' forum, saying that I believed the sacking of Steve to be a terrible mistake. I feared for the direction and future of the club. I wrote an article for the *Non-League Paper*. 'What Steve Claridge needed was cool heads and courage,' I wrote. 'Any good judge in the game knows that a manager needs a year to sort things out, a second to move players in and out and to blend them. The third, unless you have previously had vast fortunes that Steve didn't have despite what others may say or think, though he was expected to compete with the best, is then about going for silverware.'

To me, judgement at the club had gone out of the window. Steve had been sacked, quite simply, I believed, because he was too closely associated with my vision for the club. He was 'my' man and I suspected that Martyn had envied my closeness with him, one that he could never achieve as Steve was not a yes man. 'He is a free spirit and if you give him his head he will deliver,' I had told Martyn when I left the club.

'Nothing about this short-sighted decision makes any sense to me, either from the football, business or commercial standpoints,' I told the *Echo*. Martyn 'appears to be systematically dismantling everything that attracted him to the club ... Steve Claridge is my friend, yes, but hiring him was a professional, not personal, decision. I believe that the best thing to happen to Weymouth FC deserved better treatment than he has received.'

Now I was just a fan, rather than holding a position of responsibility, I felt free to comment. It had been my policy never to go on the website when chairman, as I believed it to be an independent forum for criticism and comment, and I preferred to use the local paper or programme notes to address issues that concerned fans. All bets were off with this move of Martyn's.

Martyn had no such qualms about using the website when

in power. I had suggested to him a while back, for his own good, that he should stop posting and that he would get used to football, where everyone had an opinion. It wasn't like the hotel business in which he could operate without the scrutiny of supporters, I said.

I wasn't quite prepared now for the vilification I received in return from him and tame fans who thought themselves close to him and enjoyed the titbits of disinformation he fed to them. They accused me of undermining the club. It's a bit like criticizing your parents. It's all right for you to do it but not an outsider, as I now was.

The abuse became personal. Naturally, Jamie Lyones and Duncan Stewart joined in, even making snide comments about Vikki. When Weymouth played a game at our local team, St Albans, Jack went along with some schoolfriends, only for a fan who recognized him to shout 'Ridley is a wanker' at him.

What disappointed me was the way the attacks were centred on me, rather than on the issues affecting the club. Someone even suggested I must have been on a cut of Steve's wages. And what hurt most was the revision of Steve's record at the club, that he had been a failure since the previous January, that the players didn't train enough, that he spent too much time on media work. Actually, we were still top in March until Martyn Harrison showed up. Coincidence?

But again that was football: win three games and nothing matters. Lose three, and everything is wrong. Nothing much in Steve's approach had changed. The trick as a chairman was to keep your cool, not to panic but to keep the bigger picture in mind. Martyn had listened too readily to the voice of the minority mob.

Arnold Bennett summed it up perfectly in *The Card*. He wrote, as long ago as 1911,

The great football public had no use for anything but victories. It would treat its players like gods – so long as they won. But when they happened to lose, the great football public simply sulked. It did not kick a man that was down; it merely ignored him, well knowing that the man could not get up without help. It cared nothing whatever for fidelity, municipal patriotism, fair play, the chances of war, or dividends on capital. If it could see victories it would pay sixpence, but it would not pay sixpence to assist at defeats.

What I couldn't understand was that if all this money was being doled out – and Steve received a cheque for £238,000 within a fortnight – why he hadn't just given it to Steve to spend on the team. It would surely have guaranteed promotion.

It was nasty and was to get nastier. I received calls and emails from all sorts of people inside and outside the club urging me to expose things that were going on. They were worried about the present and the future. One fan said that they were alarmed now at directors in the box at games standing up and swearing at our own players. Another, one of several, said that they no longer posted on the website because of bullying verbal intimidation, for fear of the abuse they would receive from Martyn and his acolytes if they voiced their opinions or concerns.

Martyn detested the fact that so many people, especially within the club, were still sympathetic to me and spoke to me a lot. It was one reason why, one by one, he was getting rid of them. Because of the declining mood now within the club, many still wanted a friendly voice to talk to. Steve never had one and had continued to ring me to talk things over, since I knew the players and personalities involved.

Soon, more serious matters came to light. I heard that

Martyn was revising the stadium plans I had left in place and I sought a meeting with Asda. Because of the respect Asda had for me, they said, they agreed to the meeting even though I was no longer chairman. They wanted to find out what I knew.

They told me they had met with Martyn that very morning and he was now talking about a 4000 capacity stadium with – wait for it – a hotel on it, rather than the 8000 capacity and community facilities I had envisaged. It would compromise promotion to the Football League, should we ever achieve it.

In return, Asda were interested to hear from me Steve's statement that Martyn intended to take money he had put into the club – or was guaranteeing with the bank – back out when the deal was completed. That deal signing the club over to Martyn, I recalled, had said that he would not benefit from the sale of the stadium. However, crucially, it did not preclude him from getting back what he said he was owed. And I was losing confidence in what was left of the board reining him in.

At first, Matt McGowan, who always fancied he knew the game though had been out of it for a long time, was placed in charge of the team, with Paul Buckle as head coach. Paul, though, would not have that and rightly insisted on picking it. He had an early problem to deal with when Robbie Pethick stormed out of the ground in a huff after being dropped for a match at Welling. Robbie had been a disappointment as a player, though I reckoned he would still come good, but now the board decided to pay up his contract, which had another six months to run.

Paul was told that he would get a month's trial as manager. However, at a dinner in London, I came across the Yeovil Town manager Gary Johnson who told me that he had received a call from a Weymouth director asking him to 'name his price'. This was strange, given that Martyn was telling everyone that Claridge was too expensive an item. Gary was on much more at Yeovil.

Gary's stock in the game was high. He had taken Yeovil up from the Conference to the League, and was now in the middle of getting them up into League One. He told Weymouth thanks but no thanks. He knew that he could do much better and would turn down the chance to manage Coventry City, Watford and Derby County before accepting the Bristol City job.

Instead, Gary recommended his brother Steve, who had left Chertsey Town, somewhere below Weymouth in football's pyramid, and had latterly been helping out at a Sussex League club. Gary had also told the Weymouth board that he would help out by putting some Yeovil players, unwanted by him but good enough for our level, the club's way. Paul never got the promised month because Steve Johnson was appointed manager. Paul had been canny in negotiating an extension to his contract through all this, but one look at Steve Johnson's training methods proved to him that he couldn't work with him.

He negotiated another pay-off. The board was furious. Martyn went on to the website to say that he would never trust another player. Matt McGowan, catching Martyn's disease, posted to say that a requirement of Paul Buckle had been that he trained the players twice a week and that in the first week it had not happened. He was painted as dishonest and mercenary. It did not square with the Paul I knew, who had given everything for the cause the previous season, playing with an injury for the last three months and postponing an operation until the summer. He had also taken a £100 a week pay cut to come to the Wessex from Aldershot, though he could have sat out another year on higher money with them.

Paul phoned me. His wife had been reading the website and pointed out what Martyn and Matt had said. He was angry at this lack of professionalism, this one-sided portrait. He had told Matt McGowan, he said, about the cancellation of one training session because the players were tired from a recent heavy programme, which would make it counter-productive, and Matt had consented. When the club called a fans' forum, he wanted to be there, he said, to put the record straight. But Martyn would not call one.

When Johnson took over, he immediately set about dismantling Steve's squad. The board had claimed that men like Lee Philpott, Nathan Bunce and Lee Charles were on too much money and that the wage bill should be cut. Johnson, hardly seeing the players in action, was clearly the man the board wanted to do their bidding.

Lee Philpott, a terrific influence for us, was on £500 a week, the going rate for such a player, the others on a little less. Martyn also put it about that Matt Bound was on £1000 a week. He was actually getting £675, which Martyn had sanctioned. Philpott, Bunce and Charles were also paid off and shipped out. Despite the public statements about cost-cutting being necessary because of my excesses, the costs were mounting, unnecessarily in my view.

I could not take all this propaganda and misinformation lying down but my Internet row with Martyn Harrison was simply dragging the club through the dirt, dividing fans. I grew frustrated that only a few brave souls would voice their own concerns and that Martyn's clique held sway. Though I tried not to bite, sometimes I would be goaded into responding to their uninformed view of Harrison's way of running the club. There must be a better way of getting this out in the open.

I questioned when the next Annual General Meeting would be. Under pressure, Martyn finally called it for December, some two months later than usual. As chairman, I had made a point of holding open forums for fans at the club once every three months, so that they could voice their opinions and ask questions. Martyn combined the AGM with a fans' forum. I made it clear that I, as still the second largest shareholder, and as a committed fan, would be attending and asking awkward questions.

CHAPTER 20

Rumbling and crumbling

The Annual General Meeting was to be held at one of Martyn's holiday camps, the Riviera at Bowleaze Cove, the striking old art deco building at the western end of the town. These days it was lit up at night by purple floodlights making it a local landmark. One fan on the website dubbed the event the Rumble at the Riviera and in the run-up to what was threatening to be a torrid night it stuck.

It was to be Harrison v. Ridley, they said, though I saw it as more of a battle for a club's soul; money – or the illusion of it – and dictatorship versus a more open and cooperative way of running a football club. Harrison had made his raid from the holiday camps that had intrigued Paul Theroux. I was from the town.

Many fans contacted me with information and questions they wanted asking, now unwilling to do so themselves as they feared the abuse they would get from Harrison's vociferous supporters on the website or on the forthcoming night. I had become a thorn in the board's side, wondering on the website whether all the money spent at the bar of the Riviera at the AGM would go to the club (it would not) and, with website fan support, compelling Martyn to abandon his own plans for a 4000-capacity stadium and at least raise it to 6000. As a result, the forces were being marshalled against me.

One call surprised me. It came from the Dorchester fan Rob Hodder who had been a thorn in my own side, posting on his own club's and our website that I would bankrupt the club and that our achievements had been bought. Actually, he now said, I had done a great job and he secretly envied what had happened at Weymouth in my time there. No hard feelings he said, just banter between local rivals. I accepted it, and had no hard feelings.

Then he asked me why I was doing this, when I could have simply shut up and walked away a local hero. I told him this was not about me and how I was viewed but about the well-being of the club and I feared for it. If pointing out my deep fears, as the person who knew most about the club, was to be unpopular then I would live with short-term unpopularity for the sake of long-term integrity. I saw this as my last act as chairman, to alert people to what might be in store for them. If it all went wrong in the future, I added, and I stayed silent, they would quite rightly turn to me and ask why I hadn't warned them.

Martyn's response to anything critical of him on the website was curious. Either he would reply quickly, in an attempt to nip the dissent in the bud, or he would say that he didn't understand all this, didn't need it. The subtext was that he might just walk away and leave the club in the lurch. Worried fans thus shut up. To me, he betrayed a lack of knowledge and understanding of either the game or the passions it inspired in people.

I did my homework, spoke to all manner of people in and around the club in Weymouth. It was surprising how many people were willing to talk. One fan had been doing some digging of his own and sent me a detailed report about the state of Hollybush Hotels and Martyn's business affairs.

It prompted me into taking the due diligence that I now saw that we as a board should have taken over the summer months before we handed over control of the club to

Martyn. Instead, the board had had pound signs in their eyes. I engaged a financial investigator to dig into Martyn and Hollybush's background. There were other areas, such as a timeshare business in Florida, but they did not seem – yet, anyway – to be relevant to the club.

His report did not make happy reading. From the last published accounts – more recent ones were due but were now two months late and counting, incurring an Inland Revenue fine – Hollybush were deeply in debt: £3.54 million owing to banks, £2.09 million to creditors and, intriguingly, £1.53 million to Harrison himself. This total of more than £7 million was against assets valued at £5.4 million. 'This level of gearing is, to put it mildly, very high,' the report said.

Hollybush's trading loss for the year was £354,000. This was a successful businessman? And it was curious how newspapers, particularly local ones, always seemed to append the word 'successful' to the nebulous job description of businessman.

In addition, we obtained the respective reports on Weymouth FC and Hollybush Hotels, from a reputable business information company, ICC, which ranks companies for their financial viability and is used by banks and other lending organisations.

Their report on Weymouth read:

> The latest score is 67 and this indicates a risk level for the next year three to four times less than the average rate of 2 per cent. We would expect 31.24 per cent of companies to be at and above this score. The credit limit is £120,000, which is a reflection of the score and the quite high financial strength of the company.

By contrast, the report on Hollybush stated:

The latest score is 10 and this indicates a risk level for the next year at least 10 times higher than the average rate of 2 per cent. We would expect 99.74 per cent of companies to be at or above this score. The credit limit is zero, which is a reflection of the score and the very low financial strength of the company.

It meant that Weymouth had been in much better condition that Harrison liked to portray, Hollybush worryingly worse. I wondered if he would seek to prop up his company by using the value of the football club's assets. The ground was valued at £2.2 million and could be secured for borrowing. It also meant that the controlling shareholding in the club could be seized and sold off to meet debts if Hollybush were to go into receivership or administration. Then, legally, what would Harrison's agreement not to benefit from the Asda deal or that he did not own the stadium be worth? It worried me, too, that he had taken the club's banking out of Weymouth to one that also handled his company.

A source supplied me with an advance copy of the club's detailed accounts for the period of my chairmanship. They showed record turnover of £591,468 – up 89 per cent on the previous year – and record gate receipts of £178,851, almost three times the previous season. In addition, Mel's sponsorship efforts had brought in £102,145, more than six times the previous season and bar takings had doubled to more than £62,000, while Supporters Club contributions were up also to £44,000.

There was, though, a trading loss of £240,000, which stunned me. How could this be, when the total for players' wages – the biggest cost to any football club, from Chelsea downwards – should have been no more than £450,000, including expenses and all tax and National Insurance liabilities? In fact, they were shown in the accounts to be £531,552.

I could understood a trading loss of around £150,000, which was to have been underwritten by the directors buying new shares. In reality, we had got in £102,000, leaving a cash-flow loss for the season of £48,000, due entirely to Murless, Lyones and Pugsley failing to buy shares.

Something distinctly fishy was going on here. I was also interested to see that the accounts showed Martyn Harrison being owed £338,000 by the club, when he had been claiming that he was putting in all this money as a benefactor. It had been right when Matt had told Steve that Martyn would be claiming back his pay-off from the Asda deal.

In the week leading up to the AGM, the dirty tricks campaign against me intensified. The annual accounts were given to the *Echo*, who had clearly been briefed, and they used the headline I suspected Martyn was hoping for. The club, in Ian Ridley's tenure as chairman, had lost £250,000 on last season. I wasn't quite sure how the loss had crept up another £10,000 from the draft accounts to the final ones but a quarter of a million pounds sounded so much more damaging.

I phoned the *Echo* to ask why they had not delved further into the accounts, receiving only a curt reply from the editor that the reporter who had written the story used to be an accountant. It was astonishing, therefore, I told him, that he had not taken into account the £102,000 paid into the club in new shares from new directors.

As I wearied of telling the reporter, we had always said there would be a trading loss because of the paying off debts and the costs incurred in revitalizing the club. What should count was the cash-flow figure, the actual amount the season had cost the club. And that should have been zero, given directors' contributions.

There was, I noted, no such fuss at Crawley Town, where they would announce that their loss on the season was £190,000, also underwritten by the family that controlled the club, the Dulys. But then, they had won the title and we had finished second. Such was football, the dividing line between heroes and villains so very thin. A missed penalty and a late chance . . .

Our trading loss was £90,000 more than the figures Nigel Winship had envisaged and his reputation had also been blackened. We set about finding out why this was.

Only abbreviated accounts had been sent out to the *Echo* and shareholders. As well as the full accounts, I got my hands on the appendages from the auditors. They showed that another £96,000 had been included in the accounts for future bonuses due to Steve Claridge – never paid – and tax on his and other players' expenses that the Inland Revenue *might* ask for.

Martyn, and the *Echo*, could easily have made the figures look good just by reproducing the facts of the record income. It did not, however, suit Martyn's purposes of being the white knight to show how successful the club had been the previous year.

He launched a vicious attack on me in the *Echo*, making it personal in a way that I had studiously avoided. 'Your real contribution to this club can be measured in two words, your ego,' he said. 'He screwed up, got me in to bail him out and then he is bad-mouthing me everywhere.' He had, he added, never liked me. It seemed to be that I had now to be punished for having backed Steve and questioning Martyn's methods.

He then turned his attention to Steve, who, with me, had almost bankrupted the club because of 'the most crazy player's contract in all time'. How a man who had never been in football knew that – and he should see some of them, with their side-benefit clauses – was beyond me. The majority of Steve's contract had concerned productivity. And he had delivered.

Martyn added that he wished he had sacked Steve the day

he took over the club. Steve responded by saying he wished
he had left the day Martyn had arrived. He had known he
would be in trouble when Martyn started suggesting to him,
as a response to a few fans posting on the website, that he
should play 4–3–3. A man by his own admission who didn't
know anything about football picking the team?

So I was spoiling for a fight that week before Christmas.
As Ricky Tomlinson might have said: season of goodwill?
My arse. I came prepared, detailing every financial figure
in a twenty-three-page dossier containing every salient fact
from the previous year, along with the financial investigator's report. There was, as well, a seven-page statement by
Steve Claridge about his time as manager and how shabbily
he had been treated by Harrison. 'Sometimes your face
doesn't fit with some people,' it said.

The night was a typically tacky Harrison promotion. As
I distributed the dossiers and statements – a couple of fans
ripping them up with contempt but more digesting them –
Chris Pugsley approached me with his trademark sickly grin,
hand outstretched. I could not countenance such hypocrisy
and, refusing the handshake, told him I thought he had
behaved appallingly in all this. Soon he was in conclave in a
back room with the rest of the board, devouring the dossier.
Start time was put back from 7 p.m. to 7.30.

It was good to catch up with a few friendly faces, like
Sarah Redford, Roger Mutch and Liz Bell. Many others
were afraid to approach me, knowing my opposition to
the new regime and fearful of being allied with a man now
a pariah at the club. The new manager Steve Johnson did
introduce himself and we had a brief conversation. I knew
he would not be up to the job but he was an innocent party
in the middle of all this and I wished him well. I told him
that he would need a slice of good fortune working for
Martyn Harrison.

The board, smirking, took their seats on the stage to dry

ice and the strains of that PJ and Duncan monstrosity 'Let's Get Ready to Rumble'. It prompted laughter, undermining the tense atmosphere. 'He's a cleverer man than I thought he would be,' my accountant, Roy Warren, who had come with me, would say later.

When question time on the accounts arrived, I immediately asked the auditor, John Tate, why the trading loss had gone up from £240,000 to £250,000 between drafts of the accounts. He did not know. I asked how much had been allocated for Claridge in the accounts. He did not know. And so I told him. Matt McGowan expressed surprise that I had access to the full accounts and supposedly private correspondence between the board and the auditor and asked how I got it. I wondered why the chairman of the year in question should not be allowed to see it all.

I said that the £96,000 for Claridge and the other players was a simply a figure arrived at because of Pugsley's struggle to keep a check on expenses, the club's way of covering themselves just in case the Inland Revenue came calling. I told how Pugsley, Jamie Lyones and Tristan Murless had reneged on promises of putting money into the club. The latter two, in fact, having taken shares for the work they had done while the rest of us had freely given our time. Vikki, to whom I had sold some shares – along with a few fans who had asked me for them so that they could attend – asked Tristan how much he had put into the club. He declined to answer.

Pugsley, in turn, told how he had been approached by Murless and Lyones to become involved in the board. Thus was it confirmed, in one sentence, how the section of the board unwilling to invest had been working behind my back.

Martyn put up Claridge's contract on an overhead screen to try to show how all of this was bankrupting the club and that the hiring of Johnson and paying off of certain players had to be done. He had put in £1 million, he insisted, and all the club owed him was £68,000. Really? Why then did the accounts show differently? We could not afford to live the dream any longer, he said. Now we were living the reality, he added, the club being run along business lines. We would come to see exactly how.

It almost went unnoticed when Pugsley announced that this board expected a trading loss of £350,000 on their own first year.

What Harrison didn't say was that he had been adopted by the board because he had promised no-strings-attached money and was willing to increase the wage budget. Just a few months later, having sanctioned all the signings – and with Steve Claridge still £3000 under the weekly wage limit when he departed – he was saying that it was all too much.

In the end, though, he could not avoid agreeing with me that in reality the club had lost only £48,000 during my season, that because of three reneging directors. And in the end, to my great sadness, the majority of fans appeared to care not a hoot about the financial side of the club and its vagaries, though many did seem shocked to learn from me that the club was now owned by a hotel chain.

The team – with still enough of Claridge's players to eke out a few results – had just taken eight points from four unbeaten games to move up to eighth in the table. They were going to make the play-offs. What did the long-term future of the club matter by comparison?

What hurt most was a voice at the back of the room questioning my support for the club down the years. It came from Terry Nutman, a former director and friend of Matt McGowan. At a New Year's Eve party at Matt's house a year earlier, he had badgered me to get his vice-president's season ticket restored. As a paying fan, since leaving the board following a dispute seven years earlier, he had not been near the ground. I looked to Matt on the podium and asked him to confirm my commitment to the club. He shrugged his shoulders. It was the final act of betrayal from a man I had trusted so much.

Now I could sense that people, some 300 in a highly charged ballroom, had had enough, even though there were still so many unanswered questions. They had points and pound signs in their eyes. I said I would take my leave, let fans now have their chance to talk about new signings, the need for a better public address system and cleaner toilets. I had already got Harrison to backtrack on his stadium plans, had got him to agree the true financial figures of the previous season and had stood up for Steve Claridge. It was about the best I could have hoped for. I saw it as my job, I said, to keep Martyn honest. He hated the statement. I shook his hand for the cameras, in a move I would come to regret as being untrue to myself. But I sensed the supporters needed closure on a turbulent episode.

'You are a brave man,' Roy Warren said to me in the car going home. I felt there were few left behind in Weymouth.

Yet again, I expected that to be it but the club went from bad to worse and I found it impossible not to comment. Players would ring me, tell me how awful life was under the ranting-and-raving Steve Johnson, a man clearly out of his depth and carrying no authority with the players. Martyn had told all and sundry that the club needed to cut the wage bill, then made the striker Kirk Jackson, a victim of Hornchurch's demise, the highest-paid player in the club's history on £700 a week.

Johnson caught the Harrison disease by going on to the website to take up issues with fans, one day having a go at one by saying that he seemed to be dreaming of Claridge and Ridley coming back and they would certainly not be. I phoned the club to speak to him, to ask him not to drag my name into things. He responded with a one-minute tirade of foul language. This was clearly not a man coping well with stress, as was seen when, after a 3–0 home defeat by Welling United, he sent the players out to apologize to disgruntled, departing fans.

Then the secretary Liz Bell texted me from the car park outside the club one day. 'I've been sacked' it said. I immediately phoned her. She was in tears, could think of no reason why she was being dismissed. I was outraged. Yet another good person was being badly treated. An Internet campaign led to her reinstatement, though it was only the righting of a PR gaffe. She was given a token position within the club. Martyn told the *Non-League Paper* that it was only a £50 job and he couldn't see what all the fuss was about. He later denied saying it, but the *Non-League Paper* had him on tape, they assured me.

Then two of the club's biggest assets, Lee Phillips and Steve Tully, were let go for nothing to Exeter City, Martyn calling it good business to get them off the wage bill. At last, fans began to wonder what was going on inside the club, though naturally a few close to Martyn turned on the two players for what they saw as disloyalty.

I spoke to both players and, it turned out, they could no longer stomach playing for Johnson. Some more of Martyn's acolytes accused Steve Claridge of, behind the scenes, getting the players out of the club. The truth was that Johnson had been hawking Lee around, deeming him a troublemaker, and offered him to Aldershot. Lee, who had never had an agent, had contacted Steve just the once to ask how much money he should be asking in wages from a Conference club. A troublemaker? He had a laid-back Cornish nature.

With few of Steve's players left, to be replaced by a host of players not good enough, results inevitably deteriorated. Martyn, never the most tolerant of men, eventually sacked Johnson after a run of one draw and five defeats. I did feel for him. He had just moved his family to the area, got his daughters into a local school, and was fired the day they were due to start. It showed how little feeling there was for club employees any more. The personal touch had gone, the mood unforgiving. What amused me was how Matt McGowan, who had said that Claridge would not make a manager but had been a prime mover in recruiting Johnson, now kept his head down.

The excellent groundsman, Mark Reynolds, had also been sacked. He was spotted helping out on Yeovil's pitch one night and the board would not have him moonlighting. However, since we could not pay him the full going rate for the job, Pugsley had negotiated a self-employed contract for him that would have given him the freedom to work elsewhere. Soon Mark's solicitor would be contacting me.

It pained me to see how far downhill the club was going, with a relegation struggle looming, and no manager in place. I met with Charlie Lesser to see if he was interested in trying to do something about it. He said he would think about it. Then one night I returned from dinner with Vikki at a neighbour's house and checked the website to see what fans were saying about the state of the club.

To my astonishment, Charlie had posted a message. He regretted now, he said, offering to take over the club and expecting to make money out of it. With no strings attached, he was now willing to buy out Martyn's shareholding then gradually over the next five years sell his shares to a supporters' trust so that the fans owned the club.

The next morning, after speaking to Charlie, I posted a message myself, offering not so much to swallow my pride as spit it out and help the club until the end of the season by using my contacts to help find a new manager and restore some stability. This would be on the basis of Martyn agreeing to speak with Charlie about the transfer of ownership. I spoke to Tony Adams, who had resigned as Wycombe Wanderers manager the previous November, about coming in as coach until the end of the season.

The offers went down well with fans on the website, even those who just a month or two ago were blindly loyal to Martyn but now questioning the direction of the club. They did not go down well with Martyn, however.

He posted on the website, accusing fans of having 'shit in their eyes'. He was in tears, he said. He had pumped in a fortune, he added, and this was his reward. Then he threw down the gauntlet to Charlie. He could have the club for £400,000 for his shares. But he would want £1 million back for the money he claimed to have put into the club.

I was baffled. The wage bill had been cut after the so-called Ridley excesses but now we were £1 million in debt to him? It was an offer too easily refused. Why should any prospective investor pay for the mistakes of the previous owner? But that was football and what its power brokers expected.

Martyn had also said that he was about to pull off a major coup and the next day it was announced. He had hired Garry Hill as manager, Kevin Hales as his assistant. Claridge had been refused an assistant; 'Why should we have a coach when he's getting all that money?' Martyn had said. Gary Calder was to be the new chief executive. The names were familiar: they had been the men in charge at Hornchurch when it had gone bust the previous November.

I posted on the website, saying sincerely that Charlie and I would not have made our offer of help if we had known the club had plans. I took my leave hoping the club would now fare well – prompting Tristan Murless to respond that I should go away and never come back. He would get his way.

These were men with experience in the non-League game and more fitting for a club like Weymouth. The cost of it all would be huge, but at least there would be something better on the field. So it proved. There were six wins from the last eight games and I watched two of them from the terraces, an ironic 2–0 win at home to Hornchurch and a 3–0 at Sutton in the penultimate game of the season. In the end, the play-offs were just two points out of reach as we finished seventh. To me it showed what might have been achieved had Claridge been allowed to continue in the job, and had people realised the longevity of the season and that just one string of results would be enough. Crowds? The average was some 250 down – worth around £40,000 in revenue – at 1248.

Soon it would emerge what the cost of it all would be for the following season. A newspaper contact phoned me to say that Hill had been bragging in Essex what he was getting – around £100,000 a year. Hales was on £50,000 and Calder £60,000. That was £4000 a week – around the complete playing budget of more than half of the clubs in the Conference South – just for the management team. The chairman of Barnet, Tony Kleanthous, told me that he had tried to get Kevin Hales as their assistant after their promotion from Conference to League Two but he could not match what Weymouth were paying.

Martyn decided to make the players full time, overkill at this level. 'The man from the Regent says yes,' wrote Matt McGowan on the website, announcing it before Tristan went on to say 'Eh?' Soon Matt rewrote his statement to declare that the board of Weymouth FC had agreed to it.

Players were brought in on comparatively vast sums at this level. One had his wages doubled from £350 to £700 a week. Steve Tully returned, unable to resist the increased pickings on offer. Strikers came in for more than £1000 a week, one for £1250 my sources told me, and houses in the town were rented for them all. Even the physio was put on £500 a week, up from the £175 I had negotiated with him. It totalled more than £1 million for the season. This was living the reality?

I did some calculations. Even with admission prices going

up, based on record gates averaging 2000 and record sponsorship, they would still lose at least £500,000 for the season, unless they made it to an FA Cup third round tie at Manchester United. This on top of Pugsley's projected trading loss of £350,000 at the AGM, which would now have risen with all the subsequent payoffs.

Where was it coming from? The prayer was clearly for the Asda deal to come off. Everyone continued to think that Martyn was bankrolling it. But he knew how he could get it all back.

Angry, I was tempted to speak out when my sister Mel resigned as commercial manager. She was being put under more and more pressure to raise funds and hated seeing prices being hiked for sponsors without value being given in return. She felt she could no longer do it without embarrassment. The birthday parties she ran for kids, our future support, had been stopped. Martyn did not like the noise the kids made near the directors' box while he was watching games. He also wanted an end to the community partners, believing they were getting too cheap a deal.

And seeing all these contracts being doled out to management and players but having been stalled on one of her own for eight months, in addition to her request for a pay review of her £250 a week being ignored, Mel did not want to be associated with what she described, when contacted by the *Non-League Paper*, as 'growing greed' at the club. The *Echo* didn't contact her, printed only the club's statement that she had left 'for personal reasons', which caused her embarrassment in the town, people wondering if she was ill.

Mel was always a dilemma for the new regime. She was popular with the fans and the sponsors, in the town in general, and exceptional at her job, having increased sponsorship revenue sixfold. She was pretty much unsackable. Had she not been committed to her family and the town of Weymouth, she could have worked in the commercial department of any football club, and at a high level. But she was Ridley's sister, the last real remnant of his time at the club. Better that she did not get her contract and pay rise and resign instead. It smacked, to me, of constructive dismissal.

In the summer, I saw the club lose – given my experience of the previous year – what could only have been around £120,000 on two more concerts, featuring stars of the eighties like ABC and Tony Hadley and classical acts like G4 and Aled Jones. And I bit my lip anew. 'Never again,' said Martyn once more in the *Echo*.

It was hard observing it all, reading only paeans of praise to Harrison on the website from his cronies, who had dwindled to about twenty, the rest no longer wishing to post for fear of receiving abuse. The local paper also appeared to have given up writing anything that might upset him. Privately, I heard the dissent. The speedway promoter, Brian White, phoned me seeking sympathy. The football club was threatening to close him down if he didn't pay the money he owed. He had paid it; the club had lost the paperwork.

The sight of so many players coming in may have made many fans wonder about the cost of it, all but the majority of those who still used the website were drunk on arrogance. There were polls over the summer about how many points the club would accumulate in the league. Fifty-four per cent said 101 or more, while a total of 78 per cent said 86 or more, enough to win the title. 'We WILL win the league,' Martyn announced on the website. Later, after a bad start, some of them said they were pleased they hadn't made extravagant claims in the summer.

The kit manager, Pete Dennis, resigned. He was angry that Martyn, in his Jag, had bumped into his partner Gaye's car outside the ground. Martyn's daughter Faye had got out of their car to check only the damage to the Jag before

Martyn drove off. 'I didn't like to make a fuss. I'm worried that Martyn will leave with all his money,' Gaye told me when I saw her at a game some months later. It was how a lot of people felt. Martyn was forced to pay for the damage.

Our coach, Gary Borthwick quietly left the club. He had organised the players for a fund-raising celebrity masters football tournament in the summer, then arrived at the club a few days later to be handed his P45. At that event, the club raffled a Mini. It was won by the company accountant for Hollybush Hotels.

Park Engineering came back as shirt sponsors, despite another of Martyn's companies, Style Holidays, having agreed a two-year deal. Park got it for a knock-down £15,000 since they could find no one else. It led to Mick Archer having a pop at me in the local paper for freezing them out. This was a man who rarely went to a game even when a director. It also meant that new replica kit with new logos could be sold to fans even though it was only a year since we had changed. The third strip became pink, with green flashes. No true fan of the club would ever incorporate Yeovil Town's colours.

There were some incredulous posts on the website when Martyn made Faye a director on her eighteenth birthday, but they were quickly quashed. We couldn't have Martyn being challenged or upset just in case we lost his supposed millions. It did not seem to matter any more who might eventually have to pay. But what were Martyn's motives in making Faye a director? Businesses had been known to transfer ownership for financial purposes.

There were times, I have to confess, when I hoped for things to go wrong, for results to turn, so that the club would reach its rock bottom sooner and emerge from the trauma a new, happier concern. Now I just looked on. I felt sure they would still be promoted, given the squad assembled and money being thrown about, but at what cost, financially and to the soul of the club? I was concerned, but without rancour.

They had a terrible start, stunning all at the club and leading to internal strife, as they lost three of their first five matches. I saw one, a 4–0 defeat at St Albans, and was taken aback by their ordinariness, given a wage bill of more than £1 million a year, around what many League One teams were paying.

Gradually they got their act together and rose to the top of the league, without ever really storming it as the money should have guaranteed. They even had a good FA Cup run, earning a splendid 1–1 draw at Nottingham Forest, where I hired a box and treated Charlie Lesser, and Mel and her family to an enjoyable day out.

The replay was televised live on Sky Sports, attracted a record crowd of 6500 and brought the club in around £200,000. They would need it, given the annual accounts that would come out the next month. Steve Claridge was the Sky guest pundit at the Wessex for the night and phoned me afterwards. He was sickened by the nasty chanting directed towards him from some Weymouth fans. The team performed creditably again, losing only 2–0.

I, too, was sickened by the treatment of Steve. Though I knew I had the respect of most Weymouth fans beyond Martyn's cronies on the website – and Mel even encountered Jamie Lyones in a pub, who asked her to apologize to me on his behalf and convey that he had underestimated me and what I did for the club – I no longer wanted to be associated with the club in any way. I went on the website to express my disgust and offer my shares for sale. It brought more criticism, then a swift phone call from Gary Calder. Martyn was willing to buy my shares. Two days later, at a hotel near St Albans, Gary handed over a cheque.

And that was it. It was time to let go. I was relieved.

I knew why Martyn was so keen to buy, though he did

not need the shares. A few weeks later, the AGM – which I was not now entitled to attend and ask questions – heard that the club had lost a staggering £886,000 the previous season. This was before going full time. Worryingly, the club now owed Hollybush Hotels £808,000. Still none questioned it, still all thought Martyn was bankrolling it all and did not grasp the implication that the club would have to pay back him and his company, or the bank that was advancing it all. The AGM lasted eight minutes.

Soon worries would increase. A government planning inspector did not believe the Asda deal should go ahead. No need for a superstore or a new stadium, she said. At best, the project would be delayed; at worst, the club now had no way of paying off its enormous debts to Harrison, mounting towards £2 million, huge at this level.

Powerless, I moved on. Though it could never be the same, I joined the board of my local club St Albans City, for whom I had always had a soft spot and where I believed I could help them raise more money commercially and work to increase attendances from around the 500 mark. I got more stick on the Weymouth website, naturally, and I did feel strange. I thought that Weymouth FC was like the Hotel California: you can check out any time you want but you can never leave.

Weymouth would always be my first love but they no longer wanted me and I had missed the buzz of being involved with a club, felt I had skills and experience to offer. I could not be as hands-on as at Weymouth but it was good to be around people again, led by their chairman John Gibson, who were all pulling in the same direction and without the latter internal strife at the Wessex Stadium that had replaced the harmony I believed we had created and was now rediscovering at St Albans.

What gave the move piquancy was that St Albans were among the chasing pack behind Weymouth, and even began to challenge them for the title. As soon as anyone did get close, though, Weymouth signed another player. The former Wimbledon and Bolton striker Dean Holdsworth joined for another £1200 a week after leaving his position as assistant manager at Derby County.

Weymouth were the strongest, most durable team in the league but Saints the most attractive and it was an enjoyable run-in to the season. All this on a wage bill of around £4000 a week, less than one-fifth of Weymouth's.

It got messy for me. With their tight-knit group of talented young players – they do keep you young and we had a lively bunch with such great lads as Matty Hann and Lee Clarke – and under a veteran non-League manager in Colin Lippiatt who was working wonders, St Albans kept snapping at the heels of Weymouth's expensively deep squad. Weymouth lost a game at Welling United and Saints were within a few points. Only the champions would go up automatically. The play-offs would have been a bonus for St Albans at the start of the season but now here they were going for that title. Attendances – difficult to build in an area where Luton and Watford coexisted and on which the London clubs also drew heavily – were nudging that magical 1000.

Ironies, coincidences abounded. The fixture list showed, on Easter Monday, Weymouth v. St Albans City. I agonized about going. Then something happened which made me determined to attend.

Out of the blue, the Weymouth finance director Chris Pugsley resigned and his views were plastered all over the front page of the *Echo*. 'MY FEARS FOR TERRAS FUTURE' screamed the headline, with a strap of 'Club owes over £2 million says former finance chief'.

In a pang of conscience, and maybe because he was a local accountant with a reputation to uphold, Pugsley was confirming everything I had warned about. It came as no shock to me when he was quoted as saying that the club had received a letter from Hollybush's finance director demanding that any money Harrison had put in, or guaranteed, was to be treated as loans. It should have come as a shock to fans, though.

Thus I felt sure that I would be able to go to the match against St Albans with even Harrison's blindest supporter having to agree that what I had been warning against was true and despite the superficially glossy picture of a team top of the table, there was serious trouble ahead. Instead, their reaction on the fans' message board stunned me. Pugsley was a turncoat, they said, his timing stank. The *Echo* – which had shown some courage at last – should not have printed it. I despaired. How could they be so naive?

I did go to the game, with Mel and Jack, and stood in the St Albans end, penned in by a now, in my view, graceless club determined to make life as difficult as possible for any visitors, especially ones only three points behind them. It was a cracking match, Saints playing the better football and desperately unlucky to lose 3–2, hitting the bar, a shot cleared off the line and what looked like a good goal disallowed.

As I left, I received some foul-mouthed gloating from a few home fans out of what was declared as a remarkable crowd of 5022 though looked somewhat fewer, and, to my own later shame, bit back. I was, though, simply staggered by the whole mood of the place.

Six points clear now, Weymouth would surely win the title. But there came another twist a few days later. It emerged they had fielded a player earlier in the season without international clearance and stood to be docked four points. Naturally I – 'bitter and twisted', according to the Harrison lackeys – was seen as the man who drew it to the Conference's attention. In truth I found out about it only when the St Albans secretary, Steve Eames, told me.

St Albans – as Weymouth would have done – did pursue it, though. The chairman, John Gibson, had little time for the Weymouth chief executive Gary Calder after being involved in a separate dispute over player registration the previous season when a player moved from Hornchurch to St Albans.

Theoretically then, Weymouth could still lose the title on the last day of the season if they did not beat Lewes at home and Saints, with the better goal difference, beat Weston-super-Mare at home. A shock for a club who expected to have it all wrapped up long before now. The Conference were desperately hoping that Weymouth would win, so as to avoid the embarrassment for them of the league potentially being decided in a committee room.

They got their wish. Weymouth won comfortably 2–0, Saints losing 2–1. Weymouth were indeed champions.

It would mean the play-offs for Saints and the chances were good with a bye to the final, fourth-placed Lewes's ground precluding them from taking their place. It turned out to be a gloriously enjoyable, though tense, day as St Albans beat Histon 2–0 in front of 3175 at Stevenage Borough FC. Remarkably, little old Saints were in the national Conference with Weymouth – £4000 a week, more than £20,000 a week: same result. 'Bitter and twisted?' I was delighted for both clubs, though still worried about the financial future of one.

Culling and cutting began at Weymouth. They released ten players, ostensibly not good enough they said, but an economy drive was also under way. Martin's acolytes pointed out that it had to be done, that the Conference salary cap was set at 65 per cent of income. Yet the rules also say that if a backer wants to put in £1 million a year, that can be treated as income. If he wants to put it in as loans, then it can't. Harrison clearly fell into the latter category but they were still unable to see it.

No longer able to treat the money as loans, he wasn't going to put in – or borrow – any more, and it galled me the way he now openly referred to them as loans in quotes for the *Echo* without anyone picking up on it, having always maintained previously, including to the annual general meeting, that these were not loans. He could only now hope that the Asda deal would be resurrected. But it would still be the club ultimately paying back the money, the quality of any new stadium and facilities compromised, and it was an alarming prospect.

None of it was my concern any longer, though. I got on with doing my bit for St Albans in the enjoyable tasks of summer as we prepared for bigger attendances in hosting 'big' clubs, like Oxford United, relegated from the Football League, Exeter and York City. There were ticket prices to set, a homely and intimate little ground at council-owned Clarence Park to spruce up, pre-season friendlies to arrange, dear old Neil Warnock agreeing to bring down Sheffield United, newly promoted to the Premiership, as he had done at Weymouth. It all felt comfortingly and energizingly familiar . . .

I had felt empty, bruised by the experience of Weymouth but grateful for it still. That which doesn't kill you makes you stronger. My emotions, and life, were more in balance, football back in perspective. I had taken a smashing job as chief football writer on the *Mail on Sunday* working with a good set of people under an understanding sports editor in Malcolm Vallerius – who agreed to me going on the board at St Albans – and got back to work properly, my finances gradually recovering.

As the Billy Crystal character in *Throw Momma from the Train* says at the end: 'Hate makes you impotent. Love makes you crazy. Somewhere in between you can survive.'

At the end of the day

Like the novel and the theatre, that sage of the press box Brian Glanville once suggested, English football is ever in decline. And along the path of its decline are strewn broken dreams and men. And broken clubs. If there was a time when all football clubs were happy, friendly concerns, with players and directors united in a common cause and balanced books, let us pine for it.

In reality, and in its behind-the-scenes machinations, from clubs going bust, through players behaving badly to corruption and 'bungs', there is probably nothing much new in a hundred years. Every generation thinks it is the first to experience such things. Sex, after all, was only invented in 1963. Financially, though, football on these shores has undergone a huge transformation in the last fifteen years and the game itself improved, thanks simply to someone who cried.

It was Italia 90, the most vivid World Cup in my memory. It was a cynical tournament short on entertainment, though not on drama. England went with what proved to be a vintage team that included rare talents such as Chris Waddle, Peter Beardsley and Gary Lineker. They were given little chance, however, with the game, the nation indeed, in a downbeat mood. The English game was in a trough, its hooligans having rampaged through Europe making us social pariahs. We were the knuckle-draggers who turn up at a party swinging a six-pack, terrorizing guests who are enjoying civilized company and a couple of glasses of wine.

The Thatcher government despised the game and its followers – though when it was trendy enough, and the boss was gone, such 'fans' as David Mellor and John Major would emerge from hiding to flaunt their supporters' credentials – and it had some cause, it must be admitted. The carnage of Heysel, Bradford and the darkest day of all at Hillsborough had brought the game to its knees. Stadiums were crumbling and unsafe, attendances were falling.

In Italy, I met a man who was writing a book about England's campaign. The premise was that England as a nation was washed up, paying the price for years of Thatcherism with its me-me-me consumerism that had driven deep division between the haves and have-nots and abandoned social justice. The City of London had flourished while mining communities were closed down. Bust had, inevitably, followed boom. It was all reflected in its national sport, a sorry conclusion to a century and more for a country that had invented the game, its Football Association once a symbol of all that was good and fair.

Pete Davies's *All Played Out* would indeed turn out to be a thoughtful study and a brilliant ground-breaking work. Except that a young man by the name of Paul Gascoigne had no idea about any political premise or social metaphor. The Geordie boy simply wanted to play: 'Just giz the ball, man,' he said, seizing possession and the day.

Dispelling the gloom of a nation, Gazza led England to the semi-finals, where a careless, adrenalin-charged foul on West Germany's Thomas Berthold meant a second yellow card of the tournament and a ban should England reach the final. He wept and so too did a nation, with him and for him. England lost on penalties to the Germans but in the talented talisman Paul Gascoigne, the nation had discovered some resources of pride and self-esteem amid the ruins of its reputation.

Gazza developed into the perfect icon for the laddish lager-and-video nineties. Later every footballer would come to owe Jean-Marc Bosman for his fight against the iniquities of the retain-and-transfer system and the installation of freedom of movement at the end of a contract. But way before that the path to riches was paved by Gascoigne's lifting of the sport back into the public consciousness and affection. Just as every average golf pro around the world owes Tiger Woods for raising the prize money of a tournament by his very appearance, so should footballers thank Gazza.

Two other factors combined to rehabilitate the game in the nineties. The brave and visionary Lord Justice Taylor had been commissioned to look into the game's ills following the Hillsborough disaster. Among a package of measures he recommended all-seater stadiums. Money would be made available through some government funding. Gradually, facilities improved to the point where England hosted a successful and joyous European Championships in 1996 – however, a semi-final defeat on penalties to the Germans was still the outcome.

Then there was Rupert Murdoch's British Sky Broadcasting, which decided that football was the perfect vehicle for selling satellite dishes and subscriptions. The Premier League was created. The marketing men moved in. Billions have since gone into a game that moved from back to front pages, its influence marching to the very heart of English culture.

The effects have been wide-ranging. Never before has the game been so wealthy at its top level, but never before have its finances been so tangled, especially beneath the Premiership. The short-lived ITV Digital sought to follow the Sky model by securing the rights to the Football League for sums it could not sustain, failing to recognize that the glitz and glamour of the Premiership was a market apart. When ITV Digital went bust, so too did many clubs, having budgeted for three years' worth of money that would not arrive. We were back to the haves and have-nots.

At Weymouth, we were among the have-nots but we were still linked – or certainly should have been in the brotherhood that makes the game in England deeper and more colourful than any other nation's football – to the haves at the very top.

Take Manchester United, honoured guests at the opening of the Wessex Stadium and the country's, probably the world's, most successful football club. Over the booming nineties, they became England's dominant force. With the arrival of the Premiership they capitalized on the rediscovered devotion to the game by going public. They sold more merchandise and season tickets than anyone else, all based on the legend of the Munich air disaster and Sir Matt Busby returning a decade later to win the European Cup.

It was chicken and egg; they had had to invest to fund success on the field, which then brought success off it. Now they had manoeuvred themselves into a position where players' wages accounted for around 50 per cent of turnover. It was enviable for every other club, the business model.

An American by the name of Malcolm Glazer recognized it, and reckoned there was even more money to be made, perhaps by selling even more shirts in Asia, perhaps by developing the 'brand' in the United States, perhaps with an eye on future Internet and broadband markets in, say, the barely tapped, vastly populated football fields of China. He bought the club with the money of banks, landing it immediately with vast debts.

How did that, in essence, differ from Weymouth, where a club's fortunes had been turned around to the point that a businessman with little previous interest was suddenly attracted?

Glazer's move came two years after Roman Abramovich had bought Chelsea from Ken Bates, wiping out a £100-million debt that Bates had accumulated in trying to make the club the Manchester United of the south. The Russian then invested huge, mind-boggling sums of money into surpassing United and making Chelsea champions.

How did Martyn Harrison differ from the egotistical Bates in spending vast sums – or persuading banks to – that were not coming back through the gate or in sponsorship? Or differ from Abramovich, indeed, in wanting to add a football club to his portfolio of interests, superficially for fun, though none will really know until the plot unravels further.

Bates, personally £18 million richer out of a club he had purchased for £1, such was the debt he was prepared to take on, soon returned to the game by taking over Leeds United. There, a culture of excess in seeking to gatecrash the elite of the game, overseen by Peter Ridsdale's stewardship, had resulted in horrendous financial problems. Ridsdale himself then surfaced at Barnsley, to be followed by a spell sorting out Cardiff City, where Sam Hammam, who had sold Wimbledon profitably to Norwegians thinking they were buying a Premiership Rottweiler only to discover a pup, had also been getting into deep financial trouble seeking to fulfil the Welsh club's potential as a Premiership concern.

There were other parallels lower down, at the Championship club Millwall for example. Theo Paphitis stepped down as chairman, to be replaced by Jeff Burnige. Paphitis, owner of the Ryman chain of stationery shops, had underwritten the club's overdraft for a number of years, agreeing to spending not matched by income in chasing the dream of the Premiership. When Paphitis decided he had had enough, Burnige picked up the pieces, seeking to cut the wage bill, deciding it was time for the club to address its debts and live within its means.

Burnige appointed a new, cheaper manager than Dennis Wise. His name was Steve Claridge. Football really can be a village, with everyone knowing everyone and their business. Steve, his canny football brain still in demand, had played for Brighton, Brentford and Wycombe Wanderers after leaving Weymouth. He knew he was walking into another cash-strapped club in Millwall, but relished the challenge of galvanizing another club where he had been a hero as a player.

This job lasted just thirty-six days. Paphitis did not like the way Burnige was running the club and resumed the reins, immediately sacking Steve, who then took his boots to Bradford City. As at Weymouth, he had been the victim of a boardroom coup, not given a proper chance with the controller of the purse already having made his mind up that Steve was not his bottle of Budweiser.

Then, at Stoke City, a former chairman Peter Coates was usurped by an Icelandic consortium, which believed there was money to be made if they could get Stoke into the Premiership. For several years they tried, accumulating debts. Coates sought to buy back the club, but the Icelanders wanted their money back. Why, he not unnaturally wondered, should he have to pay for the mistakes they had made? Why should any money he invested go to them rather than into revitalizing the club?

How, again, did that differ from Charlie Lesser's attempt when Weymouth were floundering to return the club to a more benevolent ownership, eventually handing it over to a supporters' trust, only to be told by Martyn Harrison that it would cost him a million quid over and above the price for the shares?

In the Conference, Telford United went bust because of an overambitious owner overstretching the club, paying wages that were too high. His company went bankrupt and the club was forced to reform in a lower division of the

Northern Premier League. The same had even happened in our league with Hornchurch ending up in the Essex Senior League.

It all carried echoes for Weymouth, who had now hired the very men whose huge salaries – and as professionals they were simply doing the best deal for themselves they could, as this hire-and-fire game had taught them and many others – had contributed to Hornchurch's demise. From Glazer through Bates and Ridsdale to Harrison, I was reminded of a witty and appropriate observation by a colleague on the *Mail on Sunday*, Pat Collins. 'I don't know where football keeps finding these people,' he wrote, 'but I wish it would stop looking.'

What was it that made such men want to play with football, take decisions that they would not take in their businesses? What turned the hard heads that prevailed in company boardrooms into soft hearts as they sat watching games in directors' boxes?

The easy initial answer is ego. Many business people toil their whole lives to make money. There is little recognition, little acknowledgement even. When you become the owner of a football club, its chairman, you are in the spotlight. From local to national paper, regional to networked television and radio, your name, face and voice are known.

It is, too, a way to quick popularity. Chuck some money at a problem and you reckon the fans will love you. For me, a key insight into Martyn Harrison's motives came when Matt McGowan said, after they had been out for a drink together, that 'the poor bloke's never had a friend in his life'.

Courting popularity may be to some extent understandable but it was, to me, the wrong motivation. Vikki often wondered why, if he did genuinely have all this money, he didn't just help out Queen's Park Rangers, who had been struggling financially for years and where Martyn claimed he had been a season-ticket holder for decades. She pointed out, too, that he was a hotelier and our land was under offer, with potential for all sorts to be built on it. I wondered if it was more to do with being a big fish in a small pool.

Football clubs are alluring places. They can be poisonous nests of vipers or life-enhancing collections of kindred spirits. In whatever guise, they are not nine-to-five-spreadsheet dull. There is, at worst, contact and connection with others, at best camaraderie.

At first, owners believe it can be run as a business like any other, until they find out its hidden vagaries: the player who has to be paid off, due to injury or form; the hiring of managers or players not in the budget, because not to do so means income falling through fans not coming to watch. The stand seats and floodlight bulbs that need replacing. They get tired of results not matching the effort behind the scenes, and the criticism that goes with it, and cannot resist borrowing to pay to keep fans happy.

A quote from a West Ham official intrigued me. In the summer, the club were in talks about a takeover. The manager Alan Pardew wanted to sign the Norwich City striker Dean Ashton for £6 million but the takeover panel vetoed any transfer moves while talks were going on. 'We appealed to the takeover panel and fortunately they understand a football club is unlike other businesses,' said the official.

I then watched the next autumn when the Heart of Midlothian chairman George Faulks resigned, accusing the new owner Vladimir Romanov – who would controversially go on to pick the team – of being a megalomaniac. I read with interest of the FIFA president Sepp Blatter worrying about clubs spending money outside their income and of the Sports Minister Richard Caborn's insistence that football start adoping a fit and proper test for those taking over clubs.

Naturally Martyn accused me of being spendthrift, arrogant and an ego-maniac. Of course, I wanted to be liked, but

I did not react with a jerk of the knee to every suggestion on a website or when I was waylaid in the club bar. I cared most about the club and its wellbeing. It was the club of my youth, a focal point of my life, not something I had come to belatedly for diversion.

I made many mistakes as a chairman. Partly out of the needs-must of securing funding, I recruited too many people to the board, and too many without good judgement or knowledge of the game, with their own personal local agendas.

I gave the manager too much rope at times, too little at others. Players' bonuses were too high, but then we should have invested in the team after Christmas to strengthen the Championship push. Then again, what is to be done when the bank refuses to extend the overdraft and directors refuse the money they had promised? In football, money doesn't guarantee success but lack of it guarantees failure. As Steve Claridge told me: 'We may have done some things wrong, but we did far more things right.'

My intentions in going into Weymouth had simply been to rejuvenate an ailing club, to do what supporters often dream of doing and sort out the club that has given them more pleasure than pain down the years.

There came an irony some six months after I left Weymouth. I was at a dinner in London attended by Ken Bates and his partner Suzannah. 'Tell Ian,' Suzannah told my partner Vikki, 'that Ken really admired what he did at Weymouth. He obviously did it from the heart.'

The strategy was quite simply to speculate to accumulate initially but above all to bring momentum, by getting crowds back and generating income, without overstretching the club. I hoped to achieve this by creating an environment in which people felt empowered to bring their talents, comfortable in the knowledge that they would be valued. I believed that people and clubs flourished in an atmosphere of trust and respect, rather than one of creative tension and fear where people could be fired at a whim.

The problem was the biggest one in football: expectation.

The Labour politician Denis Healey once said that it matters not how bad the unemployment figures are, only in which direction they are heading. So it is in football.

We were heading upwards but too quickly. I had hoped in the first season to finish around sixth: a major sign of progress and a launching pad for a promotion campaign the next time around. There came a point, though, when I – and fans, I am sure – thought we would win the league by six points. I tried to keep myself and the club humble but humility is elusive. Disappointment was huge, expectation even greater for the second season. When you finish second, anything other than first is a let-down. It is, however, sometimes impossible to explain these things rationally when the blind emotion that affects a supporter's passion for their club is involved.

Thus the strains for the second season were almost impossible for Steve Claridge to withstand. Above all, what hurt me was the treatment he received from the board and, fuelled by Martyn Harrison, a group of fans. But, strange as it may seem to the fans of bigger clubs, I have rarely come across a more passionate and expectant set than Weymouth's.

A minority of the less enlightened of our fans disappointed me, as any chairman will tell you privately and not dare to say publicly. I believe that success should be measured in making the most of resources rather than simply in silverware; in terms of doing a good job, of providing entertainment and enjoyment.

At Weymouth, no one really wanted to contemplate the cost of Martyn Harrison's headlong pursuit. I detest fans with money basking in glory at their club, then squealing when it has been frittered away. Only then do they come out and say that they were worried all along. Few want to know what could go wrong. Football is in huge denial.

Just take the Premiership. Bloated by its £1 billion TV deal with Sky, it has paid vast sums to players, often the merely mediocre from overseas. With the further riches of the Champions League, the biggest clubs have got bigger. It has even created a divide within itself, those three – Chelsea, Manchester United and Arsenal – who can win the League, those seeking to qualify for European competition and those in a third tier simply bent on surviving to retain the £20 million and more a year rather than the £1 million for Championship clubs.

But Premiership gates are falling, if only slowly, some fans tiring of the lifestyles of the rich and famous they subsidize with ticket prices of sometimes more than £50 that preclude them taking their kids regularly. Gates in the Championship are up, the competition between clubs tighter if not of the same quality. It filters down to the non-League where the experience is value for money and more intimate.

One thing that involvement in football did give me was an empathy for people in positions of responsibility. I may have little sympathy for men who do not need it such as Bates and Ridsdale, but I can see how many of the things that are said about them, and their families, are vicious and hurtful. The rise of the radio phone-in and especially the Internet forums, which have only a nodding acquaintance with the laws of libel, is a new phenomenon that can wound with ill-informed barbs. Indeed, when Steve Johnson left Weymouth his parting shot was to his critics on the website. Higher up the scale, Joe Kinnear did the same when he left Nottingham Forest as another disillusioned manager.

The difference between myself and the Bateses and Ridsdales is that I never believed there was money to be made personally. Indeed, while many chairmen and chief executives are being paid fortunes these days, I believed in time freely given to serve the club closest to my heart. Employees should be paid properly, of course, but not to satisfy greed.

What happens when the egos and personal ambitions of Abramovich and Harrison are sated, when gratitude turns to a grilling, as happened to the 'Golden Tit' of Wolverhampton, Sir Jack Hayward, and he took a back seat? When the Glazers see more money to be made elsewhere?

These days, an organization called Supporters Direct does sterling work in setting up supporters' trusts and helping committees of fans run clubs, doing so with the good of the club in mind, making sound decisions about whether to spend money on building new stands or signing a new striker. They also provide an ear and emotional support for beleaguered officials of trusts. I could have done with some of that.

There are some admirable big clubs, too, running along footballing, rather than financial, lines. 'This club is not dependent on one person for funds that come from external sources,' said the Arsenal managing director Keith Edelman. 'It can live off its own revenue.'

But then they have been fortunate by recruiting an extraordinarily wise manager in Arsene Wenger, who not only knows players and where to find them for reasonable prices, assembling attractive teams in the process, but understands the business of the game. And, most importantly, the board have stuck with him, given him time to do the job.

Just one of his pearls: 'To build a great team is not all about money. First you have to create spirit and togetherness in the squad and that is not easy.' The same applies to a chairman.

Sometimes it is hard not to be cynical when money-men and agents abound, attracted by the glamour and the pickings. And, on bad days, it is hard to avoid the conclusion that if you build it, as Ray Kinsella did in *Field of Dreams*, some bastard will come along and knock it down.

But when eleven men kick off against another eleven on a Saturday afternoon, something simple, uplifting and reinvigorating, even magical and mystical, occurs. All the politics, personalities and economics disappear into ninety minutes of the simple game that absorbed you as a kid. It is genuinely addictive.

Several fans, worried about where the Harrison era was leading, emailed me. Would I go back to Weymouth, sort it out should the worst happen, perhaps help set up a supporters' trust? Would I be willing to risk again the abuse that followed the adulation.

Absolutely not, I replied. Never. Not on your life. No way. But never say never, they also say in football. Like every man, and many women these days too, I would not want to see the club my father gave me left in the lurch, and would do my best to help.

You grieve and finally you do risk again, as I did at St Albans City. As with a cherished son, you watch him make his mistakes and when he seeks help, you hope you will give it freely and forgivingly – but only if he wants it. The game has a habit of biting and not making twice shy.

And you keep in mind something I came across in the Gospel of St Matthew, which seems to me to apply to running a football club:

'Be ye therefore wise as serpents and harmless as doves.'